D0918515

The America's Cup Challenge

THE AMERICA'S CUP CHALLENGE:
THERE IS NO SECOND

Tony Fairchild

NAUTICAL BOOKS
MACMILLAN LONDON

ISBN O 333 32527 3

First published in Great Britain 1983 by
NAUTICAL BOOKS
an imprint of Macmillan London Ltd
4 Little Essex Street
London WC2R 3LF

Associated companies throughout the world

Reprinted 1983 with corrections

Published in association with the *Daily Telegraph*

Photoset in Great Britain by
Rowland Phototypesetting Ltd, Bury St Edmunds, Suffolk
Printed by St Edmundsbury Press
Bury St Edmunds, Suffolk

Contents

Diagrams and Tables

To Hazel and the family

Preface

This is the story of a challenge for the last 'Everest' in sport. It is mainly from a British standpoint and describes the effort to win the America's Cup in 1983. The intention is a broader than usual examination of the activities of the challengers, though chiefly of one syndicate.

It is not a microscopic analysis of that one syndicate, the Victory challenge, headed by Peter de Savary under the flag of the Royal Burnham Yacht Club, Essex, England. Rather it is an account, after close and prolonged observation, of the intense and well intentioned efforts of the people who were involved with the British group in pursuit of yacht racing excellence. I was privileged to witness this from close quarters for three years, from before the official announcement of the challenge until its conclusion in September 1983.

Unnecessary controversy or criticism has been avoided, and instead the reader will find an earnest, if hurried, attempt of as honest as possible a record of the activities of the Victory syndicate. Step by step, I have followed the fortunes and disappointments of the British and other syndicates, so that the commitment of the America's Cup can be made clear to readers other than the sailing fraternity.

Because of the giant efforts made by Mr de Savary and the fortune he spent on his quest, the challenge seemed to fire the enthusiasm of the general public for sailing. The story was told continuously in the press, and its coverage far surpassed anything that has gone before in connection with the America's Cup and sailing generally. To those who have come recently to have an interest in yachting, I apologize for any technical references that annoy. Conversely, I do not apologize for the lack of any technical information that the more knowledgeable among yacthsmen might have preferred to read. In this respect I am happy to leave the technicalities to those better qualified than I am to deal with them.

To those with such knowledge I would say this: the America's Cup is, of course, about boats and sails and sophisticated equipment. But it is, above all, a story about human endeavour; a matter of great personal commitment and intense physical demands. I believe the best part of the America's Cup story to be about people and their efforts.

Tony Fairchild
Lyme Regis
October 1983

Acknowledgements

The America's Cup of 1983 was the second which I had reported, but this time I was to spend no less than three and a half months in Newport, Rhode Island, in addition to several visits in 1982 and early 1983. These were on behalf of my newspaper, the *Daily Telegraph*: every day I filed copy to London – and even on Saturdays for the *Sunday Telegraph*. I would like to thank the management and editors, especially Peter Eastwood, for their permission to write this book and giving me the assignment which enabled me to do so. To Ted Barrett, Ian Ball, Edna Jackson and the newspaper's sports room staff I am grateful for support as pressure built up.

Peter de Savary deserves my greatest thanks for his endless help and friendship. He never refused to answer a question and always met and discussed with me any point I wished to put to him. If anyone was remiss it was me for failing perhaps to put to him some questions that ought to have been asked. There can have been few better leaders of an America's Cup campaign in terms of help to an author – budding or established. I thank him also for providing a long and fascinating story.

I would like to express my gratitude to all his staff, in London as well as in Newport, for their pleasant response to regular requests for assistance, and especially to Jim Alabaster, a loyal supporter of de Savary and the Victory syndicate through all its changes; he too never refused to answer a question or to give valuable help. My thanks are due also to his delightful wife Sandy, my 'landlady' during my early visits to Newport.

I would like to mention Ian McBeth and the crew of *Kalisma*, and Glen Wales and Norman Colhoun, the 'pilots', for their kindness and assistance.

My special thanks go also to Kit and Suzy Hobday, frank and pleasant to the end, and whose help at times was invaluable;

thank you to them also for the continuance of a long-standing friendship. Thank you, too, to the KH staff, troubled not infrequently by queries and enquiries.

I would like to pay tribute to the flag officers and senior members of the Royal Burnham Yacht Club for their co-operation in England and in Newport. My thanks go specially to Frank Kemball, David Geaves, Neil Kennedy and Philip Tolhurst and to Tim Herring, whose 'hospitality' at the Ark in Newport was as welcome as his frankness.

It would be a terrible oversight not to mention the whole of the Victory squad and crew and to those who gave help and a friendly word – or more – I am most sincerely grateful.

Back on shore cheerful assistance came from Vanessa Bellamy, especially with details of *Victory of Burnham*; Alice Simms, whom I got to know later in the campaign; Pamela James; and Jane Craig for invaluable copy transmission.

Material about the 1980 racing in *Lionheart* was aided by Tony Boyden, John Oakeley, Ian Howlett, Iain Macdonald-Smith and Lawrie Smith. Stories of the middle stages of the 1983 campaign received assistance from Peter Bateman, Phil Crebbin and Ed Dubois. A number of facts about earlier America's Cup contests come from the *Guinness Book of Yachting Facts and Feats* by Peter Johnson, who also gave me advice and encouragement in writing this book for publication so soon after the events it describes.

The most sincere thanks possible go to Margaret Comley, who retyped my scrawl and without whom nothing would have been achieved.

The photographs of the wonderful 12-metre yachts, the fascinating participants and the superb racing are credited in each instance. They are from four sources: Associated Press (*AP*), Alastair Black (*Black*), Koren Evans (*Kos*) and the *Daily Telegraph* (*DT*).

T.F.

Boat names. The Victory syndicate owned a number of boats, some of whose names are confusing. *Victory of Burnham* is the ocean racer that was one of the 1981 British Admiral's Cup team. *Victory* was the first 12-metre: she was designed by Ed Dubois and launched in 1982. *Victory '83*, a second 12-metre, designed by Ian Howlett, was launched in 1983. *Australia* was purchased from an Australian syndicate after the 1980 races and was a British trial horse during the campaign. She should not be mistaken for *Australia II*, which arrived in Newport as an Australian challenger in 1983 and became, in the event, the most famous boat of all.

Queen Victoria had seen parts of the race on 22 August 1851 from aboard the royal yacht and is said to have enquired which yacht was second behind *America*. By way of answer, her signal master told her, 'There is no second, ma'am.'

William N. Wallace of the *New York Times*,
from various early sources.

'I have it and the boys are getting it now – that great desire to win. There's no such thing as being second in this, as there is in the Admiral's Cup or the Olympics. In the America's Cup, if you come second you've lost.'

Peter de Savary, December 1982.

I

America's Own Cup

No other international sporting contest has the slightest resemblance to the races for the America's Cup. Strangely it is the oldest sporting trophy to be raced between nations, yet it has the longest sequence of wins by a single nation or club. In yacht racing it is by far the most senior and sought after prize, held until 1983 by the New York Yacht Club since the schooner *America* beat the finest yachts of the Royal Yacht Squadron, as she crossed the finishing line at Cowes at 8.37 p.m. on 22 August 1851.

Until the historic races described in these pages the boats sailed off Newport, the sterling pitcher remained in New York bolted to an oak altar in its own room in the club under a case of fine heavy glass sheltered from touch, from corrosion and, for twenty contests over a span of 132 years, from the efforts of challengers to dislodge it.

In 1980, with potential challengers from four nations, there was no evidence that the cup had even suffered a tremor. Then as before the record of the Americans had been awesome. Besides winning every series from 1870, they had only been beaten in eight of the eighty-six match races sailed.

On occasions the defenders have also won with what they agree have been inferior boats, but by 1980 it was clear, with an increasing number of challenges from ever more countries, that the defenders had stepped up their preparations to a level of skill unrivalled in the history of the America's Cup; perhaps even to a level beyond which any other country could hope to rise in the foreseeable future. This improved standard by the Americans was to have at least one inevitable consequence.

It meant that in terms of cost and length of time taken in preparation by a record number of potential protagonists the America's Cup series of 1983 would provide a further batch of staggering records. Nine months before the start of the Cup event proper, in September 1983, the British syndicate involved in the series reported that its efforts, uniquely thorough for a challenge from Britain, were expected to cost $8 million. The total costs of three Australian groups and syndicates from Canada, France and Italy together cost twice as much and with the Americans building no fewer than four new 12-metre yachts and preparing with three others it would be fair to assess defence costs as at least half as much again as those of Britain: a grand total of around $30 million.

The Olympic Games or football's World Cup may cost more, involving as they do far more performers than the 250 or so crew members who may have been involved in boat tuning at the height of preparations for the 1983 America's Cup, but they are also public using 'public' money. The financing of the America's Cup challenges and defence is a private affair: between the New York Yacht Club, holder of the trophy, which organises races every three years (until 1983), and other overseas yacht clubs. Though the challenges have become more nationalistic syndicates, often multi-member affairs, have usually replaced the single 'benefactors' such as Sir Thomas Lipton, Sir Tom Sopwith and Harold Vanderbilt of the first ninety years of the cup.

The money for the challenges comes from private sources and as such must represent the biggest such outlay in international sport for just one event – a series of seven races for which, because of its increasing popularity, it is becoming as difficult to qualify as it has been to win. To breed an all-time great racehorse may cost more, but every horse has more than one competition in which to prove its greatness, and, unlike the America's Cup, there is also prize money as an inducement.

For a world heavyweight title fight, the boxers spend much more time in training camps preparing for the clash than the actual contest can ever take; the same is much more true now of the America's Cup. Not only the Americans but at least the British among the challengers devote almost two years to near non-stop practice and training. A monumental task in an unbelievable number of ways: first, the cost, not merely of boats and boating equipment but also airline tickets, staff wages, accommodation, transport, houses and house-keeping, security, safety, fuel, food, uniforms and foul-weather gear and, indeed, every aspect that can be imagined of looking after between 50–70 crew members and supporters in three bases as much as 3,000 miles apart and the various craft they sail and service in specially arranged docks.

Second, America's Cup crews in the main are still amateur; many with jobs and families to consider and seldom wealthy enough to undertake a yachting campaign just for love. If you find the people, how do you look after them for two years in various borrowed accommodation? If it takes a million pounds to mount a one-boat challenge, it would raise also a million considerations in a campaign to bring back the cup.

Individuals may take even longer to prepare for, say, a major running race; some teams, like a football club, may spend up to three years preparing for a championship clash and, of course, some professionals spend their entire lives at their sports.

But the America's Cup has always been about money, including the silver cup itself. Weighing 8lb 6oz, it stood 2ft 3ins high in a special glass case in its own room at the New York Yacht Club, 37, West 44th Street in Manhattan. Made by R. & G. Garrard, of Regent Street, London, and first named 'The Hundred Guinea Cup' – its actual value when it was made – it was one of a number given every year by the Royal Yacht Squadron. The name 'Auld Mug', often used by the Americans, was coined by Sir Thomas Lipton, five times challenger for the trophy.

Its history is long and fascinating and the subject of numerous books and articles; its modern history, the years of competition in yachts built to the international 12-metres rule – an involved and complex formula and including no single measurement of 12-metres but giving a rating of 12-metres when such facts as length, girth and sail area are calculated – began in 1958, and including the most recent series in 1983, has involved nine challenges, each more extravagant and expensive than the last.

The arms race period in current America's Cup history leading up to the participation of so many yachts in 1983, began as late as 1970, for which challenges from Australia, Britain, France and Greece were received within the stipulated period of 30 days after *Intrepid* had beaten the Australian *Dame Pattie* in the 20th Cup defence.

Though the Greeks and the British dropped out of the chal-

lenge it was still necessary to run a selection series to decide
between Baron Marcel Bich's first challenger, *France*, and Sir
Frank Packer's *Gretel II*. With the Australians winning the
elimination races but being defeated in their fourth tilt at the
America's Cup there had been much of historical note in the
series which, four years later, in 1974, again resulted in France
and Australia contesting an elimination event. Australia beat
the French then with *Southern Cross* and were to meet them
and Sweden, America's Cup newcomers, in 1977. This time the
Alan Bond 12-metre *Australia* came through to challenge and
did so again in 1980 when the elimination series involved also
France III, the British *Lionheart* and *Sverige* from Sweden for
the second time.

If 1970 was a water-shed, with extra challengers forcing an
elimination contest and the resulting improved preparations by
the Americans, then 1980 was a waterfall of Niagara-like
dimensions in bringing no fewer than 10 challengers, including
four from Australia. The total quickly reduced to seven and it
seemed fairly certain at the start of the Cup year that there
would be no fewer than five challengers in 1983 and with a
probability of seven. Not only were the chips down for a battle of
titanic proportions – with the Americans first responding to
overseas fervour with four syndicates – but money was being
spent on a massive level.

There was much that was notable from the first about the
preparations for 1983, involving as they did some impressively
wealthy syndicates in Australia, Britain and Italy; a line-up of
astonishing yachting talent in Australia, Canada and Britain and
with the challenge contenders combining cleverly to construct
a selection contest which promised to produce a challenger with
outstanding credentials. The yacht which came through to meet
the American defender of the trophy would in such a selection
contest a minimum of 55 races and might have to race in 58 if
the final selection series had to be decided over seven races.

The significance of the lengthy selection process envisaged by
the challenge contenders would not have been lost on the New
York Yacht Club's committee responsible for choosing the
yacht to defend the America's Cup. The primary reason for the
defeat of a challenger in earlier years was that it invariably
involved just one yacht financed by a successful businessman
unfamiliar with the fine skills of top sailing. The result was that

while the Americans usually were able to select a defender from a number of contenders, the challenger was not selected but merely bought by an owner wealthy and unwise enough to challenge: though since a number of challenges were brought to promote businesses rather than win the America's Cup, many of them were highly successful as advertisements or promotional devices.

In more recent challenge series, when there were still rather more 'promotion' boats than cup-winning craft produced than may seem the case, it has been the outstanding weakness of the challengers' selection series compared to that of the defender that has been a handicap. While none of the American skippers or crews ever knew for certain until the very end of their selection series which boat and combination of skipper or crew would be chosen, there was never the same degree of doubt among the challenge contenders and thus far less testing racing. Even in 1980, when there were the four challenge contenders, there were not only fewer races than for the Americans with their three defence contenders but equally if not more important, the knowledge that only the one yacht could represent her country. Nothing could stop *Lionheart* representing Britain; nothing could stop *Australia* representing Australia. While there was the knowledge that *France III* might beat *Lionheart*, as she did, and *Sverige* might lose to *Australia*, as she did, there was not the same urgency to succeed for their country among the challengers as there was for the defenders, for whom selection to represent the United States was just as important as winning the America's Cup.

In 1983, however, it seemed that it could be different, because, though the New York Yacht Club's America's Cup committee would have realized that the selection system devised by the challenge contenders was not without its flaws – designed as it was to satisfy the demands also of some less promising syndicates as those more threateningly efficient – it did suggest that it was capable of producing a more worthwhile challenger than the Americans had ever met.

For once, a Cup series seemed to threaten rather more than merely promise to be historic, and this state of affairs was brought about not just by the selection process but by the preparations made by the syndicates – in some cases uniquely efficient and for once very similar to the previously invincible methods of the Americans themselves. Certainly this was the case with Peter John de Savary*, international financier, oilman and boss of what he decided to call the Victory syndicate. He challenged through the Royal Burnham Yacht Club and this story is in the main about his remarkable campaign.

There cannot have been more thorough preparations, attention to detail and all at massive cost, in the history of seventeen British challenges for the America's Cup than those by de Savary. He had not only the ability to take in quickly most, if not all, of the fundamental America's Cup lessons but the equally necessary dedicated pugnacity of the modern-day world champion sportsman. If you happen to subscribe to the belief that to be a modern champion you have to be extremely ruthless – then you would see that de Savary had a lot of the necessary credentials.

De Savary's preparations not only promised to be better than any previously attempted by a Briton to regain the Royal Yacht Squadron's ugly urn, they proved also an agonizing thorn in the flesh of the New York Yacht Club from the day he announced his challenge in Newport in 1980 and were more comprehensive than any others attempted for 1983 by the rest of the foreign intruders into what, until the appearance of upstart Australian sailors in 1962 had been, but for brief Canadian bounty-hunting in 1876 and 1881, an exclusive 'row' between the British and Americans.

For 1983 the Australian syndicates with much experience among them built three new boats, but none had a trial horse; the Canadians and Italians had impressive trial horse-yachts but the former had a cash problem and the Italians had talent but that seemed certain only to make them the best-dressed outfit in Newport; and the French only had an aging hulk whose moment of glory had been in notching a hollow victory over the British *Lionheart* in the elimination contest of 1980.

The British were not the only group the Americans had to take seriously: the Canadians were likely to race with a compellingly competitive crew and three new craft and a return to Newport for their sixth successive series again made the Australians a force with which to be reckoned.

Not only that, the Australians were becoming as fanatical

* His name de Savary is pronounced as in 'have' and not as in 'save'.

about the America's Cup as the Americans and some saw them, rather than the British, as the most likely official challengers of 1983. But the Australians could not match the British for style: the de Savary style which had swept Newport first in 1982 as his impressive preparations began to put right the 'wrong' witnessed by Queen Victoria in 1851.

The blunt truth about the event was spelled out to Her Majesty on August 22, 1851: 'There is no second, Ma'am' in reply to a question from Queen Victoria about the yacht which was finishing next after *America* – the design of which was of major interest to yachtsmen. One, the Marquis of Anglesey, who had said of *America*, 'If she's right then we're all wrong', insisted on climbing out on to her bowsprit to watch the bow wave. After 20 minutes he climbed back on deck and commented: 'I've learned one thing; I've been sailing my yacht stern foremost for the last 20 years'. He must have been a game old boy because he was 83 and had only one leg.

The same 'game' description would apply to the British challenge by *Lionheart* of 1980, when they failed to achieve the status of the official challengers, that honour being won by the Australians. The British challenge of 1980 was once said to have been as close to the defence ability of the New York Yacht Club as British Rail was to NASA, the American space agency. The comparison may be unkind – indeed brutal – but the extent of the implied gulf between the America's Cup aspirations of the two countries may have been less exaggerated than believed.

Sharper and more astute students of the America's Cup suggest that the first necessity towards winning the trophy is to begin on a level which is at least equal with that of the Americans. This means having the same number of boats, the same approach to training and involving at least two rival syndicates. The same dedicated and prolonged preparations then would follow the same ruthless approach to rejection and selection of boats and men. In none of the challenges certainly since the beginning of the century had these fundamental requirements been applied. Indeed, while victory would doubtless require rather more effort than those listed, most of the challenges included only a few of the features established as being fundamental to success. Of course, it is possible to argue other courses and other fundamental factors, but on the basis that those tested had brought 24 successful defences, at

Fig. 1   *America's Cup challengers and defenders 1870–1980.*

In 1851, the schooner *America* (John C. Stevens and Syndicate of the New York Yacht Club) won the hundred guinea cup outright at Cowes in a race around the Isle of Wight. This cup, the America's Cup, was offered for international competition by the New York Yacht Club, after James Ashbury, owner of *Cambria*, had challenged for it in 1870. The defender always represents the New York Yacht Club. Races were held off New York until 1920, then moved to the present course off Newport, R.I.

Year	Defender	Challenger and country
1870	*Magic*	*Cambria*, G.B.
1871	*Columbia*	*Livonia*, G.B.
1876	*Madelaine*	*Countess of Dufferin*, Canada
1881	*Mischief*	*Atalanta*, Canada
1885	*Puritan*	*Genesta*, G.B.
1886	*Mayflower*	*Genesta*, G.B.
1887	*Volunteer*	*Thistle*, G.B.
1893	*Vigilant*	*Valkyrie II*, G.B.
1895	*Defender*	*Valkyrie III*, G.B.
1899	*Columbia*	*Shamrock I*, G.B.
1901	*Columbia*	*Shamrock II*, G.B.
1903	*Reliance*	*Shamrock III*, G.B.
1920	*Resolute*	*Shamrock IV*, G.B.
1930	*Enterprise*	*Shamrock V*, G.B.
1934	*Rainbow*	*Endeavour*, G.B.
1937	*Ranger*	*Endeavour II*, G.B.
1958	*Columbia*	*Sceptre*, G.B.
1962	*Weatherly*	*Gretel*, Australia
1964	*Constellation*	*Sovereign*, G.B.
1967	*Intrepid*	*Dame Pattie*, Australia
1970	*Intrepid*	*Gretel II*, Australia
1974	*Courageous*	*Southern Cross*, Australia
1977	*Courageous*	*Australia*, Australia
1980	*Freedom*	*Australia*, Australia

least they can be put forward as the proven first steps towards victory.

But, as the de Savary challenge began to take shape, here, at last, was a syndicate, it seemed as preparations gathered pace, which would restore British honour; at least to the extent of being a worthwhile challenge if not a winning one. At least an 'expeditionary' force capable of sending packing the pretenders from the 'colonies' and the wretched continentals who had muscled in on the act. Not only was de Savary apparently spending money on the same scale as the Americans, but he had encroached offensively on their sacred territory with a band of modern mariners which included some of the more talented of British yachtsmen. The presence of such world renowned helmsmen as Rodney Pattisson, the triple Olympic medallist, Phil Crebbin and Harold Cudmore gave encouragement to a syndicate which had built two new boats and bought two others for training and use as 'trial horse' craft.

Just as important, neither de Savary nor his senior henchmen ever lost sight of the fact that all of the ballyhoo which preceded the actual races of the preliminaries to the Cup series of 1983 actually amounted to anything of great significance; they knew that the only way to regain the America's Cup for Britain was by defeating the United States defender in seaborn action on Rhode Island Sound. No matter how shrill the 'fanfare', it would do no more than earn perhaps a brief psychological advantage if the 12-metre yachts of Britain and America should meet and as they squared up for the start of the first race of the series. No, the de Savary soldiers-of-fortune were well aware that all the preparations were about was to train them to be as near level as possible as the Americans in terms of yachting expertise. It was like the roadwork of the heavyweight boxer who met his rival in head-to-head combat in a ring which offered no shelter and from which there was no escape. Necessary but possibly meaningless if the other chap had carried a killer punch. There would be no hiding for the British either when they took to the ring of the open sea and it would be known in minutes rather than hours who possessed the killer punch.

As usual for an America's Cup series there was uncertainty until the very start of competition almost about actually which boats the British would face; both in terms of other challenge contenders as well as in relation to the American yacht which would come through to defend the trophy. The cup series would not begin until September 13 and neither the challenger nor the defender might be known until around September 6.

It was still a long way to September 1983 when, in early 1981, the New York Yacht Club announced the challengers for the 25th defence of the Cup in 1983; there were four from Australia, two from Britain and one each from Canada, France, Italy and Sweden. Alan Bond, making his fourth Australian challenge through the Royal Perth, was the senior on the list.

It was clear that some of the challengers would turn out to be feeble contenders, but it was equally certain, because of the sheer weight of numbers, that there was a better chance than ever before of one of them proving an exceptional challenger. The Americans may have been confident about their abilities to defend successfully the trophy they had held so securely since 1851, but the New York Yacht Club must have been aware that among those ten contenders could be one with more than usual menace in her hull. The American response however, showed that the challenges would be met in the usual, full-blooded manner. Dennis Conner, the hero of the 1980 defence, was able to raise enough money to build two and then three new boats to campaign in 1983 with *Freedom*, the successful defender of 1980. Two other American syndicates, those with Russell Long and Tom Blackaller as skippers, also planned one new boat each, while Dave Vietor was to campaign with an up-dated *Courageous*, twice a successful defender under the command, first, of Ted Hood and then Ted Turner.

The announcement, in early 1982, that the Independence syndicate of Russell Long had been wound up seemed only to reduce slightly the outstanding odds in favour of a further United States success in the 25th defence. Conner, with a new design from Sparkman & Stephens, *Spirit*, and another from Johan Valentijn, *Magic*, announced that he would begin training in May of 1982 against *Freedom*, and Blackaller, whose new yacht was being designed by Dave Pedrick, was due to begin training against *Courageous* early in the summer of 1982. At the end of that summer, Conner was to put *Magic* up for sale, gut *Spirit* and order a third new boat.

Concerning the overseas efforts, Bond had announced a two-boat campaign with John Bertrand as skipper; the second Australian challenge was organised by Syd Fischer, who was to

build a 12-metre designed by Alan Payne, and the third Australian group, the Melbourne-based *Challenge 12* syndicate, had
been approached by both the other two about joint preparations. The fourth Australian challenge did not materialize. The
Canadian challenge had been entered by Marvin McDill, a
Calgary lawyer, in the name of the Secret Cove Yacht Club,
though acceptance had been delayed because of technical difficulties; involving primarily, the land-based yacht club's ability to host America's Cup matches should their challenge be
successful.

De Savary headed the most promising British challenge, from
the Royal Burnham Yacht Club, while Ernest Juer's, through the
Royal London, was soon to founder. Yves Rousset-Rouard
headed a campaign that by early 1982 had raised half the money
towards a French challenge with a modified *France III*.

Backed by the Aga Khan and a consortium of companies
including Fiat, the Italian effort was to be headed by Cino Ricci
and their first 12-metre due to be launched early in 1982. The
Swedish challenge never looked very promising. Pelle Petterson, unable to finalize support for a boat, was expected however
to design and skipper a glass-fibre yacht. The cash was not
forthcoming and the Swedes faded from the picture completely
before the end of 1982.

For the first time, designers of the yachts for the 1983 challenge had to be nationals of the challenging countries and the
Australian Ben Lexcen, formerly Bob Miller, was again designing the new 12s for Bond. Construction had begun early on of an
aluminium boat and it seemed that the second could be of
glass-fibre. Lexcen had merely modified *Australia* in 1980 but
for 1983 he was reported to have been engaged in a quarter-
million dollar tank-testing programme. Neither could it be
ignored in connection with the Australians that two of the four
America's Cup races won by Australian 12-metres were designed by Alan Payne; though much had changed since Payne's
last effort.

Bruno Trouble, who steered *France III* to the best finish of any
French effort hitherto in the 1980 series, was to be the skipper
for the new French syndicate. His boat for 1983 seemed likely to
have a longer, thinner keel, drawn by Jacques Faroux, who also
designed the boat in which Trouble won the 1981 Quarter-Ton
Cup.

Ed Dubois, the designer of *Victory*, had had only limited experience with 6-metres and, before *Victory*, had never drawn a 12, but his outstanding record in International Offshore Rule boats seemed to make him a considerable threat even with his first design. Ian Howlett, who replaced him as de Savary's first-choice designer for the second British 12-metre built for 1983, had of course designed the 1980 *Lionheart*.

Concerning the Italian effort, Mario Tarabocchia, who had been chief draughtsman at Sparkman & Stephens since the early 1960s and had worked on the design of every America's Cup defender since *Constellation* in 1964, left the New York company in October of 1981 to design the Italian 12-metre. He was to tank test three small models of different displacements and then do another programme of testing with ⅓rd scale models. In the event Tarabocchia was replaced by Valachelli. The Canadian design work was to be in the hands of Bruce Kirby, designer of the Laser dinghy and a number of other quick boats of up to 40ft long.

Interestingly, Lexcen, Payne and Petterson were each involved in at least their third design effort. Interestingly also, all but one of the 12-metres to have defended the America's Cup were designed by Olin Stephens, who, although in semi-retirement, still worked in an advisory capacity on the *Spirit* project. Valentijn, Dutch born but who became an American national on June 1 1981 and who was co-designer with Lexcen of *Australia*, but designer alone of *France III*, said that the gains in 1980 were mostly made in the field of sails, and he hoped that he could still show in his third 12-metre that there was room for speed gain in hulls. The rejection of *Magic* from the Conner camp so early in 1982 suggested that Valentijn did not achieve his aim.

When the elimination system which would weed out the challenger proper for the America's Cup series was decided it was to provide at least 42 warm-up races for each of the seven competing yachts.

The elimination trials were to begin on June 18 and the system devised meant that the 12-metre which came through the various trials to meet the United States defender of the America's Cup in the challenge series proper would have competed in a minimum of 55 races. It was decided that the first of the trials should be a round-robin event run from June 18–28 and with each yacht having 12 races over half-size, about 12-mile, America's Cup-type courses. A win would count as one point, a defeat nothing, the same scoring system operating throughout. It was decided that the yachts would carry forward 20 per cent of the victory points into a second round-robin series, which would be held between July 4–15, again with there being 12 races per boat, six over half-size courses and six over full, 25-mile America's Cup courses.

Yachts would now carry forward into a third round-robin series 40 per cent of their winning points from the second series which, with the 20 per cent winning points from the first series would be added together after the final round-robin contest between July 22 and August 6 and involving 18 races per boat with 12 half-size and six full-size courses. All points from this series, plus the percentage from the earlier two rounds, would decide the four top yachts for the semi-final rounds to begin in August.

The semi-finals in August would again be a round-robin event involving three series each of nine races over full courses with the top two yachts going through to the final round, and the final between August 28 and September 9 would be under the same full course conditions as the Cup series proper with the winner being decided over a best-of-seven race event. If all seven races were sailed the winning yacht would have competed in a maximum of 58 races.

The main objective of this system, with some flexibility and built-in safeguards for ties or bad weather, was to give the winning yacht the same sort of intense competition as that faced by the yacht chosen by the United States to defend the Cup.

The first American trials were to be held between June 18–25, with observation races July 16–27 and the final trials from August 16 until the New York Yacht Club named the defending yacht.

The system devised by the challengers certainly seemed to have merit in so far as it was hoped to provide the eventual challenger with very good competition up to the beginning of the series proper. It was however, somewhat contrived, essentially to keep interest in the elimination series for heavily sponsored yachts from some countries which were not expected to offer much of a threat to more established nations.

The obvious weakness was that the defending nations might

have chosen a far more comprehensive arrangement than either the weather, the fitness of crews or boats would allow – with a possible chance of damage to boats or inclement weather delaying trials and forcing alterations to plans so as to bring serious discord and disharmony among more tested crews.

As the Cup year began, with the new Dennis Conner yacht still to be launched and with the new British 12-metre at an early stage of construction, there was still much that was uncertain about the Cup series. It seemed that two further challengers could be withdrawn, and all that was certain at the start of 1983 was that there had been more pre-America's Cup blarney perhaps than ever in the long history of the trophy. While it would be necessary to wait until September to learn the suspected outcome, there stayed on record the past story of America's Cup.

II

The Oldest and Costliest in Sport

The first four Shamrocks all failed – some less completely than others. But in each one of them my fond hopes were centred. With them I made four attempts to 'lift that auld mug' – surely the most elusive piece of metal in all the world so far as I am concerned – but I can truthfully say that in the quest of it I have spent some of the happiest hours of my life. Neither money, nor time, nor trouble – aye, nor disappointment – have marred my joy in the pursuit of it.

– Sir Thomas Lipton Bt, Leaves from Lipton's Logs, *1925*

It all began with the schooner *America*, a most remarkable yacht even in her own time and which was launched only on May 3 1851. She was purchased outright by a syndicate headed by John C. Stevens and consisting of his brother and four other members of the New York Yacht Club. Her dimensions were 101ft 9in long, 90ft 3in on the water-line with a beam of 22ft 6in and she cost just $20,000. After the Cup race of 1851 she was sold in England and cruised and raced occasionally before she returned to the United States during the Civil War to become a blockade runner. She later became the property of the United States Naval Academy and joined in the 1870 America's Cup match. At one time she was refurbished but by the 1940s was in a poor state of repair and was destroyed in 1945 when the roof of a shed in which she had been stored at Annapolis collapsed.

The first race for the 100 Guinea Cup started at 10 am on August 22 1851; there was a fleet of 17 British yachts, varying in size from the *Aurora*, of 47 tons, to *Brilliant*, a 392-ton three-masted schooner. The race was eastward, out to the Nab Light-ship, then to St Catherine's Point and back to the Solent via the Needles. The *America* was first to finish in 10 hours 37 minutes followed by *Aurora* in 10 hours 55 minutes.

The Cup first became an international challenge trophy in 1857 when the surviving members of the American syndicate gave the Cup, which they had won outright, to the New York Yacht Club, stipulating that it should be available for any yacht club to challenge with a yacht of between 30 and 300 tons. The first challenge was by James Ashbury, owner of the schooner *Canbria*, a 108ft two-masted yacht which arrived at New York in 1870. The race was in New York Bay and started with the yachts at anchor in the contemporary manner. Fourteen yachts defended in a single race with *Cambria* finishing 10th, 27 minutes 3 seconds after the winner, the schooner *Magic*, while *America* was fourth.

The second challenge involved *Livonia*, a 127ft schooner, again owned by James Ashbury, which sailed against only one defender, although there were four yachts available to the New York Club. Depending on the weather of the day the New York Yacht Club selected the most suitable defender. Raced in 1871, it was one of the few times that no defender was built. *Livonia* defeated one of the defenders, *Columbia*, in the third race and this was the first race ever won by a challenger and the last until 1920.

It was in 1871 that the first sustained ill-feeling between a challenger and the New York Yacht Club occurred. It was the only time that a challenger claimed to have won the series. Ashbury said that he had protested in the second race and this should have been allowed, therefore he had won two races. The New York Yacht Club ignored his point, but Ashbury subsequently sailed over the course and on a further day sailed over the line so he judged he had won four races and the Cup, but the bad feeling which resulted was one of the reasons why there was no further British challenge for 14 years.

In the intervening years, before Sir Richard Sutton with the 96ft cutter *Genesta* made the most sportsmanlike gesture in a Cup series for Britain, there had been challenges by two Canadians, in 1876 and 1881. In the second race, the first having been postponed because of lack of wind, *Puritan*, the defender, on port tack collided with Sir Richard's *Genesta* and should have been disqualified, giving the race to the challenger. The committee said so also but Sir Richard retired as well saying: 'We are very much obliged but we don't want it that way. We came over for a race not a sailover.' *Puritan* went on to win the two necessary races but by the closest of margins so far. For this series and all future ones until 1956 the challenging yacht was obliged to sail to the location of the races off New York 'on her own bottom'.

The worst of any bitterness and bad sportmanship to arise in the America's Cup was in the second of the two challenges by the Earl of Dunraven. The dispute which began with the Cup series of 1895 continued up to the point where Lord Dunraven, accompanied by his barrister, appeared at a special enquiry at the New York Yacht Club, the club committee being enlarged by the famous Captain A. T. Mahan, US Navy and H. J. Phelps, a former United States Minister to Britain. Lord Dunraven's charges were quite unproven and as he also failed to apologize, he was expelled from the New York Yacht Club of which he had been an honorary member.

The problem arose when his *Valkyrie III*, 129ft long with a sail area of 13,028 sq ft, met *Defender*, slightly smaller but which was allowed 29 seconds allowance over the course. After the first race and a defeat by 8 minutes 49 seconds, Dunraven accused the defending yacht of having had ballast put aboard after measurement. He also complained about wash from spectator boats. Both competitors were, as a result, remeasured, found to be in order and the second race was sailed.

A few seconds before the starting gun a spectator craft cut between the two competing yachts, escaping herself, but causing a collision between the two yachts. *Defender's* rigging was partly damaged by *Valkyrie* but she finished the race, although losing to the challenger.

However, *Defender's* subsequent protest was upheld and Dunraven's boat was disqualified. Two days later the third race began. Both boats crossed the starting line but *Valkyrie* turned away, hauled down her flag and returned to her anchorage. It was the end of the series, but not of the arguments.

Back in England, Dunraven wrote a letter to *The Field* in which he raised again the whole question of ballast being altered to cheat the measurement. The results of the protest case also reverberated with Dunraven making it clear that the committee had arrived at the wrong decision. The conclusion was the Earl's return to New York in December 1895 to appear before the New York Yacht Club enquiry.

The most persistent of all challengers was Sir Thomas Lipton, who restored the good feeling between British and American yachtsmen that had been tarnished by Lord Dunraven and he purposely made the Cup even more of an event that was publicized in the Press of the world. The first Lipton challenge in 1899 was by *Shamrock*, towed across the Atlantic by his steam yacht *Erin*, the first time that a challenger had been brought over in this way. It became the standard method until, in 1956, the challenger could be shipped.

The second Lipton challenge, with *Shamrock II* in 1901, was significant in that at 137ft she was the longest ever challenger, but once again lost in three straight matches to *Columbia*, the only defender to race twice under the same skipper, Charlie Barr, and in unaltered form.

But the largest and most extreme yacht ever to sail in an America's Cup match, indeed in any yacht race, was *Reliance*, the defender of the 1903 series. It was no coincidence that this was the last match before the First World War when huge, nearly untaxed fortunes, could be amassed in America and in Britain. *Reliance* was 142ft 8ins long with a water-line length of 89ft 8ins, beam of 25ft 8ins and a 20ft draft. She was built in bronze with a lead keel and the biggest sail area, at 16,160 sq ft, ever put up on a single-masted yacht.

The only Englishman ever really to threaten American dominance in the design field, in those early days, was Charles E. Nicholson, who designed Lipton's fourth challenger, *Shamrock IV*, the most successful of the *Shamrocks*. The fourth, at 110ft long, was bigger than *Resolute*, the defender she met in 1920, when three American boats were built. War broke out when *Shamrock* was on her way across the Atlantic in August 1914 and she was laid up in New York until six years later – the last time, incidentally, when the races were held off the outer course of New York harbour, near Sandy Hook. They were the last to be held using time allowance but the first to have as many as five races to decide the winner. It was the first time also that both boats had amateur skippers, another sign of the changing mode of yacht racing. The American was Charles Francis Adams, the Englishman was William Burton. The first two races were won by *Shamrock IV* and this was not only the first win by a challenger since 1871 but the first time that a British yacht had won two races in succession, let alone at the beginning of a series. *Resolute* won the next three races, by 7 minutes 1 second

– the elapsed time was an exact tie, the only dead heat in Cup history – 9 minutes 58 seconds and 19 minutes 45 seconds.

The first America's Cup series to be held on the present course, off Newport, Rhode Island, was in 1930 after a gap of 10 years when Lipton, by now an old man of 80, challenged again. He was loathe to leave New York and the publicity it afforded but the commercial traffic made it essential to seek better racing waters. The yachts were now to the Universal Rule's J class of 76ft rating, and from now on the boats raced level, with no time allowances. No less than four potential defenders, *Enterprise*, *Weetamoli*, *Yankee* and *Whirlwind* were built for the honour of competing with *Shamrock V*; the old, to be repeated, story of a single challenger against a competitively selected defender.

The winner was *Enterprise* which won four straight races and it is interesting that she was skippered by Harold 'Mike' Vanderbilt, the only man to skipper and steer three different and successive cup defenders and one of the greatest yachtsmen of all time. *Enterprise*, which had been designed by W. Starling Burgess, had many new features, including a light alloy mast and a 'Park Avenue' boom, with a wide section on which a huge mainsail took up its required shape. *Shamrock V* was another design by Charles E. Nicholson and skippered by Ernest Hird. She was beaten in four straight matches, one in which she retired when her main halyard parted. It was one of those occasions to be repeated in 1937 and 1967 when American technology in sailing leapt ahead and quite outclassed the challenger. It was, indeed, the most decisive defeat of Sir Thomas Lipton. At the end he said, 'I will not challenge again, I canna win.' The famous remark was typical of the sometime thoughts of every challenger.

The challenge that came closest to winning the America's Cup was that of the flying ace and later millionaire aircraft builder T. O. M. Sopwith. In 1934 his J class yacht *Endeavour*, designed by Charles E. Nicholson, was faster than *Rainbow*, the defender, and won the first two races and lost the last by less than a minute. Sopwith failed to sustain his early success because he was outwitted by the American helmsman and had an inferior crew. This latter problem was owing to a strike for higher pay by his professional crew before leaving England. As a result he had his Captain Williams, nine faithful professionals and a balance of amateurs. *Endeavour* carried the first quadrilateral jib, though this was spotted in trials and copied by the Americans. By this time also spinnakers had become symmetrical instead of the earlier triangular sort, sheeted to windward on the forestay.

The circumstances of this cliff hanger of a challenge were that *Endeavour* won the first race by over two minutes and the second by 51 seconds. In the third race she was leading by more than six minutes at the leeward mark but the wind went light, which British yachtsmen traditionally dislike. At this time Vanderbilt, *Rainbow's* skipper, turned her wheel over to Sherman Hoyt who, by clever tactics among which Sopwith ran to the light airs, won the third race.

What happened on the evening of that race demonstrated the sort of action the defenders were prepared to take if they thought there was a chance of losing. In spite of the ancient rivalry between New York and Boston, Frank C. Paine, owner of the Boston boat *Yankee*, was asked to join *Rainbow*. He did so with his own J class spinnaker, the finest in America. The ballasting of *Rainbow* was altered, so they changed both the men and the ship.

The most famous of all protest races, however, was the feature of the fourth race of the 1934 America's Cup. On a reaching leg *Endeavour* luffed *Rainbow*. *Rainbow*, with Vanderbilt at the helm, kept going and Sopwith bore away to avoid the serious collision that would result between the J boats. *Rainbow* kept ahead for the rest of the race and *Endeavour* crossed the line 1 minute 15 seconds later with a protest flag in the rigging. The next day the New York Yacht Club committee rejected the protest that *Rainbow* had failed to respond to the luff on the grounds that the protest flag had not been hoisted immediately after the incident. There was anger then and for a long time after. The third of the immortal quotes of the cup race was coined – all three concerned defeat – 'Britannia rules the waves, but America waives the rules'.

Rainbow won the next two races (in one of them brilliant spinnaker tactics by Paine was largely responsible) and in the final one *Endeavour* lost by 55 seconds. The hands of many of the amateur crew of the challenger were in bad shape by this time, which limited Sopwith in his choice of quick tacking and similar tactics, though their observed performance was professional in handling and said to be no worse than *Shamrock V's*.

The greatest chance that the Cup ever had of returning to the Royal Yacht Squadron, under whose flag Sopwith had challenged, was lost.

The last racing of really big yachts inshore took place in the 1937 series. It was the last of the J class and saw the ultimate yacht of the class, the defender *Ranger*, owned by Mike Vanderbilt against Sopwith's *Endeavour II*. Even in 1937 such yachts were too expensive and no syndicate was found to support *Ranger*, nor were there any other new contenders for the defence. *Rainbow* and *Yankee* took part in the trials, but *Ranger* was vastly superior. She was designed by Starling Burgess but with considerable assistance from the young Olin J. Stephens, who, with his brother Rod, also sailed in the yacht. Charles E. Nicholson had presented *Endeavour*'s lines to Burgess after 1934 and these were put in the tank with other models.

The chosen model among those tested by Burgess under the orders of Vanderbilt is thought to have been one of those to the lines of Stephens. She was 135ft 3 ins long and her mast was 165ft high. The amount of sail worked into the foretriangle was greater than ever for the measured area. The spinnaker was the largest sail ever made at 18,000 sq ft, more than 2/5ths of an acre. The hull was of steel.

During the trials, *Ranger* set a record over the 30-mile course of 2 hours 43 minutes 43 seconds (i.e. 11.1 knots). *Endeavour II* had been designed by Nicholson without the tank but using traditional yacht-design methods. She was faster than *Endeavour* and her professional crew were smarter than the amateurs of 1934. But *Ranger* was altogether faster than her rival and won four straight races, two of the margins being large – 17 minutes and 18½ minutes – she won the other two by 4½ and 3½ minutes. In the third race *Ranger* achieved the all-time record for a yacht on the windward leg; 15 miles to windward in 2 hours 3 minutes and 45 seconds.

There then elapsed the longest blank period for the America's Cup – 1937 until 1958. The reasons are obvious, the social and financial changes brought about by the Second World War.

In 1956, the United States Supreme Court allowed changes to the 1887 Deed of Gift of the Cup to reduce the minimum water-line from 65ft to 45ft and no longer to require that the challenger crossed the Atlantic on her own bottom. This enabled 12-metre class yachts to the international rule to be used for subsequent races. They had already been racing regularly as a class in both America and England before 1939. Apart from being just about half the length of the J class, they had first to be built of wood and could be manned by an amateur crew. There were some rules for accommodation but the yachts came to be designed entirely for inshore racing. By 1970 the accommodation rules had been officially dropped.

Another real chance was thrown away by the British with the first post-war challenge. The 12-metre class created by the International Yacht Racing Union, of which the USA was not a member before 1947, had been sailed far more in England and Europe than in the United States and now also the disadvantage of sailing the Atlantic had been removed. The old, old mistake of building just one challenger was again made. The designer of the first post-war British yacht was David Boyd of Scotland who was not in the business of designing yachts to modern competitive rules but who had designed the winning 6-metre *Lalage* before the war. His new *Sceptre* had a clever innovation of a huge cockpit in the centre of the boat; later the rule was changed to stop the practice. She was built on the Clyde and had trials in the Solent against Owen Aisher's pre-war 12-metre *Evaine*. However, the writing was on the wall when *Sceptre* found she had difficulty in consistently beating *Evaine*. In the United States the starting point was another pre-war 12-metre *Vim* designed by Sparkman & Stephens, where Olin Stephens was in charge of design. Altogether for 1958 there were three new 12s built in America, namely *Columbia, Weatherly* and *Easterner. Vim,* sailed by Emil 'Bus' Mosbacher, started by doing better than the others. But *Columbia* was also a Stephens design sailed by Briggs Cunningham but with Olin and Rod Stephens aboard as they had been on *Ranger*. She won the trials. She went on to beat *Sceptre*, sailed by Graham Mann under the flag of the Royal Yacht Squadron – a syndicate owned her – very soundly. The margins were 7 minutes 44 seconds, 11 minutes 42 seconds, 8 minutes 20 seconds and 6 minutes 52 seconds.

The first challenge for the America's Cup by Australia was in 1962 and it was also the closest series since *Endeavour* in 1934. The Americans did not rate the Australian effort highly in advance and only one new yacht *Nefertiti* was built, to the design of Ted Hood. The new boat with *Columbia, Easterner* and *Weatherly* took part in the trials. *Weatherly*, designed by Philip L. Rhodes and sailed by Bus Mosbacher, was selected as the defender. *Gretel*, the yacht owned by Sir Frank Packer and designed by Alan Payne was, like *Endeavour*, the faster of the boats. She won the second race and lost the others by small margins of 47 seconds, 8 minutes 40 seconds, 26 seconds and 3 minutes 40 seconds. The 26-second margin is the closest ever result in a Cup race where a corrected time was not involved, but Mosbacher saved the Cup by superior helmsmanship tactics and as a result he became the first Jew ever to be elected a member of the New York Yacht Club.

It was after the next British challenge, actually the 16th by Britain, in 1964, when *Sovereign*, owned by Anthony Boyden, was easily beaten by *Constellation*, that the Americans decided that they would not accept the challenge more frequently than every three years. The story is that although the British selection was made for the first time by a challenger in the waters off Newport, Rhode Island, after races between *Kurrewa* and *Sovereign* they were similar hulls and the writing was again on the wall because neither boat had seemed vastly superior to *Sceptre*. Amazingly, all were designed by David Boyd. There were a number of American contenders for the defence at that time and which took part in the 1964 trials. The new boats were *American Eagle* and *Constellation* and they were joined by *Columbia*, *Nefertiti* and *Easterner*. *Constellation*, designed by Sparkman & Stephens and skippered by Bob Bavier, was chosen and beat *Sovereign* with Peter Scott at the helm. The margins in four straight races were 5 minutes 34 seconds, 20 minutes 24 seconds, 6 minutes 33 seconds and 15 minutes 40 seconds. The New York Yacht Club felt its members had built new boats for nothing. Any of the US 12s or even *Vim* could have beaten *Sovereign*. British yachting prestige was at a low ebb.

In 1970 *Intrepid* became the first yacht since *Columbia* in 1899 and 1901 to defend the Cup twice running. However, she was considerably modified by Britton Chance who was not, of course, her original designer. In 1974 she was nearly selected again as the final trials were between her and the eventual defender *Courageous*. However, the trials were so close that she could also have beaten the challenger. At that time she had been modified yet again but by her original designer Olin Stephens. *Courageous*, of course, also was to win twice in 1974 when skippered by Ted Hood and in 1977 when Ted Turner was the skipper. It was in 1970, the first time incidentally that a French challenger went to Newport, that the series eventually won by *Intrepid* was to become notable for the greatest acrimony since Lord Dunraven; the first collision since Sir Richard Sutton and the first protest since 1934. In the first race Jim Hardy, the Australian skipper of *Gretel II*, protested over an alleged infringement before the starting gun but the protest was dismissed by the New York Yacht Club. It was in the third race that the collision occurred, just after the starting gun. Since the boats had touched there had to be protest and flags were flown by both sides. The Australian yacht finished first. The fat was then in the fire because in the resulting hearing the New York Yacht Club committee dismissed the Australian protest on perfectly legal grounds, but this meant the Australian win was taken from them and *Intrepid* won.

Laymen do not always realize that protests are common in yacht racing. It is the way rules are enforced, there being no judge or referee on the course. The resulting publicity, much of it ill informed, was mainly directed at the New York Yacht Club committee. (An Australian Member of Parliament said that their ambassador should be recalled from Washington and the Australian troops withdrawn from serving with the Americans in Vietnam! One result was that in the subsequent races of 1974 there was for the first time an international jury with 'neutral' members.) The third race was won by *Intrepid*, but the fourth race was won by *Gretel II* by 1 minute 2 seconds. This was the first time a challenger had ever won a race after losing a sequence of three. However, the series ended when Bill Ficker, the first Californian and West Coast yachtsman to skipper a defender, beat Hardy by 1 minute 44 seconds.

The most overtly commercial challenge was that by the Australian Alan Bond, a property millionaire from Western Australia and under 40, the youngest owner to challenge before Peter de Savary who was 39 in 1983. Bond challenged under the flag of the Royal Perth Yacht Club but the challenge was meant to enhance the prestige and value of Yanchep Sun City, a huge holiday development. His dream was to hold the next series there. But once again the mistake was made of having a single challenger, *Southern Cross*, and she was designed by a comparatively unknown designer, Bob Miller. She tuned up against

Gretel II but there were no eliminations in the American way and the 1974 challenger was the twenty-second America's Cup series and the fourth Australian one. The challenger lost every race.

When *Courageous* came to be modified for her second tilt at the Cup in 1977, after her victory in 1974, it was found that she was heavier than when she had been weighed previously and it was interesting therefore that when the first international jury came along there was also an international measurement team for the first time, showing at least that the New York Yacht Club were moving over to the general practices of international regattas.

But as other challengers came along the same mistakes and attitudes prevailed. A single challenger against the selected defender after an elimination series; a challenging owner with motives of commerce or fame as well as sport; an owner too of comparative recent entry into the world of yachting against the long-standing traditions of the New York Yacht Club and its members whose fathers and ancestors have upheld the American tradition of speed under sail; the immense resources in sailing men and designers possessed by America also.

III

A New Challenger

Lipton's challenge came as a surprise to everyone. He had never evinced much interest in yachting. He had, it is true as early as 1887, written to William Lynn of Cork, suggesting he would like to try for the cup with a boat designed by an Irishman, built by an Irishman and manned by Irishmen. But he had readily abandoned the suggestion.

Sir Thomas Lipton, it cannot be too often repeated, was a man of automatic reflexes. Looking for fresh worlds to conquer, the America's Cup looked to be as good a bet as any.

Alec Waugh, The Lipton Story, 1949

The story of *Victory* began to unfold, first in Newport on the evening of September 21, 1980; less than a month after the defeat of *Lionheart*, the first British contender for the America's Cup since *Sovereign* in 1964, and while *Freedom* was taking a two-one lead over *Australia* in the 24th challenge series of 1980. It was announced to the world's press in the Armoury, on Lower Thames Street, on the Sunday night that there would be an official announcement the following day concerning a further British challenge for the Cup in 1983. On the Monday it was made clear that the challenging club would be the Royal Burnham Yacht Club, at Burnham-on-Crouch, and that the leading figure behind the challenge was Peter de Savary, who had come on to the international yachting scene only in 1980 when he made contributions in the region of £100,000 towards the *Lionheart* cause.

The suave, balding de Savary, then 36, had been educated at Charterhouse, and had first worked in Canada as a labourer. He came to Newport with a smart, 50-foot, Italian designed motor yacht called *Lisanola*, which gave the British group their most outstanding support vessel during the 1980 campaign. De Savary made clear to the press immediately that he had really no experience of sailing beyond some dinghies while still at school. He also made it very clear that his intention was that the *Victory* challenge would be the most professional ever by a British syndicate. He explained that the challenge would begin with a new Admiral's Cup ocean-racing yacht, to be designed by Ed Dubois. His plan was to get together a nucleus of leading yachtsmen for the Admiral's Cup in order to build upon them the necessary crew and management for the America's Cup campaign, which would be based on the Bahamas, where they would be racing in winter, and on Newport. He made clear that he did not believe it would be possible to win the America's Cup by racing in Britain in the Solent.

Sitting on the Armoury platform with de Savary when he made his announcement were Tim Herring, a former Commodore of the Royal Burnham, Kit Hobday, named as the project director, Ed Dubois and Phil Crebbin, who was nominated as the skipper for the yacht to be built for the Admiral's Cup and which was also to be called *Victory*. Earlier, during an informal press briefing for the British aboard the *Lisanola*, de Savary had explained that the idea for the name of the syndicate had come from Phil Crebbin, an Olympic yachtsman in 1976 who had come up from the ranks of Britain's leading dinghy sailors to prominence in offshore racing on such top Admiral's Cup yachts as *Moonshine* and *Eclipse*. After the casual nature of the press conferences during the 1980 America's Cup series, the announcement of the challenge for 1983 was the more impressive because each member of the British contingent first stood up to introduce himself. It was evident then, and it was to become even more certain, that the Victory campaign would be a very much more business-like affair than that which had faltered in 1980. While the *Lionheart* campaign, backed by the British Industry 1500 Club and such other beneficiaries as Friends of *Lionheart*, had been short of money from the outset, the Victory group insisted that they already had more than $1½ million with which to build at least one new 12-metre and with which to buy a top American 12-metre (in the event they did not obtain one). Naturally, following the somewhat tame efforts by *Lionheart*, there was considerable scepticism about the Royal Burnham challenge when it was first announced. All that was being said by de Savary and his lieutenants had, in effect, been said by Tony Boyden and the committee for the *Lionheart* campaign.

Anyway, it had all been heard before. The British had been definitely set to win back the America's Cup from the United States ever since 1851 when the schooner *America* carried off the trophy for the famous race around the Isle of Wight. All to no avail; why should the Royal Burnham effort be any different, it was thought, even if the superlatives, such as preparations in the Bahamas, a new boat and the taking heed of all the lessons from 1980, were taken into consideration? Surely it would be just another British debacle? But within a very short time, only a matter of six weeks or so, de Savary was sweeping scepticism aside with further bold announcements that he had already purchased *Australia*, for a figure believed to be in the region of about £100,000, and had also acquired *Lionheart*, her bendy mast, sails, her tender *Chaperone* and various equipment.

Furthermore, it was apparent that a great deal of work had been done in signing on important aides for the management of the campaign in terms of marketing and advertising as well as the sailing. Crew management was to be the responsibility of Robin Fuger, for many years the man in charge of the day-to-day running of the Frenchman Baron Bich's 12-metre campaigns and Jim Alabaster, well known in the international world of sails, was to be responsible for the evaluation of sails and the technical side of the challenge. The signing up as a potential helmsman of Harold Cudmore, like Crebbin, a former British match-racing champion, and the announcement that the Olympic stalwarts Rodney Pattisson, Iain Macdonald-Smith and David Howlett were to be associated augered well, as did the news that the Olympic coach Peter Bateman and Lawrie Smith, the skipper of *Lionheart* during the semi-final races of the elimination series in 1980, were also to be involved, and that invitations had gone to various other leading figures in British yachting circles.

In addition, and perhaps even more impressive, was the announcement that attempts were being made to purchase a 300-ft long, 1,800 ton former Greek cruise liner as a 'mother' ship for the Victory syndicate and which would be converted to carry the two 12-metres on her after-deck between Newport and the Bahamas where training was to begin in the autumn of 1981. At the same time it was made clear that plans to buy an American 12 had been shelved because it was decided instead to build two new British yachts, the first of which was to be launched in the autumn of 1981. The mother vessel was to be converted also so that a sail loft, at least 100ft long, was provided below decks in addition to a workshop capable of accommodating at least one of the 12-metre yachts; there was to be a large crane fitted so that the yachts could be launched easily – or lowered to the workshop of the vessel, which would be equipped to accommodate the whole crew and supporters and visiting VIPs. There was also to be a cinema, restaurant, gymnasium and laundry. All most impressive it seemed. De Savary, who made the announcements about the two new boats in a new London club which he was purported to have bought for £2 million, was anxious also to point out that he would not be requiring any public subscription for the campaign, membership of which it was understood could be secured only by the sum of £80,000. What the management group of the new campaign would not discuss at that stage were their plans concerning the actual design team for the new boats, but which it had been explained would include Ian Howlett, the designer of *Lionheart*.

Plans were really beginning to take shape! Formal notification of the Royal Burnham challenge for 1983 had been sent to the New York Yacht Club on October 6; they were the first to get in their plans for the following challenge which it was understood at that time would also probably include challengers from Australia and France. De Savary, who felt that the two months he spent in Newport during the 1980 defence helped him to understand the requirements for a successful campaign for yachting's most coveted trophy, maintained that his own priority was in the setting up of a professional management structure and raising the necessary £2 million or so for a successful challenge. He was soon, however, to take such close interest in the sailing side as to be criticized of meddling.

De Savary, who was quick to emphasize that he was 'English born of English parents in Essex', insisted that only yachtsmen totally dedicated to winning the America's Cup would be suitable for the Victory project. He wanted 6ft 3ins tall athletes of 13–14 stone and aged between 20–30. Although de Savary insisted that he would not interfere in the day-to-day management of the boat, leaving that to experts, he was equally determined to understand the requirements of successful crewmen by taking part himself in the campaign with the Admiral's Cup

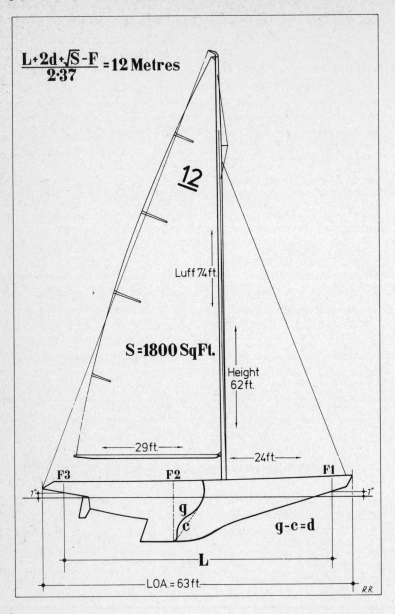

$$\frac{L+2d+\sqrt{S}-F}{2\cdot37} = 12 \text{ Metres}$$

12

Luff 74 ft.

S = 1800 Sq Ft.

Height 62 ft.

29 ft.

24 ft.

F3   F2   F1

7"   7"

g

c

g − c = d

L

LOA. = 63 ft.

R.R.

Fig. 2

Fig. 2 *What is a 12 metre?*

$$\frac{L + 2d + \sqrt{S} - F}{2 \cdot 37} = 12 \text{ metres or } 39 \cdot 36 \text{ feet}$$

The racing yacht known as a 12-metre was created by the International Rule drawn up in 1906 at a conference in London of the yacht racing authorities of eleven countries (the USA was not among them). The rule consisted of a formula whose components when calculated produced a figure of 12 metres. There were also classes of 8 −, 6 − and other sizes. The rule has had major revisions in 1920 and 1933 and numerous minor amendments on maximum/minimum dimensions and restrictions on gear and building methods. Among changes since the adoption of the class for the America's Cup (in December 1956) is the abandonment of any rules for accommodation and the permitting of construction other than in wood. Boats have since 1974 invariably been built of light alloy.

The profile of a typical 1983 12-metre shows likely dimensions and where measurements are taken. L is measured about 7 inches above load waterline and corrections for girth at these stations are applied. To find d, skin girth is measured on the surface of the hull about amidships (G) and chain girth (C dotted) is a length of line stretched from sheerline to a defined level on the keel. A fin type keel gives a bigger d and so, if displacement is reduced, some other dimensions must be decreased to get the rating; perhaps sail area or length. Freeboards are measured at F1, F2, F3 and give a mean freeboard for the formula. The figure 2·37 is a constant factor.

The sail area, S, is mainsail foot times height plus 85 per cent of the foretriangle. There are a number of limitations on the rig such as maximum mast height, minimum mast weight, position of centre of gravity of mast. The height of the forestay is limited to three quarters of mast height.

Thus every 12 is slightly different, as its designer has adjusted length, displacement, freeboard and sail area to give what he believes will be the best performance.

Comparison with other classes of racing yacht.

Type	LOA	Displacement lb.	Sail area sq. ft.	Crew
IOR 'Maxi'	76 ft	54,000	2000	20
12-Metre	**63 ft**	**60,000**	**1800**	**11**
Admiral's Cup minimum	39 ft	15,000	850	9
Half Tonner	29 ft	5,000	500	5
Laser racing dinghy	14 ft	130	140	1

yacht *Victory*. When he first went to Newport in connection with the *Lionheart* campaign, he chose to join the crew of the British 12-metre in their early-morning runs. Indeed, it was the lack of enthusiasm by the British crew for the physical training side of the campaign that led to some of his earlier criticism of the 1980 event. It was certainly clear that the crew and management of the Victory outfit would find their chief a most determined worker. 'I like work, it is my hobby; I seldom work less than a 16 hour day,' said the man who, apart from a few years with a family furniture and construction business in Devon, had spent most of his working life overseas. What was also encouraging as the Victory outfit was set up was that it was clear that de Savary did not anticipate that the campaign would fail because of a shortage of funds. With financial interest in the Middle East and the Bahamas, he was confident about the cash requirements of the project. In 1980 he was chairman of an oil corporation in the Middle East and managing director of a merchant bank, Artoc, based in the Bahamas, where he lived.

If there were any doubts about the Victory effort in those early days it was, perhaps, the apparent unqualified belief in the abilities of the Olympic, match-racing yachtsmen who had been 'signed up'. An understandable qualification that de Savary should be seeking, but there was just a fear at that time that by ignoring the traditional, ocean-racing side of British yachting, there would be the same disenchantment towards the campaign as there was with *Lionheart*. It was clear with the Tony Boyden effort that *Lionheart* and the British Industry 1500 Club had very little widespread support in yachting. It had seemed, in 1980, that for the 1983 campaign to be any more successful, it was essential that the campaign began with support on a much wider basis. But these were very early days and, in truth, there was very little with which to find fault.

Indeed, the Royal Burnham, who returned to the principal backer his cheque for £5,000 to confirm the entry of Victory for 1983 – instead, electing to collect at their club the required sum which was then sent by personal messenger by air to be delivered to the New York Yacht Club – had, from the start, set a very good example to the yachting community as a whole.

Ironically, considering the disastrous *Lionheart* campaign, there was perhaps more widespread goodwill concerning the Victory effort in its very early stage than might have been expected. It seemed that two factors from 1980, though both negative, had given de Savary and his troops more moral support for the 1983 attempt to win the America's Cup than Tony Boyden had enjoyed at his second attempt. The fact that *Lionheart* had been beaten by a French yacht, manned by those most ancient of British sea-faring foes, certainly rankled among British yachtsmen. If there was one defeat that it was essential to avenge as quickly as possible it was that by Bruno Troublé, the skipper of *France III*, and his men in Rhode Island Sound.

More important, it also seemed that it was the depth of the 1980 disaster which led to the yachting community in Britain having more theoretical dedication to a further campaign in 1983. The feeling was that while *Lionheart* may not have been by any means the most impressive or challenging of the contenders of that year, she had appeared to have the capabilities of producing a much more aggressive and rewarding effort than that actually realized in the summer of '80. True, the bendy mast, the sacking at the last minute during the elimination series of skipper John Oakeley and his replacement by Lawrie Smith, were controversial aspects of the campaign which had had a detrimental effect.

Generally, there was a feeling that better management and better preparation would have meant that *Lionheart* would have given a very much more comprehensive account of herself in what is the most seething of all international yachting cauldrons. Certainly the British yacht, launched in 1978 and worked up for the 1980 challenge with races in Sweden against the Swedish 12-metre *Sverige* and the winner of the first 12-metre world championship – a somewhat presumptuous title, it is true – should have been capable at least of a convincing success against the French in Newport.

There was a widespread feeling that 1980 was totally unrepresentative of the best of British yachting and that the sooner a further attempt was made to recover the 'Auld Mug' from the Americans, the better.

Not unnaturally there were some doubts about the suitability for the mammoth task of winning the America's Cup of a man who had no substantial background of yacht racing. It did not seem to be of any great help either, that the challenging club were also to make their international big-boat debut in the most demanding of all major sailing events. In terms of serious offshore competition, match-racing or, more important, the America's Cup, the Royal Burnham were novices, but challenge rules demand that a recognized yacht club is nominated.

There was hope at this early stage that the path would be less tortuous for *Victory* than it had been for *Lionheart* because of the stated intention in Newport in 1980 by the New York Yacht Club of relaxing the rules. The Americans, who had previously set limits on the amount of equipment and sails which could be bought from outside the country of origin of the challengers, had stated that, in future, practically anything from sails to all other yachting equipment that could be bought off the shelf in any country would be available to either the Americans or the challengers. Most important, at the time, seemed to be the possibility of the British being able for the first time to acquire American sailcloth for their challenge. There had been, for many years, wide-ranging arguments about advantages over the British equivalent of American sailcloth and certainly, even if there were no practical advantage in terms of American sail-cloth, there most certainly was a considerable psychological advantage among yachtsmen in their belief in that material.

The New York Yacht Club had pointed out that when the restrictions were removed, and it was expected that this would be confirmed in December 1980, the only requirements for future America's Cup challenges concerning the overseas con-tenders, were that the yachts must be designed by a national of the country of origin of the boat, which would also have to be wholly built in the country of origin, and that the crew and skipper must be made up entirely of nationals of the challenging country.

Of course all of these considerations were still very much in the melting pot when the early planning began for the Victory challenge. Also under consideration at that time was the legal-ity or otherwise of such equipment as the bendy mast of *Lionheart* and that copied by the Australians for their 1980 challenge. The International Yacht Racing Union had consid-ered whether to outlaw such bendy spars after 1980 and at their meeting in London in November of that year, they decided that certainly such masts would be prohibited in future on any yachts other than *Lionheart* and *Australia*. Of course, there was considerable argument as to whether the bendy mast idea really had very much merit. Certainly it had allowed bigger unmeasured sail area than before 1980, but with a decision by the IYRU that they would outlaw unmeasured sail area for future challenges by introducing various girth measurements of the sail, this loophole had been closed.

The Americans, anyway, had got over the sail advantages allowed by the bendy mast by deciding to develop mainsails with fuller roaches. This, of course, would also come under careful scrutiny with the intended new sail measurements. The American argument in 1980 against allowing further development of the bendy masts, was that if there was not a restriction on such a development, the results would be that the cost of mast development would almost certainly exceed that of the cost of a 12-metre yacht. The argument was that Americans would have no difficulty in making their own bendy masts, but that if such a trend were allowed, the Americans would take full advantage of space technology to produce the most superlative bendy masts and at superlative cost.

There were also to be examinations of the sort of materials which would be allowed in the production of masts, with the implicit suggestion that future 12-metre masts would be made entirely of aluminium.

The arguments for these amendments to the 12-metre rule, which were clearly aimed at limiting future changes to the rig, had come from the United States Yacht Racing Union, and it was the New York Yacht Club who initiated this restriction.

Even during the preliminary races of 1980, there was a suspicion that it was in fact the Americans rather than the French who had suggested and worked out the protest that was made by the French against *Lionheart*'s bendy mast. The document, which had gone to 30 pages, was, it was maintained, the work of the members of the America's Cup committee of the New York Yacht Club, who were not so much alarmed at the potential of the *Lionheart* mast, but were in fact working up the matter for a limit on the use of bendy spars at the IYRU meeting in 1980.

The reason for all this was abundantly clear in 1980. Anyone who thought that there were Americans who were not concerned about the loss of the America's Cup came in for a very rude awakening in Newport that year. On the contrary, the Americans would do everything in their power to hang on to the trophy which, it was reliably estimated, was worth at least $56 million to Newport alone in any one Cup year. No, the Americans would not easily relinquish a trophy of which they thought so highly. It is without any doubt whatsoever the most important of all yachting events in the world bar none in their estimation. Many Americans make light of the America's Cup and might even give the impression that defeat in the future would stimulate the races. But in truth, they would be very unhappy indeed if a challenger ever succeeded.

This then was the background to the events which led to the early announcement of the Victory syndicate and the plans laid out by de Savary leading up to the spring of 1981. It was going to be a long, tough road, but one which he hoped he would be able to negotiate with some assurance; provided the various bumps and pot-holes which had been encountered by his predecessors were flattened or filled in with the help of a top-flight management team and a crack crew based on the Admiral's Cup campaign which was to take place in 1981.

IV

Lionheart's Campaign

The syndicate challenged and named Sceptre *as the challenger.
She was therefore anointed and did not have to prove her metal
by going through the fire of competition. Though Owen Aisher
gladly loaned and raced his 12-metre* Evaine *against her, there
was never any possibility of* Evaine *being selected and neither
was she in competition with* Sceptre. *All her owner and crew
were trying to do was to improve* Sceptre's *chances of winning
the Cup.*

*Meanwhile in American waters, through the summer of
1958, there was the old redoubtable 12-metre* Vim, *champion
before the war on both sides of the Atlantic, together with
Westerly, Easterner and Columbia, the three new twelves,
fighting a series of match races in order to select the best to
defend the Cup. Each one was having to fight for that honour
and privilege.*

Uffa Fox, The America's Cup, *1958*

To consider seriously the attempts of Peter de Savary and his
Victory syndicate together with the Royal Burnham Yacht
Club, it is essential first to look at the *Lionheart* attempt of
1980.

The *Lionheart* challenge was officially announced on June 1,
1978, when it was explained that a syndicate was to be formed to
raise £1½ million from British industry. The syndicate, with a
target of 1500 members each contributing 1000 guineas, was to
be known as the British Industry 1500 Club and to be headed by
Sir John Methven the Director General of the Confederation of
British Industries. While Sir John, who was to die shortly before
the Cup attempt in 1980, was really a figure head, the principal
backer was Tony Boyden, a Dorset industrialist, who indicated
that there would be a British challenge for the America's Cup in
1980 even if the £1½ million was not forthcoming. Boyden said

he would himself underwrite the cost of building the first 12-metre to be launched in Britain for more than 15 years, and indicated that he was hopeful that the 1980 challenge would be based on two new boats – a trial-horse 12-metre to be bought from the United States and that the British campaign would involve about 60 yachtsmen and other experts. The intention of the syndicate was to follow a strenuous programme of preparation in Britain, followed by 100 days of tuning in the Cup waters off Newport, Rhode Island. The decision to select the boat and crew during this period in the United States seemed to underline a determined approach by the new syndicate.

It was encouraging that the syndicate intended to select crewmen from the best yachtsmen in Britain and to leave until the summer of 1980 the final nomination of the helmsman who would steer the chosen yacht. John Oakeley, unquestionably one of the most experienced and capable skippers in Britain, could be replaced, pointed out Boyden; another plus for the syndicate, it seemed. All seemed to be set fair for the best and most professional of all 12-metre challenges from Britain, especially since syndicate officials made it clear that they had already got a list of 40 leading yachtsmen from which to draw their crews.

In fact, it was the five other challenges, two each from Australia and France, and one from Sweden, which seemed to be the principal obstacle on the horizon of the new challenge by *Lionheart*, a name chosen from a competition by the *Daily Express* at the 1978 London Boat Show.

Sadly, those early ambitious sentiments were soon to turn to less optimistic predictions. It was very soon clear that far from choosing from the best of British yachtsmen, the crew would be selected from a far less comprehensive group, many with little or no experience of big-boat racing and that there were to be very few invitations actually sent out to top helmsmen with any match-racing experience. True, the Olympic campaign for 1980 and an Admiral's Cup contest in 1979 did limit the choice of Boyden and his first lieutenant Oakeley, but there were suspicions, for reasons which the chief backer and the nominated skipper would not reveal, that very few approaches of a serious nature were made to the experienced and talented yachtsmen who were available in Britain.

Worse, almost from the beginning in that June of 1978, it

seemed probable that *Lionheart* was going to be very far short of the finance required and that certainly there was little hope that the target of £1½ million would be reached. In the event, it was estimated that perhaps as few as 150 companies actually contributed the 1,000 guinea entry fee set by the syndicate.

In the end, *Lionheart* got to Newport only because of a late, determined attempt by a group who was known as the Friends of *Lionheart* – who undertook all sorts of fund-raising activities including a 'road show', the sale of tee shirts and toy lions and, perhaps even more important, the injection of something in the region of £100,000 by Peter de Savary. It later became clear that it was probably this injection of £100,000 that allowed de Savary to buy *Lionheart* for a similar sum soon after the Victory challenge had been announced.

The main problem in those early days of the *Lionheart* contest was the question of the credentials of her designer Ian Howlett. At the time of the *Lionheart* announcement, he had minimal practical experience, the only yacht afloat designed entirely by him being *Kurrewa*, a six-metre modified from a half-size 12-metre which curiously was entered for the Round Britain Race of that year. She did well and again in 1982 – certainly a rugged task for which she was never designed. *Kurrewa* had been built a few years previously for the late John Livingstone, an Australian who had lived for several years in Britain and who entered challenges for the America's Cup on behalf of Britain in both 1974 and 1977. In neither case was a 12-metre built, principally because of lack of financial support, though in both cases Howlett, 29 in 1978, was selected as the designer.

It was because of his research into the design of 12-metre yachts while at Southampton University, and then as a member of the Wolfson Marine Craft Unit, also in Southampton, that Howlett was chosen as Livingstone's designer.

For the same reasons, plus the additional research carried out for Livingstone, Howlett was chosen as designer by the new British 12-metre syndicate. Howlett had said that the two 12-metres he was to design for the new syndicate were likely to differ significantly from those he worked on for Livingstone, so the six-metre *Kurrewa* – which it was understood at the time had never been raced competitively – would not necessarily reflect the designer's latest thinking.

Howlett had also been involved in the design of two Half Ton

Cup yachts, *Gaffer* and *Priority*, that were to make their debuts that year. *Gaffer*, said to be a modification of *Priority*, was actually attributed to the Titchfield, Southampton design firm of Miller and Whitworth, which included John Oakeley and at that time, Howlett. *Gaffer* had probably a unique arrangement of a gaff type mainsail on an essentially Bermudian rig, but she and *Priority* both failed to be chosen for the Half Ton Cup as British representatives. It seemed, when Howlett was chosen, that the practical experience with ocean-racing yachts would have led to the choice of either Ron Holland, the New Zealand-born designer who lived in Ireland, or someone with more experience of bigger boats.

In the event, when *Lionheart* was launched there was a lot of praise for her, not least that she was the best 12-metre ever built of aluminium in the world. The builders were the Joyce Brothers of Southampton. It soon became clear however that though not radical in any real way at that stage – before the advent of her bendy mast – *Lionheart* probably was somewhat heavier than other 12-metres of her generation. But, despite concern about the lack of obvious intentions to choose the best available crew and helmsman and the nagging doubts over the ability of the British Industry Club to raise the necessary finance for a truly worthwhile challenge, there was some hope that *Lionheart* could be a good competitive 12 and that with luck Britain could fare reasonably well in the 1980 Cup series. There were some critics however who gave very little credence to the belief among the British Industry 1500 Club at that time that they really would win the America's Cup.

In fact, Ron Holland, it was explained in October 1978, had been asked to design a new 12-metre for the British Industry syndicate. Boyden said also at the time that Harold Cudmore, the then holder of the British match-racing championship, had also been appointed one of the helmsmen. It was understood that Holland was to design a second boat with Ian Howlett and that when the creations of both had been tank and tunnel-tested the best design would be built, if the syndicate could raise the necessary money. But all along, Boyden insisted that he still believed Howlett would come to be recognized as the genius of 12-metre design. Boyden said that the enlistment of Holland had been arranged because of implied criticism about the choice of Howlett, relatively unknown as a yacht designer. At that stage also Howlett said that the boat he was designing would not be recognized as revolutionary above the water line, though in attempting to produce a windward machine, there would be innovations below the water line. In effect that was the end of the plus side to the British Industry 1500 Club.

Ron Holland never did design a 12-metre for them, neither did Harold Cudmore actually ever sign on as a helmsman. Indeed a chance that the syndicate had to purchase or charter *Independence*, one of the America's Cup trialists in 1977, was dropped by November 1978. 'The price was too high and we are now working on alternatives,' Boyden said at the time. It was explained that *Independence* could have been chartered for a year for £50,000. 'It is a massive sum to pay in charter fees for just a year,' said Boyden. 'Much more money is needed before the syndicate could afford that sort of charter fee. But we are determined to get a trial-horse and I am certain that we shall,' he added. In fact they never really did get what could be called a trial-horse.

Later in the campaign, when *Lionheart* appeared at the 1970 12-metre world championship at Brighton, her trial-horse partner was *Constellation*, the yacht which had beaten Boyden's *Sovereign* in 1964. However *Constellation*, though a challenging yacht in her day, was something of a lost cause by 1980. It was explained by people who sailed in her at Brighton that they dare not really try to race very hard because every time they did something broke and there was just not the money to put it right. At that stage also another yacht which came along to help the British cause was *Columbia*. Again, there never was the sort of money available to make this yacht a real match for *Lionheart*, which by now was being hailed as a conquering yacht. Critics, however, were doubtful that either her success at Brighton, or earlier victories against the Swedish yacht, *Sverige,* in Marstrand, Sweden actually indicated anything of great importance.

All that seemed to be proved was that *Lionheart* had better equipment and was actually being better sailed than the yachts she was meeting on her way to Newport. It really did not prove that she was likely to be a match for the yachts that she met in Newport. Worse still, the backers of the *Lionheart* campaign appeared to have become completely myopic and unable to see that what they were doing was actually failing to prove what

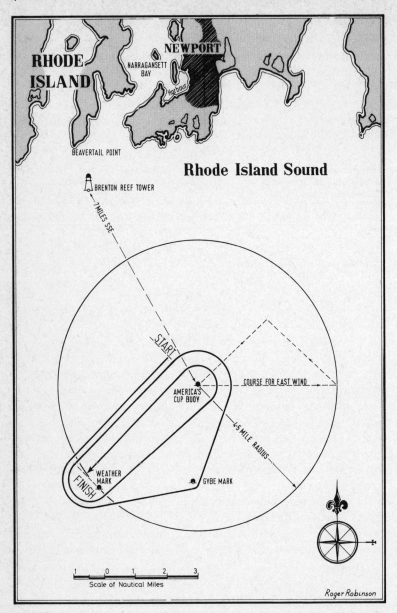

Fig. 3

Fig. 3 *The America's Cup course*

The America's Cup buoy is 7 miles south-south-east of Brenton Reef Tower and some 11 miles from Newport. The races are in the ocean away from the shore and use Olympic style courses. An Olympic course comprises a leg dead to windward (in this case of 4·5 nautical miles) starting from the America's Cup buoy, then a reach on port gybe to the gybe mark, a reach on starboard gybe to the America's Cup buoy, another windward leg, a leg down wind direct to the America's Cup buoy and a final windward leg. Total theoretical distance is 24·3 miles. Patrolling vessels organized by the U.S. Coast Guard keep spectator boats outside the course area.

This chart shows the wind in the south-west where it often is, but the weather mark is laid on the 4·5 mile radius depending on the wind direction on the day of the race.

they claimed to be proving. In some ways it even seemed that the races in Marstrand against *Sverige* and the championship races at Brighton were working contrary to the best interests of *Lionheart* for the very reason that by this stage all the *Lionheart* group were interested in was raising money. They were not learning from the races they were having.

When it was proposed, in early January 1979, that *Lionheart* should be launched by Prince Charles at Hamble on February 28, it was clear that the Americans would be able to choose for the 1980 defence series from a minimum of four 12-metres: *Courageous*, the successful defender of the trophy in 1974 and 1977; *Independence* and *Enterprise*, new yachts in 1977, and a Sparkman and Stephens-designed 12-metre which was to be built especially for the 1980 defence. With the clear fact that there would be only one British 12-metre, chances against either of the four 12-metres in America she might meet looked anything but good.

For a time there was a proposed link with the Swedes, including racing in Swedish waters as well as in Britain. This was to alleviate the lack of competition. *Lionheart* was in the end launched by Lady Methven on April 16, her initial crew was named the same day, and in a matter of a week she had her first outing.

The *Lionheart* campaign seemed to be on the up-and-up when on June 11 1979, she came to her first major test as a contender for the America's Cup challenge with a convincing victory over *Sverige* in the first of the special match-racing contests off Marstrand. Although outmanoeuvred at the start, John Oakeley and his young crew battled back in a 6–7 knot south-westerly to finish 2 minutes 5 seconds ahead of the Swedish yacht. It was a fine start. Though, in a fresher breeze, the Swedes won the second, shorter race of that day by a similar margin, the set-back did not detract, it seemed, from the significance of the earlier triumph.

Oakeley came from behind to win; the crew were equal to their more experienced rivals and *Lionheart* performed as well as could be expected on her first competitive foray since she was launched seven weeks previously. Oakeley admitted after the first day's racing that he had been inhibited at the start, being more concerned for the safety of his craft at the beginning of the series that was to continue over about a further week. Tony

Fig. 4 *British challenges since 1930*

1930 marks the America's Cup arrival in the modern era, as before then yachts were measured and time allowances applied on the difference in ratings. The races of 1930, 1934 and 1937 were held in J-class yachts which measured 76 ft to the Universal rule: these were the only three series ever to be sailed in Js. From 1958, 12-metre yachts were used. There were ten British challenges between 1870 and 1920, and there have been seven between 1930 and 1983.

Year	British Yacht	Owner	Club	Trial-horses	Result
1930	*Shamrock V*	Sir Thomas Lipton Bt.	Royal Ulster Y.C.	—	Lost 0–4 to Enterprise
1934	*Endeavour*	T. O. M. Sopwith	R. Yacht Squadron	Shamrock V, Astra, Velsheda	Lost 2–4 to Rainbow
1937	*Endeavour II*	T. O. M. Sopwith	R. Yacht Squadron	Endeavour	Lost 0–4 to Ranger
1958	*Sceptre*	Hugh Goodson & Syndicate	R. Yacht Squadron	Evaine	Lost 0–4 to Columbia
1964	*Sovereign*	Anthony Boyden	R. Thames Y.C.	Sceptre	Lost 0–4 to Constellation
1980	*Lionheart*	Anthony Boyden and 1500 club	R. Southern Y.C.	Constellation	Lost 1–4 to France in eliminations
1983	*Victory '83*	Peter de Savary	R. Burnham Y.C.	Australia Lionheart Victory	—

Boyden, who was in Marstrand for the races, also seemed well pleased with the events – a unique exercise by two countries preparing for the America's Cup.

As the series continued, *Lionheart* gradually got a winning edge which, with *Sverige* considerably modified since her elimination from the America's Cup of the previous defence series, seemed to be a good omen. It had been thought that *Sverige* had been capable of a better performance than she had shown in Newport in 1977 and was a fast boat. A *Lionheart* success, therefore, was something of a bonus. Certainly it showed that *Lionheart* was not a dog.

What was worrying, however, was that claims that there would be new suits of sails, that additional helmsmen would be added to the afterguard and that the plan was to purchase a second new mast did not seem to materialize as they should have. The new bendy mast, in fact, did not appear until *Lionheart* actually got to Newport in 1980 and far too late really to be properly tested in time for the elimination races which preceded the Cup event, and which were so important to the British crew.

Certainly the 12-metre world championship at Brighton was very much a minor exercise for almost all concerned, not least Southern Television, who at the time of the event they were sponsoring for a reported £100,000, were actually prevented from screening any of the activity because of a typically British ITV strike of many weeks. *Lionheart* won the series, but the only really significant part of her campaign was that in the two races in which she met *Sverige*, the Swedish yacht was dismasted and in a third race *Lionheart* and the Swedish yacht were in collision and ultimately the Swedish yacht was disqualified.

In the one race when *Lionheart* seemed in danger of losing to *Sverige*, the last of the series, the Swedes were prevented from an almost certain success when their mast went over the side near the finish. Shortly after the Brighton event Oakeley questioned the wisdom of persevering with the challenge unless there was much better financial backing. 'We need at least £500,000,' he said and maintained that *Lionheart* could win the America's Cup but that it was essential to have the extra money to do the job properly and that unless it was forthcoming there was no point in going to Newport. These were prophetic words and ones which perhaps should have been heeded at the time.

Certainly the amount of money of which Oakeley spoke was never raised and the outcome of *Lionheart*'s entry into the Newport arena is well known.

The only other notable happening in the preparations for Newport was first the appointment of Barrie Perry as reserve helmsman and then his resignation following a dismal showing in the Lymington match-race series of 1980. Perry won only one race in the series and his resignation was followed fairly shortly with the announcement that he was to be replaced by Lawrie Smith; another surprise, since Smith was not known as a match-race expert. While details were coming through from America that a rebuilt *Independence* had been named *Clipper* with sponsorship from Pan Am and Bacardi, *Lionheart*'s first outing with her bendy mast resulted in a broken spar. However, *Lionheart* duly set out for the United States and much goodwill went with her.

The yacht was actually loaded for shipment to the United States on June 12 1980. However, if there was drama and intrigue on the way to Newport, it was as nothing compared to the bombshells and controversy which were to be created by *Lionheart* when she got to Newport and began tuning up before the elimination series. The number of contenders had come down to four: *Sverige* for Sweden, *Australia*, *France* and *Lionheart* – the second potential challenger, *Gretel II* from Australia, having dropped out. The *Lionheart* campaign began in the waters of Rhode Island Sound, on the eve of Cowes Week 1980, when the British Yachting Season was in full spate.

In the early skirmishing, *Lionheart* was most often matched against *Australia*, although there were also short races against *France* and *Sverige*. Generally, however, *Sverige* tuned up against *France*, while there was the beginning of a joint Anglo-Australian enterprise – to continue after 1980 towards the 1983 campaign – with the Alan Bond-Tony Boyden link-up. Details were a little sketchy, since, it seems, the main backers of the four groups agreed on a news black-out. They decided it was not fair for victories by one syndicate over another to be listed, since generally the boats were practising and trying out sails. *Lionheart*, the success of which was pretty average, at that time was using the bendy mast first stepped for racing in the Solent before her departure to America and which had been repaired. But when in July it was announced that *Lionheart* was to take

delivery of a new and lighter mast which was still more bendy –
a development of the first radical spar with glass fibre top
and made by Proctors – there was, it seemed, some room for
optimism.

When the announcement was made, the *Lionheart* crew were
obviously encouraged by the result of a weekend's racing which
included seven victories out of eight races. Certainly this increased hopes that she might even go on to win the elimination
series for the four challenging 12-metres which were to start on
August 5. The mast was delayed for over a week by shipping
problems which meant that the spar was delivered to Newport
by way of Amsterdam and New York. At the same time it was
announced that as well as the new mast, which was to have a
lower centre of gravity than the first model and with more bend
in the lighter, aluminium section, a new mainsail had been cut
by North Sails, at Hamble, especially for the new mast.

Proctors, who, following design work by Ian Howlett, had
produced the new equipment, were confident that the new mast
would give *Lionheart* three per cent better lift and allow her also
to point 3° higher than any other 12-metre. There were however
some ominous signs. Boyden admitted that the syndicate was
still desperately short of money and needed at least another
injection of about £90,000 if they were not to have wasted their
time.

At that stage it was estimated that *Freedom*, by now the
outstanding favourite to become the defender of the trophy,
with Dennis Conner in charge, was considered to be at least six
months ahead of all 12-metres in terms of tuning. The *Freedom*
crew had trained hard for nearly two years and seemed never to
make a mistake, never to miss a windshift, and always to be
using the correct sails. One estimate was that it was difficult to
imagine Conner and his crew losing one race in 20.

Worse was to come. Competing against *Australia* after her
seven wins in eight races, *Lionheart* was beaten by the Jim
Hardy skippered *Australia*, by one minute two seconds over an
11-mile course and then by two minutes ten seconds over a
20-mile course. *Lionheart* had previously seemed to be superior
in light airs to the three other challengers. But it had already
been predicted that the British boat would be vulnerable in
winds of 10 knots and above.

So far as the American situation was concerned, the battle had really developed between *Freedom* and the Russell Long-skippered *Clipper*, while Ted Turner's *Courageous* was finding that she was much outclassed by her rivals. The role, meanwhile, of *Enterprise*, had been reduced almost to one merely of trial-horse to *Freedom*. While all this was developing, the feeling was that the future prospects of *Lionheart* really rested entirely with her bendy mast and the effectiveness of her new sails. There had been no clue to any other major development.

Then was to come a bombshell, which made defeat only a matter of time. On August 9, with the preliminary round-robin races of the elimination series still to be completed, John Oakeley, who had been skipper since the spring of 1979, was sacked. His place as helmsman went to Lawrie Smith, then 24 and known only as a most promising international dinghy sailor. In a brief statement, made public on Sunday August 10, the British Industry syndicate stated only that Oakeley had had too many responsibilities, and had been replaced because of the pressure of the competition. It has been increasingly found that it was impossible for one man to combine the responsibilities of the organisation with total command of all aspects of racing *Lionheart* – and the pressure of an America's Cup competition.

The statement merely added that the syndicate believed that *Lionheart*'s performance would be improved by having a helmsman supported by a navigator and tactician, rather than a single helmsman-tactician, which Oakeley had been.

Oakeley commented: 'Naturally I am very disappointed, altogether, I have given two and a half years of my life to this campaign.' He insisted that he had made it clear when he committed himself to the *Lionheart* project that he would have complete control of the boat. He felt that the *Lionheart* management had failed to honour their original agreement. It was announced that Iain Macdonald-Smith would be joining the crew as tactician, while Ian Howlett would be navigator. *Lionheart* finished the round-robin series the third best of the four contenders, behind *Australia* and *France*, but ahead of *Sverige*. The round-robin result meant that *Lionheart* would be paired against *France* in the semi-final rounds of the elimination series to find the challenger proper, while *Australia* would meet the least successful of the contenders, *Sverige*. The line-up was considered to be more in favour of *Lionheart* because by being third best in the elimination preliminaries, she at least avoided having to meet *Australia* in the semi-finals, which it was thought would have led to the elimination of the British yacht. The scores at the end of the round-robin contest were:

Australia, 6 wins, 3 defeats; *France*, 5 wins, 4 defeats; *Lionheart*, 4 wins, 5 defeats; *Sverige*, 3 wins, 6 defeats.

Lionheart prepared for the start of the semi-final races with the new sails, a second new mainsail, two genoas and a spinnaker – all produced by the North Loft at Hamble. But of main interest still at that time were the reasons for the sacking of Oakeley, which Tony Boyden was to spell out to some British journalists. Boyden paid some compliments to Oakeley, stressing that he was satisfied that when Oakeley was chosen he was the right man for the job. He had also done considerable amounts of invaluable work in preparing *Lionheart* for the competition but, said Boyden, the skipper had too many responsibilities. He was unable to deal with them adequately and as a consequence *Lionheart*'s prospects began to suffer. As well as problems over Oakeley's responsibilities for racing *Lionheart* – sails, starting and crew management – Boyden indicated that the decision to dismiss Oakeley and to replace him with Smith went much deeper. More expert assistance was required in the *Lionheart* afterguard, and it was felt imperative that *Lionheart* should have a tactician; this Oakeley would not accept. The syndicate chairman insisted that advice to Oakeley concerning sails was ignored; that attempts to persuade the skipper to make fuller use of sophisticated navigational aids had also met with failure and there was disagreement over crew management, standards of physical training and attendance at drinking parties. According to the campaign committee there was also some indiscipline aboard *Lionheart*, with a lack of a properly co-ordinated chain of command. After a race, said Boyden, the skipper was often too tired and too physically exhausted to answer questions from the campaign committee and to take control of important tasks, or to make decisions that were essential for the welfare of the boat, her crew and equipment. Perhaps most damning of all was the argument, according to the syndicate chairman, that deputations of the crew had approached the campaign committee, expressing discontent with the situation aboard *Lionheart* and, in short, insisting that they wanted a new skipper.

Boyden accepted the blame for the developments: 'I appointed Oakeley and I agreed to the terms he made.' But he insisted that the decision to sack Oakeley, though a unanimous agreement among the campaign committee, was made reluctantly.

It was stated after Oakeley's dismissal that the former *Lionheart* skipper would remain in Newport to act in an advisory capacity to the campaign committee. But, within days, Oakeley had packed his bags and was returning to England. Before he departed he answered the charges that had been levelled against him, and he maintained that he held no animosity towards his former crew-mates and, more determinedly, stood by his belief that he had been right to be in sole charge of racing the yacht.

Oakeley insisted that his demand, agreed by the campaign committee when it was first set up, to be in sole charge of the boat – racing without a tactician or navigator opposite to what the syndicate came to prefer in Newport – was the right one. He believed that only the helmsman could be sure of what sails should be used or how they should be set, and that manoeuvring or tacking was decided best by the man at the wheel. He rejected arguments that a tactician and a navigator are essential members of the crew claiming that this belief by the *Lionheart* syndicate was old fashioned and more appropriate in the days of *Sovereign*.

'When the campaign was first launched, with Tony Boyden in control my view was accepted,' said Oakeley. 'When the British Industry 1500 syndicate was formed, with various other committees, the idea of an afterguard became the favoured one.'

Oakeley claimed that on a clear day, a navigator would work for only 5 minutes during a 5 hour race; if it was foggy a navigator might be involved for 4 out of 5 hours. Though Oakeley agreed that a navigator was an advantage if it was foggy, and that on a clear day, a tactician was useful to make long-term suggestions, he said neither crewmen were essential all of the time.

For this reason, Oakeley claimed the arrangement worked out between himself and Lawrie Smith, when the young dinghy sailor was aboard as reserve helmsman, was ideal. Smith took care of navigational duties when they were necessary and gave tactical advice when appropriate. In Oakeley's belief it was possible to combine the duties of the two men and save also an extra 180lb in the fine end of the boat. Oakeley said: 'We always went better when we had just two people in the afterguard.'

Concerning charges about insufficient attention to crew training, Oakeley said it was established before the crew went to Newport that the training would be the responsibility of one campaign committee member and the team doctor. 'My responsibility was solely to take disciplinary action should it be necessary – and all of this was carefully charted beforehand. I admit to being surprised at the crew deputations to the management of the British Industry 1500 syndicate, but with 16 people in the squad it would be impossible for one person to satisfy all of the team.'

Oakeley said he was disappointed that Boyden did not tell him about the crew deputations. 'And I was disappointed that the crew did not approach me with their complaints,' said the former skipper, who shrugged off suggestions that he was at fault in joining his crew at late night drinking parties.

The crew began training at seven every morning, were then afloat on *Lionheart* for most of the day and often worked until nine or so at night on duties concerned with the yacht, said Oakeley. 'It was exhausting both mentally and physically and I think that to have a successful crew they must be happy as well as enthusiastic. I had to stop them becoming mesmerized by the task. They had been at it a long time and they had to have a break. I think it helps to have some time away from duties concerned with the boat. If we went to some parties it was to help the crew forget their problems. I think I would do the same again,' said Oakeley, who also denied that he had had any problems concerning health or fitness.

He said that he had never been fitter and though he had suffered from asthma since he was three, it had never affected him in any major regattas. On the question of poor communications between the skipper and his crew and between the skipper and the campaign committee, Oakeley squarely blamed the *Lionheart* management for using two houses in Newport.

The syndicate chiefs lived in one house and the crew in another, he said. 'If we had all been together all of the time as I wanted, there would have been no problems. I agreed to have one meal a day with the committee, as they requested, and had breakfast with them for perhaps two weeks. But I was never asked anything more important than what I planned for the day

Victory of Burnham *started the British campaign, but was later involved in a serious rating upset.* D.T.

Early days: Peter de Savary and Alan Bond at Cowes in 1981. D.T.

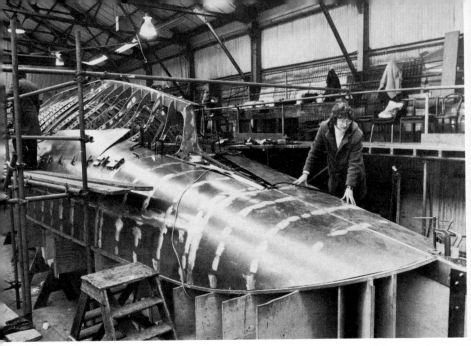

Ian Howlett supervises the building of his design, Victory '83 *at Fairey Allday, Hamble.* D.T.

The dock used by the British yachts at Newport. Here are seen Victory '83, Australia *and* Victory. Kos.

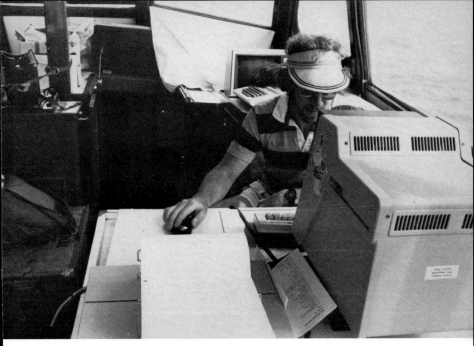

Monitoring equipment and a computer on a support craft in early practice. Kos.

Polar diagram print-out gave clues on where performance needed improvement. Kos.

Ed Dubois. His Victory *design was said never to have been properly tried against her successor.* Kos.

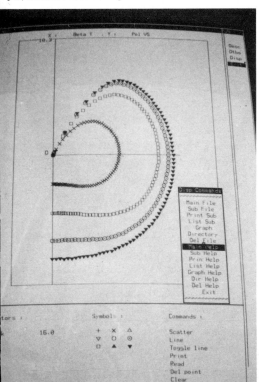

Early elimination was the fate of France's helmsman, Bruno Troublé. Kos

Phil Crebbin steered de Savary's racing boats from 1981 until a late stage in the trials. Kos.

The brains of a 12-metre. Navigator, helmsman, mainsheet trimmer, genoa tailer. Black.

Advance *arrives in Newport from Australia.* Kos.

Like Challenge 12 *each engineless racing yacht has a capable tender.* Kos.

Above. *Defence contenders: the two yachts of the Defender-Courageous Group.* Kos.

Right. Challenge 12 *gets the feel of Rhode Island Sound.* Kos.

Below. *The newest of the American boats,* Liberty, *skippered by Dennis Conner.* Kos.

Victory '83 *hard on the wind, reveals the complex deck arrangement of a 12-metre.* Kos.

Every syndicate tried to keep out strangers; sometimes seriously, but not always. Black.

ahead, and concerning lack of communications on the yacht, I don't believe there was ever a problem when I was aboard.'

Concerning the question of differences over the choice of sails, Oakeley also denied that he was at fault and pointed to the lack of action by the *Lionheart* management as the cause of the problem. Oakeley said that as long ago as 1978 he had asked for an up-to-date suit of 12-metre sails to be bought for use as comparison, but they never were. 'I was then asked to make a suit of sails at my loft, which I did. They were not perfect but they surprised a lot of people. An order for one suit of sails was subsequently placed with another loft and the order was acknowledged. But I could not get the money from the syndicate and the order had to be cancelled. When we knew we were coming to Newport, I was asked to submit a list of my requirements with regard to sails. I did and the total cost came to £94,000. I was told we could not afford it and trimmed the list to one valued at £50,000. I was told that even that was too much. It was then finally decided that Miller & Whitworth would make some new sails and that Norths would also provide some. The new bendy mast then added to sail difficulties, but I think the only real problem in the end was that we lacked a really heavy mainsail. But the committee insisted, against my advice, that I used new sails when we were not winning at practice races. I wanted to save them for the competition proper. So I was forced into using and repairing sails that I would rather not have used. What really hurt was that while this was going on, the committee had ordered sails from another loft without telling me about it. This hurt especially because I had asked two British companies to supply new cloths which the management said we could not afford to buy. And despite having to work all the time on a shoestring, I think we did especially well to come as far as we did. I don't take credit for that. We were as good as we were because of the crew – who have been marvellous,' said Oakeley at the time.

Looking back on all the turmoil that the dismissal of Oakeley caused, perhaps the two most important reasons for his sacking were race starts and choice of sails. What it came down to was that Oakeley, from the very early races in Marstrand right through to practice races and the round-robin contest in Newport, did not always display the sort of aggression on the starting line which his campaign committee thought they had found in

Lawrie Smith. Smith took the helm from Oakeley during some of the races for practice from Newport and some of his aggression was so sharp that it led to demands from the Australians to the British camp that he should ease off.

The other problem was that the sails which Oakeley was making, though perhaps satisfactory in most ways, were not the same as those which had been provided for most of the other contenders from overseas, and for the potential defenders. Lack of expertise, probably in the *Lionheart* camp, meant that Boyden and his committee felt that they would be better served with sails which were more similar to those being used by their rivals. The question of whether Oakeley's sails were suitable will never be answered; like the question of how *Lionheart* would have fared had the original skipper been retained. Because the decision was taken to go for North sails, and because they felt that in Smith they had a man who gave them a better chance of winning through winning the starts, the campaign committee obviously came to the conclusion that they should part company with Oakeley.

What was more disappointing than the dismissal of Oakeley, a most popular yachtsman, was that the probable true potential of *Lionheart* was never known at that time. If the campaign committee made a mistake in dismissing Oakeley, it was perhaps that it was not done sooner. Surely the evidence that led to the dismissal must have been clear long before *Lionheart* went to Newport. Had Oakeley been dismissed before the yacht was shipped to the States, and Smith or another helmsman given the chance to familiarize themselves with the craft, then *Lionheart*'s potential might have been more considerable. But the trouble was not so much the dismissal of Oakeley, sad and controversial though that was, as the fact that the new afterguard team with the new sails and a strange mast to work with had no time in which to come to terms with the difficulties on the boat; let alone the difficulties that were to face them in competition.

The truth is that the die was cast long before the yacht got to Newport. There should have been much more practice, especially in the area of starting and match-racing, and unless the vast sums of money that are necessary to ensure the intense preparations with a trial-horse – and all of the sails and equipment that are equally essential in such a cause – were available then any future campaign seemed likely to be similarly doomed. It was all such a pity. *Lionheart* might, despite being an estimated 6000lb heavier than any other 12-metre at Newport in 1980, at least have given a much better account of British yachting expertise. (Though by 1983 she was tried again and found lacking in performance.) Even the manner of her elimination was disappointing, coming as it did after a doubtful disqualification in the sixth race against the French. What began so promisingly with two first places in the two first races against the French, became an uphill and impossible battle. In 1980, as in all previous British challenges, taking on the Americans from a basis of just one boat meant there was next to no chance of success. The question after Newport was whether the British had finally appreciated all the lessons of the America's Cup – 1980 and before – and whether de Savary and his Victory syndicate could launch the truly professional and dedicated challenge that was essential.

For the record, the *Lionheart* quest began in earnest on August 14; the new afterguard won the start and the British yacht went on to beat *France III* in the first elimination race by 2 minutes 26 seconds, a telling success on the 24.3 mile triangular course in Rhode Island Sound. Her luck changed in the second race on Friday, August 15. Despite finishing easily ahead of the French – leading by a mammoth five minutes at the end of the first reach – *Lionheart* was disqualified following a collision at the start. The collision, details of which were provided for the protest committee largely by video recording, actually occurred shortly before the start and the jury found that although *Lionheart* had created an overlap she had not allowed the French sufficient room in which to manoeuvre and she was therefore disqualified.

The reason for the French trailing by such a wide margin at the end of the first beat was that the collision had carried away the aerial by which their Decca navigation system operated. Despite the disqualification, however, the message to *Lionheart's* strong-hearted supporters seemed to be that the boat and crew were in good trim and excellent spirits and confident for the battle which lay ahead.

Although a blow, the disqualification did not seem quite such an important aspect as the superiority of *Lionheart* on the water. *Lionheart* had been favoured with the light breezes of up to 10 knots in which she had previously performed best, but the belief in the British camp was that they could beat the French in stronger winds, and that the disqualification was not a disaster. It was also predicted by a spokesman for the British campaign committee that the young skipper and helmsman of *Lionheart* would not hit another 12-metre again.

There were no collisions in the third meeting between the two boats and the result, of course, was that not only did the French go on to win that but in the fourth race also won convincingly to lead the British 3–1 in the best-of-seven race series. The defeat in that fourth semi-final encounter meant that *Lionheart* had to win the next three consecutive races if she was to contest the final for the challengers. *Australia* meanwhile had taken a 2–0 lead over *Sverige* in the other semi-final, although trouble was also to dog them as *Lionheart* began a cliff-hanging sequence of races before her final unhappy defeat again in a protest room as a result of yet another collision.

First there was a lay day and then north-westerly winds of more than 35 knots prevented racing in the fifth scheduled race of the eliminator and the decision certainly amounted to a stay of execution for *Lionheart*.

When racing did recommence, on August 22, it produced a most exciting finish, the British 12-metre completing the course less than a second ahead of her French rival. *Lionheart* nosed ahead literally on the line as *France III*, which had led throughout, tacked and covered badly to let through her rival by a matter of feet. The French were subsequently to claim – hinting even at the possibility of sabotage – that their problem in that fifth race had been a faulty, British-made winch. There were also protests and counter-protests and undoubtedly more store set by the *Lionheart* success because of her serious difficulties with a damaged boom before the start.

After first having had a request for a lay day refused and the further plea for a two-hour postponement turned down, the crew put up a brave fight. *Lionheart* had been only 15 seconds astern at the first weather mark, but in the 10–15 knot northeasterlies she dropped 21 seconds by the gybe mark and her chances then seemed to be fading.

But *Lionheart* fought gallantly on the second weather-leg and at times seemed to be getting on terms. Alas, at the end of the leg the French were still 33 seconds ahead. However, all was not lost and the British came back to win by just 1 second and it was on the following day that the first of the new British challenges for 1983 was announced; the information being that Boyden would challenge again.

The decision on August 25 that there was insufficient wind for the 1980 elimination series to continue, led to all sorts of acrimony between the race committee and competitors and, more sadly, claims and counter-claims between the British and the French of unsporting behaviour during the second victory of *Lionheart* on the Friday. But the decision to abandon racing did appear to be premature. The south-westerly breeze that filled in at 13.30 was expected to freshen and it seemed worth starting a contest, and certainly the British crew were disappointed with the decision to abandon.

The *Lionheart* campaign to qualify as the America's Cup challenger, charged with nail-biting tension since the semi-final of the elimination series against *France III*, had further high drama on August 27 when the crucial sixth race of the series began. There was another collision!

In the opinion of most observers the British yacht had the right-of-way and the collision was the fault of the French; the belief then was that *Lionheart* had only to complete the course to win.

As the two 12-metres jousted before the start, with *Lionheart* on starboard tack, *France III* gybed, apparently misjudged a manoeuvre and hit the British yacht, which, like her rival, promptly hoisted a protest flag. The subsequent details are well known: *France* went on to finish ahead but though the British were astern, it seemed perfectly clear that the protest would go against the French and the series would be standing 3–3.

It was not to be. *Lionheart* was disqualified and her consequent exit from the America's Cup challengers' elimination series completely stunned the crew when the jury announced their verdict in the early hours of August 28. The record books will show that *Lionheart*, the first British contender for an America's Cup challenge since 1964 was beaten 4–2 by *France III*.

Lionheart had been beaten by 54 seconds in the sixth race but it was three separate video recordings of the incident which led to the international jury giving the French the verdict. They were to go on to meet *Australia*, winner against *Sverige* in the other semifinal in the decider of the elimination series.

Sadly, it had been an acrimonious as well as an unsatisfactory semi-final; altogether there were four protests, three collisions and three disqualifications. The French protest over the fifth-race collision resulted in the French disqualification. *Lionheart* was twice disqualified for collisions. On the water *Lionheart* and *France III* each finished ahead in three races. If France in any way deserved to win the right to take on Australia in the final of the series to decide the challenger, it was probably only because of superior crewing and tactics. As in the past – and just as lamentably – the British were just not properly prepared for the more professional opponents they encountered; and if the British had not learned in that mission to retrieve the trophy that nothing less than a totally dedicated challenge, with full-time commitment and based on at least two boats, would stand any chance of success, then the story seemed likely to be repeated in any further attempt.

Australia went on to beat France convincingly and in truth was beaten just as convincingly by the Dennis Conner-skippered *Freedom* in the America's Cup series proper, which began a fortnight after *Lionheart*'s dismissal. The Australians did win one race but again when analyzed it really did seem that the Australian success was based only on the fact that the Americans had been caught out by a wind shift just short of the finish of the race that the Australians won. Certainly *Australia* was a competitive boat in light weather, but there seemed to be little doubt, especially with *Freedom* suffering various forms of unexpected gear failure, that it was only in those conditions of extreme light winds that Australia stood any chance whatsoever.

V

A Victorious Series and a Launching

Many of the lessons from 1980 appeared to have been appreciated by the de Savary Victory syndicate when they began their
preparation for 1983. Since he himself and a few of his principal
lieutenants had been closely and actively involved with the
Lionheart campaign – or other America's Cup syndicates – de
Savary was well aware of the shortcomings that had beset the
organisation of the 1980 British attempt. It is not surprising that
he adopted what might have been considered an arrogant pose in
suggesting that he could do very much better. Nor was it
surprising, as a very successful businessman and banker, that he
should indicate that he would be basing his campaign on
efficiency and first class advice. Whatever his assessment of the
events generally which led to the defeat of *Lionheart* on the
waters of Rhode Island Sound, there is no doubt that de Savary
was entirely certain about the lack of aggression and uncertainty which surrounded the British efforts when competition
began.

However, though Boyden may not, because of the failures of
his two challenges, rate highly even among the list of failed
British challengers, his importance as the inspiration of re-
newed British interest in the contest cannot be ignored. Without
Boyden, the fallow years – when America's Cup was ignored by
British yachting – might have been considerably longer.

But while de Savary seemed to understand the America's Cup
and what it would represent if a challenge was to be a serious
one, the same could not be said of the proposed challenge by
Ernest Juer, who made his announcement of joining the Newport fray at the beginning of 1981. He was to challenge through
the Royal London, at Cowes. True, he may have been putting up
something of a smoke-screen, but Juer's first words did not lead

to much optimism about his prospects. He considered that he would have just one boat; would use a crew based mostly on his ocean-racer *Blizzard*; that accommodation and preparations would not be taken seriously and that the principle objective would be to win by just being jolly good sailors. But when Juer made his announcement, all that was real about his challenge was that he had paid his necessary entry fee by the time the April 1 deadline was reached for challenges. This was sad because a second British syndicate would have completely altered the likely eventual performance. The Juer challenge proved nothing but a feint.

Perhaps the first significant upset, though it was certainly denied that it was such at the time, was the announcement on January 9 1981 that the group were to scrap their scheme to adapt the Greek cruise liner as headquarters for the crew and support team. The reason given for the decision not to go ahead with the plan was a report by behavioural experts which it was said warned of the difficulties of long-term confinement of a crew and supporters in cramped conditions. De Savary said that the mother ship plan had presented diverse and unexpected problems one of which had been berthing. So at Newport the crew were to be accommodated in one or more houses and in Nassau, at an hotel.

The building of the first new boat for the challenge entered by the Royal Burnham began in May 1981 and Ed Dubois, then drawing the lines for his first 12-metre, was confirmed as the designer. It was also suggested that Johan Valentijn, the Dutch designer of the 12-metre *Australia* and *France III*, would act as a consultant. Ian Howlett, the *Lionheart* designer, was to design the second yacht, the building of which was to begin in May 1982. (In the event it started in December.) It was still proposed that training with *Australia* and *Victory* would begin in the Bahamas in October 1981 and continue until March 1982, when activities would be transferred to Newport.

Whether it was the problem of finding a suitable yard to build the boat or some other, there was no doubt that the Victory America's Cup campaign had slowed down by March 1981, when certain people had already been stood down. Unofficially, it seemed that the group had also told the New York Yacht Club that they had scrapped their plans to build a new 12 in 1981, and that Valentijn would be involved only for any necessary altera-

tions to the *Australia* 12-metre which he had designed with Ben
Lexcen. Alleged threats from the New York Club about the
possible involvement of Valentijn were understandable when it
was learnt that he was shortly to take up American citizenship
and become the official designer for one of the groups being
founded to build a defence contender. He was lost to the Victory
syndicate, anyway.

At that early stage there was still plenty of optimism in some
quarters about the prospects of the Victory group. Indeed, de
Savary said, in April, that there had been no less than 350
applications for crew and support places. Physical fitness, an
aspect of the *Lionheart* challenge which had been severely
criticized by de Savary, was clearly to be a major consideration
in 1983, with Billy Walker, a former British heavyweight boxing
champion, named as being responsible for getting the crew fit.

Earlier, when it had been suggested from Australia that they
might build at least six new 12-metre yachts as potential challengers in 1983, the Royal Lymington were announcing their
list of competitors for the Lymington Cup, the match-racing
series which had become the more significant because of British
involvement in the America's Cup. As well as Dennis Conner,
other overseas skippers invited included Pelle Petterson, Dick
Deaver and Bruno Trouble, with a further invitation going to the
1981 winner of the American Congressional Cup match-racing
series, upon which the Lymington event is based. With two
former Lymington winners, Crebbin and Cudmore, and with
John Oakeley and Lawrie Smith in the line-up, the Lymington
series promised to be especially significant. Unfortunately the
Royal Lymington's plans were upset in that neither Conner,
Petterson nor Trouble were to take part, but the Victory campaign seemed still to be forging ahead. There was much optimism when the ocean racing yacht *Victory of Burnham* was
commissioned at Hamble on April 25 by Lady Methven, wife of
Sir John Methven who, before his death, had been head of the
British Industry 1500 syndicate.

Outlining his plans at the launching de Savary had said that
the initial model for the first of the two new 12-metres which he
was planning to build would begin tank-testing in May and that
a yard to build the first of the 12's would be signed up within a
matter of weeks. Tests, in co-operation with the Wolfson Unit
at Southampton University, were to continue for at least a year

before the building of the second 12-metre, a development of the first. Working on the designs were Ian Howlett and Ed Dubois. It was the news much as before, but with the essential difference that deadlines seemed ominously to be extended with each announcement.

With practically all shore facilities, apart from living accommodation for the crew, already arranged for the Victory campaign in Newport, it was said training would begin there in September 1981 with *Lionheart* and *Australia*. Although de Savary admitted, at the time of the launching of *Victory of Burnham*, that he was not sure that *Lionheart* had so far performed at her best, it seemed that the 12-metre he would be building first would most resemble *Australia*. Indeed, it was indicated that when training began with the new boat in Newport in 1982 she would most probably race against *Australia*, with the two boats able to swop sails and equipment so as to be as sure as possible of the potential of the new boat – *Lionheart* was being edged to one side. It seemed, according to the design team, that the new boat would be 'a state of the art' design and much lighter than *Lionheart*, estimated now to have been about 10,000lb heavier than the other 12-metres racing off Newport in 1980.

A significant comment by Mr de Savary at the time was: 'We hope to demonstrate with the ocean-racer just launched that we can run a boat successfully in a highly competitive season of racing.' *Victory of Burnham*, designed by Dubois to the International Offshore Rule Mark III, soon was evident as a most outstanding ocean racer and the campaign by de Savary and his team was one of the most impressive in the history of the Admiral's Cup. An excellent omen for 1983, it seemed, until a rating scandal involving de Savary's yacht burst upon the ocean-racing scene in the early part of 1982.

Victory of Burnham, the beautiful blue yacht which either won convincingly or featured prominently at the front of every race in which she competed both before and during the Admiral's Cup trials of June 1981, was never disgraced. Indeed, so impressive was the performance of the yacht and her crew, led by Phil Crebbin, that there can never in the history of British selection trials for the Admiral's Cup have been a yacht more certain of selection than this de Savary entry. Although there were doubts until the final selection race about the composition of the British team, there was never any doubt that *Victory of Burnham* would be a member of that team. She had seemed an inevitable choice long before the trials began and it was as a consequence that her subsequent involvement in the rating scandal was the more shocking!

But first the Admiral's Cup: the leading contenders, finally, for the British Cup trio were Brian Saffery-Cooper's *Dragon*, Robin Aisher's *Yeoman XXIII*, David May's *Mayhem* and Chris Dunning's *Marionette*. It seemed that the team would be composed of *Victory*, with the other possible combinations being either *Mayhem* or *Dragon* with either *Yeoman* or *Marionette*. In the event the selection came down to *Victory of Burnham* with *Yeoman XXIII* and *Dragon* and with Robin Aisher uniquely named as team captain for a third time.

Only a little more than a week after the choice of *Victory of Burnham* for the Admiral's Cup, it was announced that the first 12-metre *Victory* was to be built of aluminium by Souters of Cowes. Work on the hull was to begin in August and the keel, on which tests were still being carried out, was to be moulded in October. By July, the drawings of *Victory*, scheduled to be launched in February 1982, had been submitted to Lloyd's Register for approval. After local trials in the Solent, the yacht would be shipped to Newport. It was stated that crew training and familiarization would begin in September 1981, with competition provided by either an American 12 or a leading overseas contender. It was this continual delaying of important developments which sapped the credibility of de Savary's America's Cup aspirations.

As well as falling behind its stated deadlines, the *Victory* syndicate was also rejecting *Lionheart*, the yacht which they had bought so eagerly and which it had been argued would feature prominently in the build-up plans. In fact, by the beginning of 1982, *Lionheart* was reported to have been sold. While, on the one hand the de Savary squad were earning friends with the triumph of their ocean racer, they were fast losing others and credibility in the 12-metre arena. *Lionheart* may not have been an ideal trial-horse for 1983, but better surely, it was argued in some quarters, than nothing; and a vehicle at least for possible crew members to use for familiarization.

Victory of Burnham, meanwhile, continued to go from strength to strength. At the time of her selection it had seemed that she was perhaps more certain to be top boat in the Admiral's Cup series than were the British team to win overall. Predictions had to be reconsidered, however, after the Solent Points race run by the RAF Yacht Club in July and in which most of the overseas teams competed. With *Victory of Burnham* first, *Yeoman* second and *Dragon* ninth, Britain had the best team showing and seemed certain to have a very good chance of success in the international event which is widely recognized as the world championship of ocean racing.

But still, with something like six teams capable of victory, in the 13th Admiral's Cup which began on July 30 1981 only a vintage performance by the British seemed likely to secure the trophy won in 1979 by Australia. And after calms, strong tides and some mistakes by the organizers, the Royal Ocean Racing Club and Royal Yacht Squadron combined to render the first of the Admiral's Cup races a near farce – and, with the British only 10th out of the 16 international teams competing, success did not seem likely to come easily. This performance by the British boats was not so typical. The British team as a whole and *Victory of Burnham* in particular performed outstandingly in the subsequent four races to win impressively but *Victory of Burnham* was denied the title of best-boat-of-the-series only by one point to the New Zealand yacht *Swuzzlebubble*. Though denied the title of boat-of-the-series, *Victory of Burnham* was a near unanimous winner of the Champagne Mumm Prix d'Elegance for the smartest of the Admiral's Cup yachts, an award decided by an international panel of judges. There was no doubt that de Savary and Crebbin had shown with *Victory of Burnham* that they were capable of mounting a worthwhile America's Cup challenge. At this point, hopes for 12-metre success were high.

Of particular influence aboard *Victory of Burnham* during the Admiral's Cup was Johnson Wooderson, the former European Flying Dutchman champion, who was Crebbin's afterguard partner at this time of the best result of Crebbin's yachting career. Indeed he was a near winner of the title of Yachtsman of the Year as a result of his showing with *Victory of Burnham*. It was a pity therefore, when the names of the squad for the America's Cup competition were announced, that of Wooderson was not among them.

It was during Cowes Week and a halt in the Admiral's Cup

competition, that de Savary and Alan Bond, whose *Apollo V* was a member of the Australian team in the international ocean-racing series, staged from Osborne Bay at Cowes, an event which in a miniature way mirrored the activities of the America's Cup at Newport, Rhode Island but which, while absorbingly fascinating to many, was considered a disgraceful stunt by others. De Savary and Bond staged a race for a £10,000 bet in a match-race series with *Apollo V* and *Victory of Burnham*. The clash, dubbed the 'pot-of-gold' contest because of the wager being struck in gold coins, had to be completed within three and a half hours.

Though the start was prompt at 08.30, with a surprising number of spectators arriving in craft of all sizes and types, the light, easterly breeze died soon after the yachts had completed the first leg of the 12-mile course and that effectively was the end of the match. But, with *Apollo* well ahead and beginning the final weather leg of the Olympic-type course, it was certainly a moral success for the Australians.

Crebbin had the best of the pre-race manoeuvring, but Hugh Trehearne, with similar steering responsibilities at Cowes for Bond, snatched the initiative within a minute of the start to take the weather station in *Apollo*. *Victory of Burnham*, unable to squeeze through to leeward, could only tack when Trehearne chose, and with *Apollo* laying the mark from her first tack after 19 minutes, she led by 36 seconds at the first mark. As the wind died, returned at zephyr strength from the west, died again and then veered – and as the flood tide took a grip – the race was doomed. The Australians stayed ahead, at one time leading by nearly four and a half minutes, and were well in control when the time limit expired with the two contenders just beginning their final beat. The rival owners agreed that they would race again one day, probably for the same £10,000 purse of gold coins.

The match had shown the need for strict preparations. Crebbin had flinched when it came to the point of starting. He was well able to take command in Admiral's Cup-type races, but clearly would need more practice in the area of match-race starts. A temporary decline of de Savary and his 12-metre ambitions really began at that time in Osborne Bay with Bond on top. The race itself was of little significance in terms of Newport in 1983. What was significant, however, was that from that point in 1981 until early 1982 there was next to no apparent action in the 12-metre field. De Savary, absent for part of the Admiral's Cup series, was to appear only fleetingly in Britain between the summer of 1981 and January 1982, and in his absence the 12-metre syndicate which he had set up so ambitiously was faltering badly without his hand at the helm. There had always been some concern about his choice of lieutenants. There was plenty of good yachting brain and brawn, but what seemed to be lacking, and what over the years had become so important in the 12-metre field, was the need for strong, determined and inspired management. It was essential either to put your campaign in the hands of a master such as Dennis Conner, or to have a back-up squad with great flair – or better, both. However good were de Savary's lieutenants at carrying out day-to-day administration, there was no doubt during that six-month period after the 'crock-of-gold' caper – seen by many as cocking a snook at the establishment – that major decisions were not being taken. Or if they were, they were not seen to be taken and they were deemed retrograde in that the originally stated *Victory* schedule was down-graded.

Work had not even begun on the building of the 12-metre by August, although the metal for the yacht, the first 12 to be built at Cowes, had been delivered. With plans for preparations with *Lionheart* and *Australia* in Newport abandoned for the autumn of 1981, with no crew named for the 12-metre campaign, with Crebbin, the nominated skipper, still to race a 12-metre, and de Savary forever absent, it seemed that there were some doubts about the future of the syndicate. Top yachtsmen who might have been considered for places in de Savary's squad were now beginning seriously to question whether the syndicate really had the money to proceed. They pointed, not unnaturally, to the termination of the plans for a cruise liner mother ship, they pointed, equally naturally, to the fact that the programme had now fallen seven months behind its stated schedule.

It was to become clear later that at the time de Savary was in fact master-minding the purchase of two major oil refineries in Houston and was dealing with what was reputed to be one of the biggest ever single financial undertakings by a foreign concern in Manhattan – for the St James's Tower – and did have good cause to be out of the country. But, though there may have been some minor activities in the 12-metre camp in Britain, the yachting fraternity could see only the steam escaping from the Victory machine.

Even when the Victory group returned to active sailing, in Darings for a match-racing series from Cowes on a cold October weekend, the main comment was that the crews had to pay for their own cost of accommodation. Crebbin was the leading helmsman after the first series, contested also by Chris Law, Lawrie Smith, Simon Tait, Andy Cassel and Larry Marks. The Daring series was organized principally by Tim Street, a well-known Dragon helmsman, whose Army duties at that time allowed him time to join the Victory administration for twelve months. The match-racing in Darings was a useful exercise and resulted in a second series involving David Howlett, Tom Richardson, Colin Simonds, Philip Tolhurst, Richard Roscoe and Edward Warden Owen. After a series of protests, Richard Roscoe got the overall verdict from Edward Warden Owen.

While the Daring exercise had done little to sharpen match-racing talent, it was a valuable exercise in that it drew together all sorts of yachting talent from all sorts of areas and renewed interest in the project at a time when the credibility of the Victory campaign was in serious decline. At the time, the Victory group would have argued that they had nothing to gain and all to lose by racing 12-metres in Newport. The probability, without serious preparation, they said, was that they would have been beaten by whomever they raced against. Better, they claimed, to rest on the laurels of the Admiral's Cup triumph rather than lose face in a not too important tune-up series in 12-metres against tested opposition in Newport. It was commendable, however, of the Royal Corinthian at Cowes, the Daring class and certain stalwarts of class and club, to give up time and to take the trouble to foster interest in 12-metre competition in general and British prospects in the America's Cup in particular in the absence of de Savary. Important also, in the opinion of the critics of de Savary and the Victory effort, was the fact that the plan to build two new 12-metres had been shelved. While Souters were now allowing a glimpse of the building of the first, there was considerable scepticism about whether the second was any longer a probability. No one had ever succeeded with just one boat and de Savary appeared to be heading down the same blind alley. A further blow to British hopes was the abandonment of Victory's plans to continue match-racing practice inland and the shelving of an idea to borrow, or purchase, two 6-metres to race during the winter of 1981–2.

De Savary however had argued convincingly that the idea for the second 12-metre had been amended rather than shelved. He insisted that the proposal to go ahead with the second 12-metre could be re-activated immediately if it was decided that the first yacht was not suitable for the task ahead. He said that had he decided not to allow his design team to take comfort in the knowledge that there would definitely be a second boat; which could have encouraged the consideration that it was unnecessary to make absolutely certain that the first 12-metre was the best that they could produce. Only when he had seen how the first boat performed would be make a decision about a second boat – and about who would design it. The de Savary argument seemed sound, especially when in mid-January 1982 the Victory effort was put back in perspective. Preparations with the new boat would begin from Newport in May with *Australia* as the trial-horse; the boats would be transported across America to be raced from Nassau in the winter and would return to Newport in 1983, by which time there would be a second new boat if it was deemed necessary. Shore facilities, for the crew and the yacht, were confirmed.

'And whether we build a second boat is not a question of finance,' emphasized de Savary at that time. 'The only question about a second boat will be whether we are convinced that she will be better than the first.' A lot of design work had been done already and the group were ready to proceed with a second boat if necessary, he insisted. Sails for the two boats, the first *Victory* and *Australia*, had been ordered from Hoods and from Norths and they would be interchangeable between the two.

The syndicate also showed their determination to get things right, with plans worked out with French and Italian challenge contenders concerning the elimination series for 1983. Representatives of the clubs, the Royal Burnham, the Yacht Club de France and the Yacht Club Costa Smeralda had agreed a common course of action at a meeting in Paris in late January and their plans, imaginative and comprehensive, were to be put to the other challenge contenders including the Australians. The Royal Sydney Yacht Squadron had been nominated by the New York Yacht Club to be responsible for the organization of the elimination series in 1983 and would be known as the Challenger of Record.

It was suggested that the elimination series would begin with a round-robin event with each yacht racing against all the other challenge contenders over a half-size America's Cup course. Racing, which it was expected at that point would involve eight contenders – from Australia, Canada and Sweden as well as Britain, France and Italy – would be staged from June 10–30. The first round-robin series, essentially to give challenge contenders more and tougher competition than previously, would be followed by a second similar contest which would eliminate four yachts. There would be at least four rounds, each yacht racing against all of the others at least four times; the first three rounds over half-size courses, the final contest over the full 24.3 mile course and with racing taking place from July 5–26.

The semi-final races for the challenge contenders, from August 1–15, would essentially be a best-of-seven-race series, but with tougher requirements than in the past. First, the series would not end if one yacht won four straight races; the full seven races would still be sailed and in order that a winner achieved at least a required two-race advantage, up to nine rounds could be staged. The final of the elimination series would be run from August 18–September 3. The New York Yacht Club required the challenger to be named by September 8, with the defence of the trophy scheduled to begin on September 13. Significantly, the three European countries involved in the America's Cup challenge – Sweden, surprisingly, did not take part in the discussions – decided to form an International 12-metre class association in order that a body other than the New York Yacht Club could discuss possible changes concerning the 12-metre rule at future meetings with the International Yacht Racing Union.

Emphasizing that the syndicate were back on course, it was confirmed that HRH Princess Michael of Kent was to name the new yacht during her scheduled launching at Cowes in March and shortly after the names of the squad, who would begin preparations in the United States in May, were also revealed.

The full squad was to be – Skippers: Phil Crebbin and Harold Cudmore. Afterguard: Derek Clark, Adrian Jardine, Andrew Spedding, Edward Warden Owen. Crew: Mark Preston, Kelvin Rawlings, Jim Barry, Colin Edge, David Miles, Richard Clampett, Richard Furse, John Best, Jonathan Layfield, John Caulcutt, David Powys, Bru Pearce, Bill Bullard, Oliver Stanley, Alex Wadson and Edward Danby. Joining in June: Peter Baines and Nigel Brookes. Trial Helmsmen: John Oakeley, Chris Law, Colin Simonds, Rodney Pattisson, Lawrie Smith, Iain Macdonald-Smith and Peter Bateman.

The team announcement was not only premature, but was partly inaccurate. A number of the crew were not available, withdrew, or were eliminated for one reason or another. The team announcement seemed also to spark perhaps the first dispute of the campaign, and one which was to have long-term repercussions. Phil Crebbin wrote something in the order of a 15-page letter setting out complaints and conditions, and basically the touchpaper was the choice of a crew, over which, it seems, he had little control. There was only one casualty among the afterguard listed, namely Edward Warden Owen, who was unable to accept the invitation because he had too recently taken up a position with a new sail loft in Britain. Kelvin Rawlings, Jonathan Layfield, John Caulcutt and Peter Baines were among those in the crew who did not show up in Newport in the early days. The alterations with the crew emphasized what was to be one of the biggest problems throughout the early days of the campaign, namely the choice of suitable people for crew. Not only did the campaign begin with a crew which was not necessarily the first choice, but was apparently not even the first choice of all the people who chose the crew. Nevertheless, the disagreement over crew selection was but a tiny ripple upon the de Savary 12-metre pond compared to a tidal wave of upheaval which followed the revelation, just three days before the launching of the 12-metre on March 25 1982, that *Victory of Burnham* was the centre of a major international yachting storm involving a measuring discrepancy.

It had been discovered in Florida, where *Victory of Burnham* had been racing for Britain in the Southern Ocean Racing Conference of 1982, that there was a substantial error in her IOR rating which had therefore given her an immediate unfair advantage in all the races in which she had competed. The Royal Ocean Racing Club set up a special enquiry to establish how the error occurred, but it was especially embarrassing on the eve of the unveiling of the America's Cup challenger by Princess Michael of Kent at Cowes, since it was inevitable that *Victory of*

Burnham would face a humiliating disqualification from the Florida series.

Worse, there was an alarm at that stage that the discrepancy could have made a difference to the even more important result of the Admiral's Cup of the previous year and would cause not only a major upheaval for de Savary but also for the Royal Ocean Racing Club who run the international team series.

The situation was potentially the more explosive also because in the previous year in Florida there had been a major scandal following the discovery of two American boats with major rating discrepancies, which was actually put down to cheating and subsequently led to long bans from international yachting on the owners of both yachts; and there were protracted appeals after that.

Although the rules of the Admiral's Cup included a clause which meant that protests over ratings could not be retrospective – protests over ratings had to be entered before the series began – the discrepancy in *Victory of Burnham*'s rating could have such an effect on the outcome of the series as to force the Royal Ocean Racing Club at least to consider handing over the trophy to the country which had finished second in the international series – namely the United States. The reason for the alarm was that the rating was no less than 1.4 ft too low – a gross error.

The discovery, reaffirmed in the United States by a representative of the Royal Ocean Racing Club who went there to measure the yacht, brought automatic disqualification from the Florida series in which *Victory of Burnham* had been third on points. Fortunately, when the RORC announced that there would be a special enquiry set up to look into this discrepancy, and rating rules in general, it was established that calculations had shown that even allowing for the rating discrepancy the British team would still have been easy winners of the Admiral's Cup, originally won by a huge, 98-point margin. Allowing for the difference of 1.4 ft. in the rating, there would have been only a 19-point difference in the team total.

The RORC. made clear that they would call on whatever technical experts were necessary to establish how, why and what had happened in connection with the discrepancy and Keith Ludlow, then the club's rating secretary, emphasized that neither de Savary nor Dubois were responsible for the discrepancy. The significance of Ludlow's comment at the time was lost upon the general yachting public who did not know the details surrounding the error, but it was no less of a surprise, when on July 2, the details of the rating enquiry were revealed.

What the enquiry, by David Edwards, Brigadier Sir Frederick Coates and Sir David Mackworth, made clear was that the discrepancy occurred because of a failure adequately to recheck certain measurement queries after the yacht was first measured. References were made to the rating office, it was alleged, by both Dubois himself and one of the Admiral's Cup team selectors that certain aspects of the rating should be rechecked. This was not done and the further outcome was that the system was to be amended after thorough examination. Ludlow then resigned from his post. But none of this was known when the 12-metre was launched.

Phil Crebbin, who has a Master of Arts degree from Cambridge, and who pioneered the world's first shared logic word processor run from its own mini computer before he turned to yachting for a career as well as enjoyment, said that skippering *Victory* in an America's Cup campaign was the second most important thing he had ever done. The only more important factor would be winning the America's Cup, added *Victory's* skipper.

He indicated at the time of the launching that he was determined to dedicate everything for the next 18 months to winning the America's Cup. 'I believe we can match the Americans technically and I am sure that they are no better than we are as yachtsmen. But we must, of course, get everything right. It is not just a question of the right boat: there is the enormous task of looking after the crews, of producing the right environment for them in which to train and relax. There is the question of attitude, at working at a rational programme for training and racing; of keeping the crews motivated and bringing them to the peak of determination at the right time. I believe we might have the right boat; I hope and believe that we have selected the right people to sail her. I believe that we shall prove a formidable force.' *Victory*, the first 12-metre to be built at Cowes, did contain a number of original ideas but at 65 ½ ft long overall, 45 ft on the waterline and with a displacement of 55,500 lb, the blue and golden coloured aluminium yacht came somewhere between *Freedom* and *Enterprise* in length and displacement.

The yacht, like most 12-metres at that time, was clearly something of a compromise, being small enough to have good manoeuvrability but at the same time big enough to be competitive upwind. One of the most interesting aspects of the yacht, though full details were kept secret at the time, was the keel, which though conventional in sideways shape, 'was different in section shape,' admitted Dubois. Noticeable, above *Victory*'s waterline, there was increased overhang aft but reduced overhang forward. The deck layout was conventional, though the primary and mainsheet winch systems were developments of those used in 1980 aboard *Lionheart* and *Freedom*. The winching system, with chains replacing gear boxes, was considered more efficient than that of 1980 which was used on *Lionheart*, and which like the system employed on *Victory*, was produced by Lewmar. There were two steering positions on *Victory*.

Commenting on developments, de Savary himself said at the time that the odds were on building a second boat. Plans were well advanced, he said, all materials were being considered and discussions were in progress with three yards about construction.

VI

How Exactly Do *They* Do It?

These seasons of 1893 and 1894 stand alone in the memory of English yachtsmen because no large American Cutters, or, as the Americans call them 'sloops' have visited our shores since those years. It was commonly said — and it is still said — that American yachts are faster than English yachts. That may be true. I do not know. We always get beaten in that peculiarly one-sided contest known as the America's Cup, so perhaps that is proof that English cutters are not so fast as Yankee sloops...

Brooke Heckstall-Smith
The Britannia and Her Contemporaries (1929)

The Royal Burnham's challenge prospects for 1983 became much more urgent and impressive once de Savary and his team moved to Newport in the early summer of 1982. That is not to say that everything was correct or even satisfactory, though generally speaking there was more in favour of the Victory group than against; the cloud of controversy surrounding the disqualification from the SORC of *Victory of Burnham* and the subsequent findings of the special enquiry set up by the Royal Ocean Racing Club, still hung. The enquiry was incomplete when the team went to Newport.

On the credit side, and a most appropriate word in view of the vast financial outlay most obviously being made by de Savary, were the impressive results that the major expense had brought in relation to the compound where *Victory* and her trial-horse were based. Before he left to work for an American syndicate, the compound at Newport Yachting Centre was the province of Robin Fouger. New piles had been specially driven in and extra pontoons provided to accommodate not only *Victory* and *Australia* but the various support craft which de Savary had brought with him to Newport. These included, most notably, *Kalizma*, the 1906-built craft formerly owned by Elizabeth Taylor and named after her children Kate, Liza and Maria. *Kalizma*, on offer for $1,900,000 before she was bought by de Savary, seemed from her arrival to be likely to be one of the most talked about craft ever in Newport in 1983, expected to be the most extraordinary of America's Cup years. Miss Taylor is estimated to have spent $2 million on improvements on the vessel in 1968 and de Savary spent about another $1 million on further modernization. It is rather the history of the 147 ft craft, built at Leith in Scotland six years earlier than the *Titanic*, which makes her such a fascinating vessel. With at least three other names before Miss Taylor changed it to *Kalizma*, the vessel began life as a sailing yacht before being motorized and doing duty with the Royal Navy during two world wars. At one time she was damaged in action, the bridge being blown away with a number of the crew killed, and on another occasion she was partly sunk. The yacht was first called *Minoma*, then *Curtynia* and *Odysseia* and during the ownership by Miss Taylor she was dubbed 'Cleopatra's barge'.

In addition to *Kalizma* and *Victory* and *Australia*, de Savary had in Newport the 55ft 40-knot Magnum *Lisanola*, a Fairey Huntsman, a 46ft speedboat and various other smaller craft; as well as three houses, an apartment for crew members, an executive jet aircraft and a seaplane.

The support craft were just an integral part; more important were the workshops and the especially installed hoist, features which put the compound in a special category of impressiveness – in as much as it was the best in Newport. It was here too that Jim Alabaster, for long the chief negotiator, planner, administrator and part-time press liaison officer for the Victory syndicate had his base and where, in time, Bob Pegler, the Met man and Dr Graeme Winn ran the computer system for the group. De Savary was able to keep an eye on matters from a fifth floor penthouse suite in one corner of the compound. Visiting oil men from around the world, many of whom were delivered to and returned from Newport by de Savary's own aircraft, must have been impressed by the psychological warfare which resulted from the lining up of all the de Savary 'hardware'.

The presence all over Newport on moving and stationary objects of the Victory bulldog mascot 'Winston' – known by some of the Americans as the 'bloody dog' – was another feature of the battle of wits that had begun between the British and American camps as soon as de Savary's men arrived in Newport. What caused most trouble was the daily 'spy' boat sent by the British to watch American preparations which involved first the tuning by the Dennis Conner camp of the new *Spirit* and *Magic* against *Freedom*. There was much unhappiness about these tactics, and the Americans alleged that at times the British surveillance craft got so close as to be a real nuisance. The immediate outcome of the early skirmishing was that Bob McCullough, Commodore of the New York Yacht Club, and de Savary had lunch together on board *Kalizma* with McCullough clearly stating he would prefer the British to desist in the business of watching what the Americans were doing and de Savary making it equally clear that the challengers would retain the right to prepare for their challenge for supremacy by watching what the champions did; a common practice in all major sporting events. There seemed to be two points of view about the value of the surveillance of the Americans; Cudmore, Crebbin, de Savary and those more closely involved with the early tuning of *Victory* clearly felt that there was far more to be gained than lost. They obviously thought that what they learnt, in terms not only of sail technology but crewing techniques, more than made up for any possible repercussions.

Now the challenge with *Lionheart* in 1980 had enjoyed certain advantages and indeed privileges through friendly relations with the American camp. These could be lost in 1982 and could prove to be more of a disadvantage than anything that was learned from the close observation that was going on during the summer of 1983. Thus de Savary really needed to look to the safety and future of his financial empire in case certain members of the New York Yacht Club should decide that, in order to clip the wings of this 'upstart Brit', they would take steps perhaps to threaten some of his financial interests in the United States. To his credit, de Savary was not troubled by such threats and it would appear that he was justified in taking the stand that he did. The only question was whether, in the early scrutiny, the British boats had infringed good sportsmanship by getting too close to the American boats. It was obviously a source of continual disagreement between the two camps and de Savary forecast that there was going to be a similar surveillance of the American efforts when they moved to San Diego for their winter training. (It turned out to be no more than a forecast.)

Certainly there was no question but that it was potentially a situation which could get out of hand and it was quite clear that this was one of the areas where it was necessary for there to be a clear appreciation of the situation by those in command in Newport. It was this issue perhaps as much as anything that emphasized the total lack of experience in the America's Cup field of de Savary and his lieutenants and seemed to highlight the need for a strong No.2 – someone in Newport to slot between de Savary and his troops. De Savary insisted that he was the mastermind, that he intended to be in Newport for most of the summer preparations, and it was obvious from the sort of gentleman that he was that he would be taking a very active role in preparations – there was no need for a 'deputy'. The worry was that his undoubted business acumen may not have been the advantage that the campaign needed. What might have been more valuable to them was someone with wide experience of an America's Cup campaign and who could quickly ensure that the activities were put back on a regular and sensible course at the first sign of any problems.

Returning to the plus side and the one which on balance probably had much to commend it, it was pointed out that as well as being an excellent camp – with excellent morale and outstanding determination displayed by the crew and back-up team – there was just as much eagerness for practically everything to do with the British effort ashore as well as afloat as there was in the surveillance of the American efforts. It was especially commendable that training had begun in Newport by the beginning of June and the fact that the boats were tuning together very soon thereafter was another major advantage and one which was almost unknown in all previous British efforts in the America's Cup. Whether it would bring victory in the America's Cup seemed at that stage to be no more certain, however, than when de Savary announced his America's Cup plans in 1980.

The British were the first of the challengers to be in Newport in 1982, though it was expected at that stage that the Canadians, who had been training in Florida with *Interpid* and *Clipper*, and perhaps the French, would come to race in the latter part of 1982. The Australians, meanwhile, had been launching the first of what was expected to be at least three boats, the Italians were still building their boat and doubt about whether the Swedes

Fig. 5 12-Metre Yachts at Newport 1983

Nationality	Name	Owner	Club	Skipper	Designer	Builder
U.S.A.	Freedom	Maritime College Fort Schuyler Foundation Inc.	New York Yacht Club		S & S	Minneford Yacht Yard (1979)
	Liberty			Dennis Conner	Johan Valentijn	Newport Offshore (1982)
	Defender	Defender/Courageous Syndicate	New York Yacht Club	Tom Blackaller	David Pedrick	Newport Offshore (1982)
	Courageous			John Kolius	S & S	Minneford Yacht Yard (1973)
Britain	Australia				Ben Lexcen	Steve Ward (1976)
	Victory	Peter de Savary and Victory Syndicate	Royal Burnham Yacht Club	Rodney Pattisson Lawrie Smith Phil Crebbin	Ed Dubois	W. Souter (1982)
	Victory '83				Ian Howlett	Fairey Allday (1983)

Country	Yacht	Syndicate/Owner	Yacht Club	Skipper	Designer	Builder
Australia	*Australia II*	Alan Bond	Royal Perth Yacht Club	John Bertrand	Ben Lexcen	Steve Ward (1982)
	Advance	R.S.Y.S. Syndicate	Royal Sydney Yacht Squadron	Iain Murray	Alan Payne	Aquacraft (1982)
	Challenge 12	Alan Bond	Royal Y.C. of Victoria	John Savage	Ben Lexcen	Steve Ward (1982)
Italy	*Azzurra*	Aga Khan & Azzurra Syndicate	Yacht Club Costa Smeralda	Flavio Scala	Andrea Vallicelli	Officine (1982)
France	*France III*	Yves Rousset-Ronard	Yacht Club de France	Bruno Trouble	Johan Valentijn & Ben Lexcen	Michael Dufour (1979)
Canada	*Canada*	Marvin McDill & Secret Cove Syndicate	Secret Cove Yacht Club	Terry McLaughlin	Bruce Kirby	McConnel Marina (1982)

would actually build a new boat was confirmed when they stood down.

Certainly the Americans could not fail but recognize that there were certain aspects of the British effort which could represent a major threat to them, although they considered then that they had very little to worry about when they surveyed just the one British boat capable of making a challenge. As well as having two new boats *Spirit* and *Magic*, the Fort Schulyer syndicate had *Freedom*, the previous winner, ready to tackle whichever of the two boats being served by Dennis Conner proved to be the fastest, while the syndicate being run by Tom Blackaller, had *Defender*, designed by Dave Pedrick and rather similar to *Victory* before she was launched, and the older but twice successful *Courageous*. *Defender*, late on the scene, was in action by midsummer. All of this added up to rather more in terms of an impressive fleet ready for America's Cup action.

Australia was found to be in a much worse state of repair and seemed likely to need regular maintenance throughout the campaign, than had been expected. In fact, some of the crew felt that it was questionable whether *Australia* represented as big an advantage as thought when she was bought. Also it was alleged that she was not delivered with all the equipment aboard that had been expected; though in the end, everything that was thought to be on *Australia* when she was purchased did find its way back on to the boat. She was, however, a feather in the 'hat' of the British camp because she was the boat from which it was possible to measure as a trial-horse how fast or how challenging new boats were even if she had been soundly beaten by *Freedom* in 1980.

Unfortunately, it was discovered that *Victory* was not quite such a perfect craft as obviously de Savary had hoped and as those who were on the side lines had been led to believe she might be. There was some distortion, it was reported, after the building and there was a lot of work to be done in Newport on fairing before the craft would begin her sailing trials. Be that as it may, when she did go afloat for the first time at least she certainly did look a beautiful craft, a quality so regularly associated with her designer Ed Dubois. It was also something of a worry to the British whether they would be able to get in what they considered to be a vital 150 days of sailing while in Newport in 1982, and as well as some worry about the boats, there was concern also about sails, with the suggestion that because major developments were expected by the beginning of 1983 it was essential that all evaluation of sails was completed by the end of 1982. The biggest question of all facing de Savary, it was argued, however, was the suitability of the personnel taken to Newport and from whom the crew of *Victory* would be chosen.

In all areas of the Victory syndicate rumours were forever rife, criticism practically non-stop, doubt endless and scepticism essentially total until well into 1982, and it was concerning the crew that there seemed to be the biggest doubt. Perhaps because of the undoubted disappointment that was felt among the British yachting public over the quick elimination from the 1980 series of *Lionheart* – and despite the success with *Victory of Burnham* – there was a reluctance to become involved with the 12-metre *Victory* until it seemed certain that de Savary would make a better effort of his challenge than Boyden and the British Industry 1500 syndicate had. Though a number of well-established and respected yachting stalwarts had courted de Savary when the *Victory* project was first mooted – and when the first appeals for crew members went out – the squad first taken to Newport was widely considered to be short of 'class' hands. This shortage of top-calibre crewmen did underline the natural gulf that existed between American and British 12-metre camps in terms of attracting the right personnel.

First and biggest of the problems facing the British was that in the deep recession of 1981–3, there were few people in Britain who could give up the time and their jobs and dedicate themselves unaided to an America's Cup challenge for about two years. Of course, if de Savary had been prepared to pay good wages it is possible that he might have assembled more of the sort of people he needed than those present in the Spring of 1982 were widely considered to be. But for a number of reasons, not least of which was the fact that even an attractive salary was not likely to tempt some yachtsmen to forfeit good careers for a scheme which, judged by all that had gone before, would end in one form of disaster or another, not even money would have attracted the right people.

The make-up of the crew and shore personnel did give a feeling that, if there were not exactly two camps, at least there were two distinct points of view. It seemed at first that yachting 'heavies', as they were termed, resented the servicemen who can have been in no doubt in those early days that their presence in the main would depend on how long it took de Savary to get together better trained yachtsmen. Nevertheless, it did seem that those most likely to be sent home early because of a failure to match up to the requirements of their boss were some of the more experienced yachtsmen who perhaps were not so ready to come to terms with the discipline that was being instilled and who felt that because of their rather more established skills in the field of yachting they should therefore be allowed more leeway.

To this end, there were three graphs for every member of the team: one to illustrate physical training progress, another which outlined behaviour in the base camp and a third graph which was drawn up from information relating to aspects of crewing. De Savary made clear that he was not expecting a 10-out-of-10 scoring in all fields, though he did expect a better than casual effort. There was naturally much discussion about how things would work out in relation to the squad members coming to terms with life in the United States and it did seem inevitable that there would be numerous changes among the personnel. And this seemed the more likely unless someone was appointed to act as a buffer between de Savary and his troops. Not one of his lieutenants was sufficiently more authoritative than another to be considered as first lieutenant, although Lt-Col Tim Street had presumably been appointed with this in mind.

In addition to the crew, there was the vitally important question of the skipper and afterguard. Crebbin, of course, had been nominated and named as skipper at the start of the campaign, though in reality de Savary obviously had the right to terminate any agreement as he saw fit.

Though announced as being Crebbin's No. 2, or tactician, Cudmore, whose earlier roles in Newport seemed to have been as skipper of *Australia* and the man responsible for crew training afloat, was unofficially considered to be on equal footing. The two seemed to work well together and there were obviously a number of very good points in their favour as an afterguard duo for the challenge ahead. Though Crebbin and Cudmore had much deeper 'pedigrees', their selection obviously had much to do with their status as arguably the two best and most experienced match-race skippers in Britain. But as de Savary and the crew got down to the business of training it was clear that there were more than rumblings about the need to bring in someone of similar stature fairly early on in order to push the first-choice afterguard. To this extent, de Savary obviously favoured the enlistment of Lawrie Smith, who had been approached and was available provided the terms were right: those, Smith made clear, meant that he would be interested in being in Newport for any length of time only if he was steering a boat. He certainly would have no wish whatsoever to go there as a winch grinder, was his comment.

It is possible to discuss at almost unending length the various complexities, difficulties, the lines of encouraging achievement and the doubts which were all too evident in the Victory Camp in those early days in Newport. But problems were bound to emerge as a completely new crew came to terms with something which was totally new to all of them. Despite all of the difficulties however, the over-riding impression in early 1982 was that although the Victory effort might not win the cup, like so many that had gone before – it was still likely that it would represent the finest and most dedicated of all British challenges.

De Savary can have been under no illusion whatsoever of the daunting task which faced him. The clear implication was that the Americans would be no less strong and maybe even stronger than ever before. *Magic* and *Spirit* were not a great success, but yet a further American boat followed. Be this as it may, the lesson that had to be learned was that while challengers may begin where the Americans had begun their defence three years previously, the defenders began preparations for the subsequent challenge somewhere in advance of where they had left off winning the last. Certainly this seemed to be the case when the Americans began their opening trials to evaluate *Spirit* and *Magic*, which subsequently led to a further boat, *Liberty*. Yet *Victory* was a development of *Australia*, built for the 1977 challenge.

Victory's mast, one of four that was to be available for the preparations for the America's Cup, was stepped at the beginning of June 1982, almost ten weeks to the day after the launching of the yacht at Cowes, and she began trials almost immediately with *Australia* which had been used since the arrival of the crews in May for team training. 'Rule Britannia', played loud enough to reach a large section of the Newport

waterfront at the time when Britain was embroiled in the
Falklands conflict, greeted *Victory* as she was finally secured in
her campaign berth. With the Americans, or more correctly, the
Dennis Conner crew, already into their training routine, the
series of gales and strong winds which prevented *Victory* having
her first outing at sea were the more annoying, and it was not
until June 6 that the yacht, which had cost some £300,000 to
build, slipped her moorings to go sailing for the first time. Her
trial-horse *Australia* had been dismasted a few days previously
and so it was just for an hour, because of expected strong winds,
that *Victory* was at sea alone for her first outing.

The second trip, a few days later, was just as short. Soon after
her first tack into a freshening breeze of around 20 knots, and
under mainsail only, the port runner support pulled out. The
yacht, looking majestic with the foam from her bow wave
reflecting impressively in the super gloss finish of her blue
topsides, was just about to pass under Jamestown Bridge into
Narraganset Bay when the incident occurred. Crebbin promptly
turned for home and repairs to the first of the teething troubles
that were to be expected. But the short outing was still long
enough to raise hopes that the yacht would give an outstanding
account of herself. Despite the delays and irritating early break-
ages, the preparations in Newport for the summer of 1983
America's Cup campaign proper were encouraging and promising: encouraging because though the trials were some weeks
behind those of the Americans, they had begun efficiently and
realistically.

Though it was then far too early to consider seriously whether
Victory or her successor could beat the Americans, there were
those ready to put bets on a British victory by the end of the
summer. This was unduly optimistic, but de Savary, who,
during the summer had become known simply as PDS, was able
to claim that the British had completed more hours of sail
training in Rhode Island Sound than the Americans. One of the
reasons for this was the trouble that the surveillance policy of
the British had brought and which had probably, it was thought,
led to Dennis Conner cutting short some of his plans, perhaps
neglecting others and certainly being prevented from doing just
as he wished because of the 'spy boats' – about which he seemed
to be more than irritated.

Surveillance, which was an emotive if not explosive issue in

Newport from the arrival of the British and the staging of their first 'spy mission', led to a serious deterioration of relations between the Conner and de Savary camps from the very beginning, when it is said that the British surveillance craft at times went between the two American 12s that were training at that time. On more than one occasion, it is alleged, the craft passed between the tender and one of the 12s. As relations deteriorated so the involvement of Bob McCullough, a former winner of the America's Cup, in trying to limit or halt surveillance became more regular and frenzied.

Even before McCullough first went to Newport to see de Savary, Derek Clark, one of the British race tacticians and an Olympic sailor, was warned that unless he gave up continuously watching the American yachts he would 'have both of his arms broken'. Whether the allegations are true may never be known for sure but the clash does illustrate that the disagreement between the Americans and the British was acute. In those early days the British tried not to allow too much of what was going on to become public because they did not want the Americans to know that they felt they were learning as much as they were. The situation thereafter was that McCullough and the New York Yacht Club continued to make contact with the Royal Sydney, the Challenger of Record, with the Burnham and probably other challengers trying to get agreement that the Deed of Gift of the America's Cup precluded such activities as surveillance by the British, with whom the New York Yacht Club were also in constant touch.

The British continued to ignore the threats, though it was noticeable that as the Royal Burnham became more involved so de Savary was more diplomatic in his attitude towards the surveillance and was quick to insist on a 200-yard limit. He actually stopped the observer boats over the period when officers of the Royal Burnham went to New York to discuss the surveillance issue with McCullough. The answer by the Fort Schuyler syndicate, which owned *Freedom*, and Conner was to have a tender with special responsibility to keep the British spy boat at bay. By the end of August, as the Victory group had perhaps a month of training left before departing for Nassau for the winter of 1982, there was even an accusation that a succession of engine failures on British craft used for surveillance work might be due to interference.

Matters came to a head when the surveillance team, which on that occasion happened to be Clark and Dubois, reported that they had been rammed by the *Freedom* tender and a blank round had been fired from a small starting cannon in mock annoyance by the tender of the *Defender* syndicate.

Interestingly, the members of the Royal Burnham's America's Cup committee who had been considered a possible 'weak link' in the surveillance issue in as much as the New York Yacht Club were thought likely to be more successful in getting it banned by negotiating with the Royal Burnham than by dealing with de Savary direct, were to prove in late September that they were in fact very much behind de Savary. Indeed, they might have been described as having 'declared war' on the Americans in general and the New York Yacht Club and McCullough in particular after the Commodore had attributed one of the difficulties to the lack of experience with America's Cup procedures on the part of de Savary and the Royal Burnham. 'The Royal Burnham', said McCullough, 'came to Newport this time without any past experience in competition. They told us in effect, "we want to observe the United States boats at close range", and their attitude was that it was done in other sports. Then they just went out and did it. That's where they got themselves in trouble.' McCullough insisted that the New York Yacht Club were trying to get the matter resolved amicably.

David Geaves and Frank Kemble, respectively Commodore and past Commodore of the Royal Burnham, were quick to hit back at the criticism. In their view, differences had arisen over the surveillance not so much because of the inexperience of the Royal Burnham, but rather because of the fact that the New York Yacht Club would not stand still and come to an agreement. What upset the Royal Burnham most was that the New York Club were ignoring the fundamental rule of the America's Cup that all conditions for the contest were by 'mutual agreement'. While Kemble insisted that the Royal Burnham were trying seriously to achieve mutual agreement over the surveillance issue, it seemed that most of their efforts had been snubbed by McCullough. Kemble also pointed out that the surveillance had not been subversive but overt. There had never been any suggestion of spying, though this had happened in previous America's Cups, and there was therefore a precedent for such a thing. 'We are observing, not spying, on the Amer-

icans,' said Kemble, making the point that the *Victory* preparations were being constantly spied upon by the Americans. The
Burnham Flag Officers were determined also to make clear that
the Royal Sydney Yacht Squadron had agreed to nothing except
that there should be a code of conduct. Certainly they had not
agreed, alleged the British, as had been maintained by the
Americans, that the Challenger of Record had agreed to preclude
observations of preparations. Geaves maintained that negotia-
tions with McCullough over the issue had failed because the
American shifted his ground every time there was a discussion.

Through all of this de Savary insisted that the belief that the
whole of the New York Yacht Club or indeed that the whole of
the Fort Schuyler syndicate were against surveillance was not in
fact the case. He maintained that he was in regular contact with
officials of both the New York Yacht Club and Fort Schuyler
syndicate who intimated that it was de Savary who had their
support on the surveillance issue. Certainly observers in Newport got the impression that a lot of Americans considered that
there was nothing wrong with this and, indeed, there were those
who clearly thought it was all rather fun and especially enjoyed
the suggestion that Conner was upset by the surveillance.

The surveillance issue came to an end in Newport in 1982
when the Americans and British stopped training and packed up
their boats and camp to go to Nassau from where, they had
indicated, they would be making arrangements for surveillance
on American winter preparations in San Diego. In the event this
proved impracticable.

Anyway by this time de Savary himself seemed to be coming
to the belief that there should be some agreement on some of the
American training being in private. The issue seemed to revolve
around the consideration that though it was normal practice for
teams to be spied upon by their rivals as they prepared for a
major event.

The teams that were spied upon in public did at least have the
ability to carry out some of their training in private at their own
headquarters. The American view was that they should be
allowed some privacy to train in Newport. This seemed to be
tacitly agreed to by de Savary, although he took some time to
make this public because he obviously felt that if he gave ground
a lot more would be sought. While the attitude of de Savary to
surveillance was understandable, there being a need to know

not only what the Americans were up to but to be able to imitate some of their more successful systems – not to mention possible psychological advantages – the attention given to the American reaction was less understanding in some quarters than it might have been.

Actually the response of the Americans to British surveillance was clumsy to an almost alarming degree. Clearly firing starting cannon; having what can only be described as bulldozer protection boats; making known the fact that they had approached the Coastguard and the question of facts about immigration forms were a sign only of a lack of preparation to deal with a rival as cunning as de Savary. All of the 'tricks' were being won by de Savary. Even though the British may not have been succeeding in anything like the way they intended with surveillance they definitely maximized the benefits to the obvious disgust of the Americans.

What must be realized, however, was that McCullough and the New York Yacht Club's America's Cup committee obviously found themselves in a very difficult position. If they stood by and allowed de Savary and his British camp to get away with what they wanted, a dangerous precedent was obviously being set for successive Cup campaigns. It was an escalation of cost and time that would be bound in the end perhaps to tell against them. If more and more overseas contenders spent more and more money to go to Newport to begin their preparations they would be forcing the American camp into what might prove even to them an unacceptable 'arms race'.

While the Royal Burnham and the New York Yacht Club were discussing the surveillance issue, which de Savary announced would be known henceforth as monitoring, there were a number of important announcements by the British camp in Newport, where some important advantages were claimed. Most important, perhaps, was the opinion that *Victory*, at the end of the summer, had the edge on *Australia*, although a number of modifications which were planned for the winter had still to be carried out. The group also claimed that at every level, from sailcloth to the number of sails they had at their disposal, they were either on a level footing or ahead of the Americans in the area previously overwhelmingly dominated by them.

Significant also was the decision by de Savary to delay, until at least Christmas or a point up to two days before Christmas, the decision to build a second yacht and meanwhile to bring *Lionheart* out of mothballs for training purposes while modifications were being made to *Victory*. How *Lionheart* was available when it had been claimed by the Victory syndicate that she had been sold brought about an answer involving complex financial deals. Be that as it may, there is no doubt that the decision to 'reprieve' the boat built for Boyden had much to commend it.

Long before a decision was announced – or perhaps even made about reactivating *Lionheart* – the Victory syndicate obviously believed, as they began the sailing campaign with the new 12-metre, that *Australia* was the faster of the two boats they were sailing against and there were some beliefs that the condition of *Victory* was considerably worse perhaps than the syndicate would have had it known. However, as the end of their training approached, there had been a shift of emphasis to the fact that the British yacht was faster now than the trial-horse. The alterations to the rudder and trim tab of *Victory*, which had been carried out in late July/early August, had brought the better handling characteristics as required and the mast of the British yacht, the position of which was altered and was not back to its original position, was giving the sort of performance that was required.

Clearly, some of the performances of *Victory* may have been made to appear worse than they were for reasons of security but were problems because, as de Savary argued at the time, the only way to be sure that *Victory* was any good was to make sure that *Australia* was being sailed at her very best. The argument was that more attention had been paid to getting *Australia* to sail well by having perhaps a slightly better crew aboard in order to get the best out of her because, it was maintained, there was no way that the threat of *Victory* could be evaluated without knowing that *Australia* was being sailed well.

In the opinion of the Victory syndicate, *Australia*, with better sails and better rigging than she had had at the time of the 1980 America's Cup defence, was faster and more competitive during the trials of 1982 than she had been two years previously. Although John Bertrand, the nominated skipper for Bond's Australian challenge in 1983, had been given the opportunity of sailing *Australia* as indeed had Pelle Petterson, the Swedish skipper, the Victory syndicate did not report whether these visiting skippers agreed with their assessment.

If *Victory* was the faster of the two boats it was strange that plans were made to fit her with a new keel at the end of the summer training. It was insisted that this was part of an original programme and in no way related to any decision on a possible second new boat. Ed Dubois, her designer, in Newport to look over planning alterations from time to time, said he was entirely happy with the progress of the yacht. It seemed that the shape of the keel first fitted had made the yacht difficult to sail to windward in light winds and calm seas. *Victory* was said to be faster in light weather than *Australia*, against whom she had proved faster downwind. But in stronger breezes and steeper seas she was apparently more difficult to sail to windward than *Australia*.

According to Angus Melrose, who was in charge of the impressive *Victory* sail loft in Newport, the group certainly had as many sails and expected to have as many new ones in the following year as any of the other syndicates, including the Americans. The sail wardrobe towards the end of the summer of 1982, and before new sails were made for the final trials and the move to Nassau, included seven mainsails, 21 genoas and 16 spinnakers, while some 30 others of various types had been rejected. Melrose, who was on special leave of absence from Iain Macdonald-Smith's North loft in England, claimed that the Victory group had done more sail testing with new sails than any of the other syndicates and there was no doubt that their sails were competitive with those of the best 12-metres in the world. Two main factors had contributed towards the breakthrough, the relaxation by the New York Yacht Club of the rules which previously permitted challengers to use sailcloth only manufactured in their country of origin, and production by a British company of a cloth currently considered the best in the world for mainsails. Now, not only did the British have access to any sailcloth previously available only to the Americans, but their observations meant that they knew much more about the sails used by Conner in the defence in 1980, and also exactly what he was testing and using in the summer of 1982.

The development concerning sails was perhaps one of the most encouraging announcements to be made in Newport because it had always been a cry among British yachtsmen that they had had to work with inferior sails in the America's Cup and certainly the amount of confidence that emanated from the loft of Melrose and his assistants in Newport in 1982 suggested that it was real rather than imaginary that the progress in sails was important.

De Savary delayed ordering the second boat and his view anyway was that there was no need for the boat to be available until April 1983 in Newport and that providing her deck layout was identical to that of *Victory* there was no other problem. It did seem to be quite a compelling argument although even the argument that with the Americans now known to be planning to build their fourth boat, *Liberty* (the third in fact for Conner) they could wait until the Americans had built their new boat and incorporate any design characteristics in a new British boat, was also a little difficult to accept.

What was encouraging perhaps was that as well as closer involvement by Dubois who had one of his associates, Chris Temple, working more or less full-time on design requirements in Newport from about the middle of the summer of 1982, there was closer involvement also from Ian Howlett, whom de Savary was quick to point out had been employed by him since 1980. With the close attention of these designers it appeared that de Savary was trying to provoke competition between Howlett and Dubois in the hope that one of them, in the extra time that was being made available, or the two of them together, would come up with a proposal which would, if not exactly guarantee a faster boat, at least give the impression of producing a yacht more suitable for cup racing than *Victory*.

It seems that some of the more respected of the yachtsmen now involved more or less full-time in the Victory campaign, and who included the triple Olympic medallist, Rodney Pattisson, did get together to meet de Savary at the end of the summer of 1982 to promote the idea that there should be a second boat but there were certainly others in the camp who appreciated that to look after yet another boat would be somewhat difficult. However, it would have been difficult to get odds on anything to do with a second new boat, of either extreme; namely, whether there would be one or whether there would not be one.

The decision to bring *Lionheart* out of mothballs to help with the 1983 challenge series seemed to be almost the de Savary masterstroke of the summer. Not only did it mean that he had two 12-metres to use, namely *Australia* and *Lionheart*, while

Victory was undergoing her major modifications, but it also injected further competition into the Victory campaign; especially as it was decided that *Lionheart* should be skippered by Lawrie Smith and that as far as possible old members of the *Lionheart* crew would also be in Newport to sail the yacht. Ian Howlett was back in Newport to oversee the facelift for the yacht and certain modifications were also considered which might make her more competitive, though it seemed that initially she would be used solely for training purposes.

The main bonus of the decision, it seemed, was that it brought to Newport additional yachting talent in the shape of Smith whom de Savary had always been known to rate very highly. Interestingly some old 'loyalties' were re-encouraged by the announcement that *Lionheart* was to be brought back. A number of people who had been associated with the 1980 yacht were very excited at the prospect of 'showing *Victory* what it was all about', although, in the end, all that was proved really was that *Lionheart* was a very fast boat in a straight line, but when it came to tacking – and certainly in the area of match-racing – she was not competitive. In a private match-race series between *Victory*, the responsibility of Crebbin and Cudmore, *Lionheart*, who had Smith and Pattison as the afterguard team, the later boat was an easy and convincing winner. *Victory*, meanwhile, had finished top also in the second World 12-metre championship, again boycotted by the Americans although compared with the event at Brighton in 1980, it was significant in as much as, in addition to three British boats – *Lionheart*, *Victory* and *Australia* – the French and the Canadians with *Clipper* also took part in the event. The series, unlike that at Brighton, was a fleet exercise and although *Victory* did not win every race she was a handsome winner in the end.

The close-down at Newport for the winter coincided with the announcement that Peter Bateman, at that time joint managing director of the Hood Sailmakers Ltd in England and a former Olympic coach, was to be coach to the Victory syndicate; but with the strong suggestion that he might in fact be the 'No. 2' between de Savary and the rest of the group.

Bateman's principle role was to sharpen British crew members who were still relatively inexperienced in 12-metre yachting, though it was obvious that his sail-making background would be invaluable so long as it did not lead to serious disagree-

ment between the two big lofts involved in the event. Whether
Bateman, who earlier in the summer had taken part in the
Round Britain Race as crew member to Chay Blyth on the
trimaran *Brittany Ferries*, which finished second, would be the
tough guy that the syndicate required remained to be seen.
Certainly his appointment seemed to be a plus factor for the
syndicate as they packed up their boats in Newport and headed
for their winter quarters at Nassau.

It was just before Christmas 1982 that de Savary, in Nassau,
came out with his public warning to the American yachting
establishment to end what he alleged was a campaign of dirty
tricks and deliberate subversion against the British syndicate of
1983. De Savary, his anger said occasionally to be bubbling to
the surface, explained that he felt the time had come to speak
out. He hoped that straight talking would clear the air before the
12-metre syndicates of six nations began the heats to select the
challenger and defender. He claimed that harrassment of the
Britons, subtle and not-so-subtle sniping and tactics designed to
make things difficult for them if not force them out of the
contest altogether, had been apparent throughout the trials off
Newport during the summer of 1982 and had still to abate at the
start of 1983. These actions, he said, had been directed against
him personally, against his global business interests, the Victory syndicate, the Royal Burnham Yacht Club and others. He
identified the men behind the campaign as a few particularly
influential members of what he chose to call the American
yachting establishment mafia. All had been closely associated
in recent years with the defence of the Cup.

'Until now I have not reacted to all this as I perhaps should
have,' de Savary said. 'I am issuing them with a warning. If it
happens again I'll start to play the same game and play it slightly
rougher. I'm used to dealing with Africans, with Arabs, with
Latin Americans and I happen to be in the roughest and toughest
business there is: international oil. If the gloves have to come off
I can give as well as take. The New York people have said they
will find a way to defeat me although there are a lot of people in
American yachting who would like to see them lose to us or
somebody else. They have said they want to see us discredited;
see us do as badly as possible. They have come out and said in so
many words to me personally and I have been told the same
thing by friends who happen to be members of the New York

Club. They have even gone as far as to say that had they realized
that members of the Royal Burnham were other than gentlemen
they would never have accepted our challenge. They seem to
have the impression that I rented the Royal Burnham just to
make the challenge. In fact, I was born in a village three miles
from the Club, I learned to sail there and my father was a
member for more than 40 years.'

Listing some of the examples of the American difficulties put
in his way, de Savary said there had been unexpected problems
which had arisen in the United States in sorting out immigration matters during the summer. 'Why were all these Britons
working in Newport for the syndicate without immigration
green cards, that sort of silly thing.' Efforts which were made 'to
see that the Coastguard gave us trouble', the subversive digs, the
stuff they tried to drag up and feed to the Press about the Victory
syndicate's close-range surveillance of the American 12s. The
orders which came down from the New York Yacht Club had
prevented the competing American syndicates from entering
their boats in what the British had expected would be a friendly
international regatta in Newport. (There was no allegation that
they had wanted to race.) The Americans had requested the
Royal Sydney Yacht Squadron, the Challenger of Record, to
re-write the rules to disallow the surveillance of a rival's boat:
'the idea was that this rule would be applied retroactively, but
the Royal Sydney are fair-minded people and they wouldn't hear
of it.' De Savary also remarked that rumours had been fabricated
about poor morale within the British camp. While making these
charges about American pre-race procedures which clearly were
inspired to a very large degree, if they existed, by the surveillance problem, de Savary declared he would observe potential
American defenders in the winter. Meanwhile from October
1982 to March 1983 the British skippers and crews at Nassau
sailed race after race in their syndicate's 12s.

VII

The Investment Increases

The Victory syndicate had never been intended as a one-boat challenge. De Savary had always insisted that a second 12-metre would, if required, be built. Yet as late summer 1982 became autumn and the existing British 12s trained at Nassau, the time appeared to have passed: time, that is, for building and tuning up a real challenger.

On October 7, de Savary stated that he could leave the decision to build another boat until as late as Christmas. This time scale was certainly not endorsed by any of his competitors who already had their challenging boats sailing, though in the case of the Australians and the USA no final choices had yet been made from those boats available.

This statement was a smokescreen. *Victory* was already being stripped of equipment to fit on to a new Ian Howlett-designed hull. Ed Dubois had not felt able to devote much of his time to the challenge. He had plenty of other work; ocean racers, single-handed sailing projects, production cruisers. It had been common knowledge for some time that the professional relationship between Dubois and de Savary had become strained over the reluctance by the designer to commit himself wholly to the 12-metre project and to spend most of his time in the United States. De Savary had actually stated, openly at times, that he had insisted that Dubois should spend more time on the project and only the arrival of Chris Temple as a permanent 'ambassador' in Newport had seemed to keep the partnership alive. Matters had obviously come to a head during a major meeting of the principal lieutenants of the Victory syndicate in Newport at the end of the racing series in September when, ill-advisedly perhaps, Dubois had decided to ignore the *Victory* 'inquest' and instead visit another client. At the meeting which Dubois missed there was a spirited demand that de Savary should build a new yacht.

According to a number of sources, it was decided by certain of the senior syndicate chiefs in Newport that it was imperative that they should lead a serious campaign to make de Savary realize that in their opinion the Dubois-designed *Victory* was not suitable for an America's Cup campaign and that another yacht should be built. Indeed, it seems that only Crebbin and Cudmore considered that there was any merit in proceeding with the alterations to *Victory* rather than going ahead with a new boat, although, in reality, they too had maintained throughout that a second new boat would be desirable.

Not long after the meeting in Newport, Crebbin was happy to state that in his opinion *Victory* would prove a worthy challenger; that although she may not have been the best 12-metre ever built, the modifications were likely to make her sufficiently competitive for the elimination series, and possibly for the America's Cup. Cudmore was certainly singing the praises of the yacht designed by Dubois in Australia at the very time that it was being revealed in Britain that a second boat was to be built. The reason for the switch may never be known, but it did seem at the time that a blunt announcement by two of the key afterguard members of the de Savary campaign, Pattison and Smith, that they would not continue with the preparations unless a second new boat was built, had considerable influence. De Savary had certainly come to respect the dedication of the quietly spoken Pattisson, whose physical fitness, despite being one of the older members of the squad in Newport, led the *Victory* chief to remark on one occasion that the triple Olympic medallist was the only member of the group who could be trusted to do his best in the boxing ring against Mohammed Ali if asked to undertake such an impossible mission.

There were, obviously, a number of other key considerations which led de Savary to order the new boat. There was the discovery that modifications begun on *Victory*, and which would have taken at least until Christmas to complete, would prove more expensive than first estimated; there was the major consideration also that Howlett had designed what was described as a 'blitz machine', when he drew the lines of the 6-metre in which Erik Maxwell won the world championship of that class in 1982; there was the fact that the expensive modifications to *Victory* might have led the New York Yacht Club to question whether she was an American or a British 12-metre. Considering that no one could say precisely how fast *Victory* was, a larger version of the Howlett 6-metre was obviously an attractive proposition.

The absolute truth of the strength and weaknesses of the Dubois boat may never be known. The problem was that some of the team obviously thought reasonably highly of the boat and tended to overstate her strength, while those with fewer loyalties to the yacht were inclined to exaggerate her weaknesses. What did seem certain was that she was never as good as the leading members of the Victory syndicate would have liked, not as bad as her detractors suggested.

The most serious charge against *Victory* was that she did not actually constitute a 12-metre yacht. Even if this were true it did not necessarily amount to a serious problem. It would not have been especially difficult to make the boat a 12-metre by reducing sail area, for example. Much more important was the problem, if it was indeed true that the boat did not measure as a 12-metre, of how much modification was needed, and of how much it would have cost to make the yacht a 12-metre.

The de Savary version was that although it would have been possible to have challenged with *Victory*, the syndicate had known in their hearts that they had some aces up their sleeves that they were not using and they wanted to go into the America's Cup series leaving nothing undone that could have been done; thus the need for a second boat.

It was expected that the new boat would be completed by late February for delivery to Newport, to begin racing on May 1. According to de Savary, that would leave plenty of time to sail her for six weeks before any competitive racing was necessary. However, when building began on the new boat it was announced that a number of new techniques were being used in the construction: she was being built upside down, designing was partly by computer and some ideas from aero-space were being used in the preparation of the aluminium plate, it was claimed.

Beyond commenting that he had used a 'different recipe' from the one for *Lionheart* but had incorporated the 'same ingredients of low resistance, high stability and high sail area', Howlett offered no further explanation about his design which was, however, understood to be 'fairly conventional'.

To take on the building of a new boat at such a late stage had seemed an ambitious project and that it was taken on may have been inspired by the fact that Conner decided at the last moment to build a third new boat. The difference was, though, that while the new Conner boat would be built and taking part in trials on the west coast of America by February and would have had perhaps three months of trials by the time she returned to Newport, the new British yacht was not to be launched until the end of March and would not be sailing until May, and then only for a few weeks. Thus she was at least three months' behind the Americans in terms of preparation, an impossible lead to recover before racing began.

The new boat was named *Victory '83* by Princess Michael of Kent, at what must have been a uniquely lavish ceremony for such a class of yacht, at Hamble on March 30. The crew however did not shine when competing in the Lymington Cup series just ten days later. Cudmore and Crebbin made not a few mistakes, some of them fundamental, the crew members themselves did not look as sharp as might be expected of yachtsmen who had been in a serious training for a year, and the winner in the event which was shortened by weather was the Australian John Bertrand, skipper of *Australia II*. The best excuse that might have been offered for the failure by the Victory team to excel as never before at Lymington was that perhaps they had had too much training and that they had become too specialized in the handling of 12-metres. In fact, there had been considerable serious friction between de Savary and Cudmore over style of leadership and the type of chain of command thought necessary for the Victory campaign. And, indeed, the first step to dispense with the services of Cudmore had already been taken. What is more, Crebbin had not entirely made up his mind, it seems, whether to return with the Victory group to Newport for the resumption of training in May '83. He had become disenchanted with the 'style' of the syndicate in Nassau, a melting pot in more ways than one.

And what an astonishing ceremony was the launching; a replica in ice of the America's Cup itself, a choir, the band of the Royal Artillery and what were cruelly described later as 'performing seals' – some members of the crew doing press-ups for the crowd at the command of their 'chief' – not to mention a luncheon with Prince Michael and the Princess at the top table after a champagne reception. There can never have been a more extravagant launching ceremony for a 12-metre. Whatever the eventual outcome of the races, it was now very clear that de Savary was intensely committed for 1983. Yet, as always, when there is ostentatious wealth, a suspicion existed, that there was ultimately something 'shady' about de Savary and his business dealings; for instance there was de Savary's connection, however tenuous, with the Ambrosiana Group through the Nassau-based Artoc Bank and Trust of which he had been managing director, which did not help.

In a frank appraisal of his business interests a year before the challenge series was due to begin, de Savary had admitted that some of his commercial involvements were having a lean time, but he insisted that the Victory campaign would suffer no financial restraints. 'When I said that I would underwrite the $8 million it was expected the Victory challenge would cost, I meant that I would underwrite it,' he emphasized. The assertion came at a time when business generally was going through a difficult period; not only in Britain but worldwide.

At the naming ceremony of *Victory '83* de Savary reminded his guests that he had fulfilled all of the major promises he had made about the Victory campaign up to that stage, though the sumptuousness of the party, of course, had nothing to do with winning the America's Cup. Considerable financial backing is necessary to win the Cup, but it cannot actually be bought.

What the ceremony did demonstrate very clearly, however, was that de Savary and his syndicate did have more substantial resources than had been believed, even as recently as nine months previously when de Savary had publicly responded to repeated doubts about the stability or viability of his empire to support an America's Cup campaign. There had been the Ambrosiana involvement and doubts about the substance of the de Savary 'fortune'.

Concerning the two oil refineries – in Houston – de Savary had said that because at the time it would have meant a loss of some $500,000 a month to operate them successfully he had put them into 'chapter 11'; part of the United States bankruptcy legislation which enables a company to take early rescue steps when getting into financial difficulties.

Lawyers and accountants take stock of a company's assets and liabilities and together with creditors and interested parties produce a plan for future stability. This sometimes means creditors losing some of their security but ensures that the company isn't bought up by someone else. The courts have to approve the solution and the company usually emerges intact from the procedure, unlike British receivership which is usually embarked on at a later stage of the problem. The Victory chief explained that the two Houston refineries were then being reorganized and restructured, with the aid of US government grants, and would operate again after nine months, when it was hoped the business would go forward into a better market.

He acknowledged that the total liabilities of one of his refineries were about $100 million but claimed that assets, plant and machinery meant that there was still a surplus. He admitted that so far as the second refinery was concerned the balance was slightly less than equal. He said at the same time that there were 'good things as well as bad', giving as an example a telephone company in Dallas from which he made 'a profit each day of $50,000 more than whatever he made the previous day'.

But while he was always most forthcoming if asked a specific question about his business interests, de Savary made it clear that he could not discuss the whole; understandable, of course, because it would enable his rivals perhaps to take advantage of him and would anyway render his value as an 'agent' that much less if his revelations enabled the people he helped to help themselves in the future.

The exact extent of his business empire, or how it was formed, remained in question during the Victory campaign. Therefore it seemed more and more probable that his interests were considerably wider than imagined, his wealth much more extensive than realized and most of what might have been 'shady' had probably belonged to his early years as an embryo tycoon. And it was not perhaps until he took delivery of his second 12-metre that the Establishment was finally prepared to acknowledge that he was, after all, a man of real substance. The rumours about de Savary continued, of course, but they seemed more likely by the start of the Cup year to be no more than that. Though to some observers it still seemed more likely that his wealth was accumulated to the greater degree from his activities on behalf of Middle East oilmen – the second most important step perhaps on his route to being a multi-millionaire. His first step was becoming involved with the massive expansion in Nigeria when oil was first a boom product in the West Africa state. He had managed to put together a total of £15,528 in borrowed capital.

In a part of the world just emerging from hideous starvation, de Savary maintains that he recognized food as the obvious commodity in which to deal: one of the earlier rumours about the man was that he built his empire on trading in cement. He admits that his first scheme went badly wrong. The moment de Savary's cargo – a large quantity of foodstuffs he had acquired for a good price in Buenos Aires – was hoisted from the hold of a ship berthed in Lagos 'Produce of South Africa' was to be seen stencilled on almost every crate. There were cabinet officials on hand for the first shipment of food, and the decision was made to burn everything from South Africa. He stayed in West Africa, however, and moved into shipping, chartering a 10,000-tonner and acquiring three smaller cargo ships at bargain rates. By 1973 the obvious business to be in was oil and de Savary plunged into the uncertain waters of international oil chartering. 'That took me from West Africa to the Middle East and the Middle East took me back to the US and Europe,' he summarized.

His success, he said, rested largely on his good fortune in being a man with a nimble mind who happened to be in the right place at the right time: the Persian Gulf years when OPEC was busy quadrupling the price of oil. With billions flowing in, they needed outside help in recycling the profits into dollar and Eurodollar investments. De Savary saw his chance.

There have been some setbacks, including a deal involving Nigerian and Canadian metals. His marriage to a Canadian girl ended in separation several years ago despite two daughters, Lisa and Nicola, aged 15 and 10 at the time of the 1983 America's Cup and whose names provided the inspiration for *Lisanola*, one of his more personal yachts. Employing for his business transactions just twenty people, it is said, he has offices in London, New York and Houston as well as Nassau, his headquarters for seven years before the Cup challenge – at which time he had involvement in about eighty business projects. They included oil deals in the Persian Gulf, agricultural interests in Central America, refineries and the telephone company in Texas and the $105 million St James's Tower in Manhattan. Shipping and aeroplanes also came into consideration though de Savary insisted that he does not deal in arms. What came through most strongly during the build-up to and the conclusion of the 25th America's Cup, however, was the popularity, forthrightness, charisma, drive and apparent honesty of Peter John de Savary. Not a member of his staff nor anyone who was known to have done business with this dynamo of a man had anything but good to say of him.

If the campaign was on a sound financial base, the command structure in early 1983 was less so. For instance: who was in control after de Savary? In Britain the proclaimed order was that Kit Hobday was the vice-chairman. But for the crew there were more 'chiefs'; Bateman and Andrew 'Spud' Spedding, 'promoted' in Nassau, as well as Alabaster, Cudmore and Crebbin. Pattisson and Smith may have been among the 'front bench', but not only were they not 'ministers', they were not even 'staff', it seemed. Though nominated by the de Savary syndicate for the Lymington Cup, neither put in an appearance, which did seem significant. But then the general public did not know at the time of the power struggle that was now going on within the group.

It may also, at the time, have seemed like an especially astute move by Pattisson and Smith to have avoided Lymington in view of the disappointing performances of the senior 'pairing' of Crebbin and Cudmore. Whatever de Savary's views may have been about the absence of Pattisson and Smith, he can have been nothing but disappointed at the showings of his 'star' pair. The outstanding performance of Law, until then only an occasional 'visiting' helmsman in Newport, in beating Bertrand – he did not, in a truncated series, meet Cudmore – led to instant conjecture about whether he would be joining the de Savary circus or replacing one of its 'tightrope walkers'. Law was at that stage embarked on his fourth Olympic campaign, this time in the Soling class (he had been a British reserve in 1972 and 1976 before the enforced boycott of the 1980 Games by Britain's yachtsmen). In the event he joined the Victory crew in Newport as mainsheet trimmer, taking his family and leaving his job. At the end of five weeks he returned home, stating there was no place for him in the team.

Bertrand was in control of the *Australia II* campaign which, unlike de Savary in connection with the Victory effort, syndicate chief Alan Bond did not believe required his personal attention at every training race. Bertrand, considered to have improved since he was a visitor to Lymington in 1982, was thought to have benefited from being left alone by Bond. He was more confident. Law, not fully involved, was also sailing like the real, aggressive Law. No de Savary influence here.

Not the same though, with Crebbin and Cudmore. Crebbin may not have changed much; he was always quiet and introvert. But Cudmore did seem to have lost his aggression. From being perhaps the most talked about match race helmsman outside of the United States, he was, at the time of Lymington 1983, fast becoming the most quickly forgotten match-race 'expert'. He finished next to last in the 1983 Congressional Cup, held in the USA a month prior to the Lymington series; then he was sixth to Bertrand's second in a similar contest in New Zealand.

So the stage seemed to be set for some changes at the top; if only de Savary could bring himself to sack some of his seniors. This he had avoided throughout, seeming to prefer his performers to come to their own conclusion that they no longer had a future with the Victory outfit. Yet 'war' between the pairings of Crebbin and Cudmore and Pattisson and Smith was not only failing to bring the sharpness de Savary obviously sought, but might have been thought to have a detrimental effect in other ways. Certainly, it seemed that, if de Savary was to go after the services of Law he ought to examine his methods and his staffing. Further, his own 100 per cent involvement in the actual tuning had always seemed suspect in the absence of a real 'buffer' between him and his crew.

In Cudmore's view the role to be played by de Savary should have been more passive; merely a man to stand on the dockside 'keeping the cheque-book dry' – a phrase, it is said, which so angered de Savary in the days of the *Victory of Burnham* that those of the crew of that Admiral's Cup yacht who subscribed to the view never were offered places in the 12-metre campaign.

And whatever de Savary may be he is clearly not passive. If this was how Cudmore hoped to distance his boss from the campaign then he badly misjudged the Victory supremo. Indeed, so far from being merely a drawer of cheques from the dockside is de Savary that he was throughout the campaign looking for a way to be in the crew of *Victory* as the 'crew boss'.

Now for once, de Savary had acted with regard to staff. He had fired Cudmore over what was officially described as differences over strategy and policy. It was a major step and one which, it is

claimed, was taken amicably, and did *not* involve a confronta-
tion. There was an understanding that Cudmore would return if
he was required.

Cudmore did not return to the Victory campaign after leaving
the group in Nassau while equipment was being transferred to
Newport and while he was competing in the Lymington and
New Zealand match-race events. The actual parting of the de
Savary and Cudmore ways is said to have taken place on the
telephone. Cudmore was due to meet de Savary in his London
headquarters; instead he telephoned from New Zealand and, in
effect, was told neither to bother to call at the London office nor
to return to Newport in April 1983.

Though there is no room in a team for continually diverging
views, the loss of Cudmore meant an immediate thinning of
match race and top yacht racing talent. Harold Cudmore was
one of the hopes that took a British success out of the realms of
fantasy and now he was gone and his great potential for beating
Australian and then American helmsmen was gone with him.

The British camp still remained the only one with no nominated helmsman and it can hardly be said that the plan to keep
everyone on their toes at once was succeeding if an important
member of the team left one month before the first races began.

Cudmore had wanted to cut the lavish establishment of more
than eighty and leave a lean hard team with back up and then
campaign a boat as he had in so many successful Admiral's Cup
and Ton Cup series in recent years. But de Savary did not agree at
all.

Many of the *Victory* squad crew, staff and relatives deplored
the loss of Cudmore even though his ideas would have resulted
in the departure of some of them.

Soon after 1983 training began at Newport, *Victory* (from
1982) was back in the reckoning. Gear previously stripped for
Victory '83 was reinstalled or replaced. *Victory* was needed to
tune up *Victory '83* and, should the latter prove a disappointment, then could even become the challenger. The trial-horse
Australia was also in use for tuning but under the rules could
never be the British challenger. As for *Lionheart* she was hauled
out in the shed at Cove Harbour and her performance was no
longer regarded as of interest. Maybe she never did have that
suspected potential; her designer Ian Howlett would have to
accept that fact, though *Victory '83* was already designed and

built as a successor with no time at all to test her enough for major alterations to the hull.

For three weeks *Victory '83* sailed only against *Australia*, then she came out of the water at the end of May for a major repaint. Launched again in early June she had seven races against her trial-horses, but no one could admit to any one boat having overriding superiority on the water. But then the Victory syndicate judged she had the highest potential and must be the boat to go forward to the first races for the challengers.

VIII

Two British Blunders

In April and May of 1983 the atmosphere in the British camp at Newport was more charged, more brittle, less friendly and perhaps even less sure than a year previously. It had required a major, concentrated effort by the crew to get *Victory '83* ready to sail by May 1. As well as the paintwork and fairing which required attention, there was the fitting of practically all of the gear, from winches and mast to instruments, cleats and, to make matters more difficult, there had been a mishap in Le Havre as the vessel was en route from Hamble to Newport via New York. The French had dropped a container on the transom, so that needed attention and resulted in some veiled allegations of sabotage.

There was the added problem for the crew that the boat was at Cove Haven, 35 miles and 45 minutes north of Newport by car, so they had to be on call from soon after 6 am up to 8.30 pm each day from the arrival there of the yacht in mid-April to the delivery of her to her racing berth in Newport on April 30.

Such pressure seemed to tell, because there was a much more uneasy feeling among the crew. The departure of Harold Cudmore from the scene and the impending arrival of Chris Law did not help. There were those among the crew who, not surprisingly, set great store by the talents and inspiration of Cudmore, and some had joined the *Victory* squad because of his presence. He had won the affections and respect of a number of others with his humour, and his sailing and leadership abilities. Not surprising, therefore, that there should be some feelings of insecurity among those who had closer affinities to Cudmore or, more especially, felt that they might be threatened also by the arrival of Law as 'a mainsheet trimmer'. But as we know his stay was short.

On April 24, a chain of command chart was published and

showed a different emphasis to the structure in Newport in
1982. Genial Jim Alabaster, who had effectively stood between
de Savary and the squad, was now responsible for liaison in such
matters as film production, press and public relations and squad
social activities. No longer did he have a say, apparently, in
sailing matters.

Andrew Spedding, still included as a navigator, had really
taken control of shore support, maintenance and rigging; Jane
Craig was responsible for accounts, administration, insurance,
travel and clothing; Tony Cudlipp had taken over from Tim
Street as chief of domestic, transportation and communication
questions and de Savary had brought in Alice Simms, his personal
secretary, from Nassau.

Surprisingly, in many ways, the crew had changed but little
and, after the first, brief sailing trial of *Victory '83* on May 1 –
with de Savary himself doing most of the steering and with 14
others aboard the craft with him, there was still no real answer
to the question about who would be on the boat when it came to
racing. The total crewing squad at the time was: Brian Bennett,
Bill Bullard, Andy Burnell, Richard Clampett, Derek Clark,
Dennis Cooke, Andrew Cooper, Ed Danby, Michael Domican,
Colin Edge, Chris Law, Chris Mason, Ian McGowan, Russell
Pickthall, David Powys, Mark Preston, Kelvin Rawlings,
Michael Smith, Andrew Spedding, Barrie Thomas, Jerry and
John Thompson, Alex Wadson and David Woolner.

Several had other responsibilities. Clark was an instrumenta-
tion specialist; Thomas was in charge of PT and medical matters
and Mason and Pickthall were listed also as sailmakers. Peter
Bateman ran the sailing programme. Angus Melrose was the sail
boss, Howlett was in Newport as design chief, Bob Pegler was
there as the resident met. man and Bryan Willis appeared as the
rules expert. The workshops 'employed' Wayne Lawrence,
Chumley Prime, Robin Prior, Stan Rae, Stephen Sinclair and
'Staff' Lynham. Annie Allsop and Sue Griffin were respectively in
charge of housekeeping and catering with the assistance of John
Allen, David Grimsland, Marina Johnson, Robert Jones, Sara
Baerselman and Katherine Townshend. Vanessa Bellamy had
switched to press and PR with Suzy Pearce and in Newport it
was Sue Heron and Donna Cooper who were responsible with
squad wives for 'merchandising' under Nigel Massey. The list
went on and on: Dr Graeme Winn and Peter Weinberg dealt with

computers; Keith Rimes photography; Stella Clark race recording and Catherine Cardona-Gilbert had become assistant to Jane
Craig. Franklyne Clarke and Dick and Rick Weller drove the
tenders.

The chart looked fine; on glossy paper and reasonably cleverly
developed, it would, to the casual observer, have seemed a very
impressive document. To the better informed among the yachting establishment, however, it was clear that there were a
number of worrying factors. Most of all the fact that there was
an afterguard made up of only three members, but no one was in
full command at sea.

This was potentially a considerable weakness and there clearly was disenchantment by a number of the crew about this
inability to come to a decision about the afterguard. Some were
not so keen at this stage to be involved with a campaign which
could falter in the same ignoble way as *Lionheart*. One of the
sort of not infrequently heard remarks in Newport at the beginning of '83 was 'bring back Cudmore or otherwise we have got
another *Lionheart* on our hands'. Now in late May there was
a palace revolt. The leading crew members pointed out at a
meeting at Victory House to Peter Bateman that they were not
at all satisfied with the way matters were being run and wanted
more urgency in the campaign. They considered changes to be
absolutely essential if *Victory '83* was to be in a position even to
qualify, let alone win the America's Cup.

Yet with all of the tenders, living accommodation opened, the
mother ships back in Newport and new uniforms being issued it
seemed unthinkable that *Victory '83* would not come through
to the final of the elimination series, even if she didn't win a
place to meet the American defender of the trophy. The crew
had muscle and expertise and had now been blended into a very
physically fit, determined and dedicated bunch who worked as
hard afloat as they did ashore, sailing and repairing, working and
playing. There was also the back-up personnel, the sail-makers
with, at the beginning of the year, 120 sails tested and another
$500,000 ready to be spent on the *Victory* wardrobe if necessary.
A workshop, though, perhaps short of the very finest workmen
that British boatbuilding could offer in the way of technical
personnel for repairs and such like, still worked very well and
the Victory campaign squad knew how to repair a mast overnight, how to cope with all sorts of difficulties in a way that few

if any of the other overseas contenders did. Yet Australia would certainly be able to match this when the action really began in earnest.

On the debit side de Savary misunderstood that although he was controlling the financial side of the effort, although he was the man who was putting so much effort into it, and was providing the basis of the enthusiasm, he could not sail a 12-metre on his own. He needed not only the brawn of the crew but their loyalty as well. He was not doing himself a favour therefore in ignoring his crew; in surrounding himself with friends and business associates or visiting personnel to Newport rather than the senior members of his sailing squad. Because loyalty was bound to be a two-way factor in such a major undertaking, it sometimes seemed he was a bully and the crew, in some instances, did not seem to like this characteristic in their boss, although, in truth, at the start of 1983, they seemed still to be giving him the benefit of the doubt. Yet at times it was evident that de Savary somehow wanted to skipper the challenging 12 from the shore. This may have been because of his enthusiasm and drive, but it was misguided. Only a team of eleven sailors could ultimately win the Cup. It seemed to be a very finely balanced thing. While on the one hand the crew were clearly ready to follow him wherever he led, were prepared to give everything they could in the interest of de Savary and their country in connection with the America's Cup, they had, it seemed, come nearly to the end of their tether. Make a wrong step, a major wrong step, Mr de Savary, they seemed to be saying, and some of us are likely to be packing our bags and making our own way home, not worrying too much whether we get a return air fare from you or not.

As for the leading helmsman, Crebbin returned to Britain after the winter training during Christmas with misgivings about the wisdom of going back to America. With a new young wife, perhaps the enchantment of an America's Cup campaign had become a little dulled. Undoubtedly he was not too happy about the way things were being run. He obviously felt that he had been slighted to a certain extent. Certainly, although de Savary may have dealt with the matter in a tough way because he was looking only for the very best – and it can be understood that if he had decided that Crebbin was not the man for the job the best thing to do was to get rid of him – it does not alter the

fact that it seems to have been less than wise not to have taken
Crebbin more into his confidence and kept him better informed
about his own intentions than he apparently did.

As for the boats, *Victory* and *Victory '83* were clearly behind
the Americans in terms of preparations in May 1983. The
official and not very persuasive line was that although they were
behind, however, as they began the summer of '83 they felt that
the amount of racing that they faced for the elimination series
would certainly put them on a par with the Americans whom
they hoped to meet at the end of the summer. *Victory '83* met
her trial-horse *Australia* for the first time in an informal way.
The 12-metre yachts came together as they passed under Newport Bridge into the sheltered Narraganasett Bay. In about a 10
knot north-easterly, the pair sailed cautiously to windward;
Australia to weather and pointing slightly higher than *Victory*
which seemed to heel more. It was not an auspicious start. The
trial lasted little more than an hour, the boats breaking off then
for calibration tests. It did show what has been known for
almost as long as 12-metres have been racing for the America's
Cup, that the difference in speed between the very fastest and
the very slowest is very little.

Work now began to strengthen the jack and the area at the foot
of the mast of the new boat. It took a further three days of vital
time.

Meanwhile, Melrose continued to organize the sail inventory,
which consisted of three mainsails, nine genoas, eight spinnakers, and two staysails, all interchangeable between *Victory*,
Victory '83 and *Australia* and chosen from 120 tested up until
May 1983 and continually being renewed or reconsidered as
more sails came along at the rate of around 10 sails per month.
The business of the sails was especially interesting because of a
particularly daunting situation faced by the challenge contender. There was no doubt that the Americans were at an
advantage in not having to take part in an elimination series –
being able to keep their better sails until the end. Also the
challenge contender with the biggest wardrobe of sails enjoyed a
similar advantage because of the length of the elimination
event.

What was uncertain at the beginning of 1983, however, was
exactly what sort of sails other people would have. Everything
had seemed fairly certain at the end of 1982 when, in common

with probably all other challenge contenders, Britain had begun by producing a sail wardrobe from the best type of sails that had been used on *Freedom* at the end of 1980; behaving like the Freedom syndicate themselves, it seemed. During winter training when *Freedom* was out of sight and when it was not so easy to establish what other overseas competitors were up to, people had obviously gone their eight or nine separate syndicate ways and could have come up with all sorts of different sorts of sails. Again, however, the British were fairly confident; they felt that if they did not have the right sort of sails, they at least had the expertise and facilities quickly to imitate the styles that had been developed by their rivals if they seemed to have any particular promise.

Incredible though it may seem, by early June *Victory* and *Victory '83* had still not met in a race. Nor had crews been allocated to them. An A and B list posted at Victory House seemed to solve the latter problem, but its existence was denied to the press! On June 15 the two yachts raced. Crebbin was at the wheel of one, Pattisson the other.

What transpired was that there was not an inch of difference in the speed of the two boats upwind and as de Savary was calling for a proper race and a run downwind to demonstrate the advantage the newer craft held over the older one off the wind, the mast jack aboard *Victory* failed and so ended the first clash of two British-built 12-metre yachts designed by different designers for the same owner, racing in the America's Cup waters of Rhode Island Sound. The lateness in building *Victory '83* was now glaringly apparent. Doubts about the relative merits of the two boats – and there definitely were those who believed that the Dubois boat was the more promising – would remain. Disappointment over the hopelessly short time the two boats spent racing had to be tempered by the knowledge that had *Victory* won the race it might have led to a misguided late decision to put *Victory* in the trials rather than *Victory '83*. The latter had purposely been better prepared for the trials.

There was confusion over the purpose of having built two yachts. Crebbin said *Victory* was slow downwind and would be used only as a modern test-bed for sail evaluation and crew training during the summer. Yet, at the same time, the syndicate were seeking clarification on whether they could enter both 12s in the trials and, whether, if one won the elimination series, the other could race in the Cup series! The rules governing the elimination series and the Cup event are quite different; the vital condition governing the former is to eliminate six yachts and there is no stipulation that the victor should compete in the America's Cup.

The only thing demonstrated in this race was de Savary's greatest mistake up to that stage. To have gained the real benefit from having a choice of two 12-metres with which to have been able to challenge, he needed to have finished the modifications to *Victory* much earlier. They should have been completed in the autumn of 1982 and the boat then taken to Nassau to race against *Australia*. *Victory '83* should have been launched five or six months earlier and then invaluable racing would have taken place in Nassau. It would have cost no more. The American syndicates had no less in the winter.

The second main blunder of the British effort was directly related to all this. Despite the comings and goings and the much touted squad system, there were in mid-June only three helmsmen, Crebbin, Smith, Pattisson and not enough back up for them to campaign two 12s anyway. Any ideas that lurked that *Victory* could be worked up to be raced if necessary seemed to be dispelled when the elimination series got under way. The problem would be, as the trials showed, keeping one boat and crew in daily racing trim. The demands of such a competitive summer would be such, it seemed, that there would be time only to service the requirements of one racing yacht. Her trial-horse would get only nominal, imperative action.

So *Victory* lay in the dock she had previously dominated as the main British 12-metre hope. It was a sad situation that here was a boat which could be potentially the best 12-metre in Newport, yet, because of delay and indecision, would not be raced.

IX

Racing and reality

The Brits continue to think money and management will win. They bring in new sails by the boatload (another twelve new ones this week), doodle with their fleet of three boats, play musical chairs with their twenty-two crew members, alternate skippers (while a third waits on call) and generally make most of the other mistakes that fledgling contenders make; the same ones that Baron Bich developed to a fine art in his first go in 1970.

– America's Cup Report *(weekly)*, July 2

Several challengers in the history of the Cup came back more than once, but only Sir Thomas Lipton challenged five times. No one came anywhere near this record until Baron Marcel Bich came for his fourth and last unsuccessful attempt in 1980 – he never any year got past the eliminations. But with *Australia II*, Alan Bond arrived in Newport in 1983 for *his* fourth America's Cup campaign. Like his previous boats, the new 12 was designed by Ben Lexcen (he changed his name from Bob Miller by computer selection which arrived at the most uncommon two-syllable word suitable for a name). As helmsman, Bond had his 1981 Admiral's Cup skipper, Finn bronze medallist, Finn World champion and sailmaker John Bertrand. His boat on arrival had been sailing and racing for a year with the Australian summer immediately behind him, and that had been filled with competition that really mattered against the other two Australian contenders.

During that summer there occurred the financial demise of the Melbourne syndicate which was running *Challenge 12*, also designed by Ben Lexcen. Bond wisely came to the rescue and the Melbourne boat was kept racing. He knew the necessity to have serious competition to prepare for the coming battle with the defenders – even if his counterparts in Britain, France and the others either did not or could not.

Challenge was thought to be a formidable yacht, but she never had the talent and the support of *Australia II*. This showed in the hard fought Australian trials and special match regattas and she came to Newport in a better state of work-up than her compatriots, the other challengers or even the defenders. If the Cup could have been held in May or June she would undoubtedly have won! But September was the date and the Americans were well aware that they had more than three months' racing in their own waters before they had to meet *Australia II* at the start line.

Ben Lexcen's concentration of his undoubted talent led him to a rather different 12-metre hull to the others in Newport. It was radically different when compared to the almost boringly conventional shape of *Victory '83*. While the others were very fast fighter bombers, *Australia II* was a jump jet. Her straight line speed is good, and her turning and tacking ability even more impressive. The 12-metre rules demand a relatively heavy-displacement boat; if displacement is reduced, then sail area – under the rule – has to be cut and this does not pay. The America's Cup boats therefore look nothing like the IOR boats that most of the world's big boat racing is done in. Instead they have clumsy bustles between keel and rudder into which displacement is poured. The bustle slows down turning. Lexcen removed the bustle from his design and put the displacement on to the bottom of the keel, so that it bulged each side and especially forward. The shapes of the bulges are critical, and were researched by the designer at one of the few ship test tanks in the world that could cope with such problems – the Wageningen basin at the Netherlands Aerospace Institute. (The fact that the work was being done in Holland led to queries later.) On the bulges were matched a pair of low aspect ratio anhedral fins. They give an advantageous end plate effect (like the deck does to a deck sweeping genoa sail). The whole combination was judged at an early stage to be effective and no other 12-metre had anything like it. Putting on fins later was not a possibility for the others as the whole hull weight and shape distribution were part of the design and the sail area which matched it. Designers like Howlett and Pedrick had been left way behind!

As for Alan Bond, his ambition to win was even more important than the design of *Australia II* (it is well known that a faster boat certainly has no guarantee of winning the Cup races). In 1974, 1977 and 1980 he spent $12 million, but his determination remained after three very clear defeats. A former sign painter who had emigrated from England at the age of nine with his parents, he made his initial fortune in property. Now, through the $185 million Bond Corporation, he has western Australian and international interests in mining, oil and many areas of Australian industry. He owns racehorses, through subsidiary companies, and acquires French impressionist paintings. Most of the summer, like de Savary, he stayed in Newport to back his cool, consistent and very experienced crew. His experience told him that all must be concentrated on winning match races: not for him outsize establishments with wives and children, parties to out-do other nationalities, or frequent appearances in front of television. The press he left to his executive director, Warren Jones, who was quoted as saying, 'We train like commandos. I first came here in 1974 and it was a lot of fun. Now that has gone. The whole thing has become deadly, deadly serious.' Correspondingly the *Sydney Sun* editorialized: 'Alan Bond may be more self appointed than elected as our flag carrier, but a lot of Australian prestige in the world rides with him. If he wins, we win.'

The soundly experienced crew and supporters included many men who had competed in the 1977 and 1980 campaigns. These, incidentally, were men whose attitudes had changed from a purposely brash Aussie style in the earlier years to a more modest, determined stance as affected by the defenders. This was the line up: a stronger factor than any facet of yacht design.

Chairman	Alan Bond
Executive director	Warren Jones
Project manager	John Longley
Designer, yacht and sails	Ben Lexcen
Director and relief helmsman	Sir James Hardy
Trustee and race controller	John Fitzhardinge
Sports psychologist	Laurie Hayden
Computer	Glen Read
Secretary	Alison Baker

Public Relations	Lesleigh Green
Sailing	John Bertrand (helmsman and sail designer), Hugh Treharne (tactician and sail designer), Grant Simmer (navigator), Will Baillieu (grinder), Colin Beashel (trimmer), Rob Brown (trimmer), Peter Costello (grinder and sewer), Ken Judge (trimmer), Skip Lissiman (trimmer), Scott McAllister (bow), sub Damian Fewster, Brian Richardson (grinder), Phil Smidmore (mast)
Tender	Phil Judge (skipper), Newton Roberts (1st mate)
Sailmakers	Tom Schnackenberg (co-ordinator), Ken O'Brien, Mike Quitler
Maintenance	Ken Beashel, Steve Harrison, Mark Reid

The first round of the challenger eliminations was a round-robin, each boat sailing three times against every other. It began on June 18, a foggy day. Less than a week later, it was apparent that, at this stage, *Australia II* was the best of the seven yachts. She lost only one of her twelve races, to *Challenge 12*, on the last day of the series.

Although almost everybody knew somebody who knew exactly what the Lexcen 'secret' looked like, and in some cases could even do sketches for you, few seemed to know anyone who had actually witnessed the 'device'. It was, it seemed, all typical Newport, where rumours abound in an America's Cup summer to the extent that almost by the time you reach the south end of Thames Street a 'secret' you told someone at the north end will have beaten you there. That the Australian keel had been tried in various forms and discarded – that this or something else had given the new yacht a better-than-average turning ability was beyond dispute in the prevailing conditions.

Alan Bond's fourth challenge culminated in the highly tuned Australia II, *steered by John Bertrand.* Black.

Above. *When not racing, a 12-metre is kept suspended clear of the water. Such measures are one reason for the expense of a campaign.* Kos.

Left. *This is what they both came for, but the leader here,* Victory '83, *went on beyond the round robin races which saw* Challenge 12, *steered by John Savage for the Royal Victoria Yacht Club, Melbourne, eliminated.* Black.

Below. *They sailed for France, but Yves Rousset-Rouard's 1980 boat never looked a winner.* Kos.

Left. *From the earliest, American hopes were with Dennis Conner.* Kos.

Below left. *Gary Jobson, back for a third America's Cup campaign as tactician on* Defender. Black.

Below. *Tom Blackaller, skipper of* Defender, *designed by David Pedrick.* Kos.

Above. *Alan Bond: his fourth America's Cup challenge is only equalled by Sir Thomas Lipton early in the century. Kos.*

Above right. *Syd Fischer: a record three Australian yachts found him managing* Advance. *Her extreme design failed. Kos.*

Right. *Australia's best: John Bertrand, world Finn champion, sailmaker, ocean racer and top helmsman. Kos.*

Above left. *Rodney Pattisson, British Olympic gold medallist, was a mainstay of the* Victory *'83 afterguard.* Kos.

Above. *Lawrie Smith was main British starting helmsman in his second America's Cup campaign.* Kos.

Left. *Once at Newport de Savary kept himself in the limelight and his sailors relatively faceless.* Kos.

Yet again! Australia II *leads* Victory '83 *in one of their many encounters.* Kos.

Heading for the start, a 12-metre crew has a hundred tasks. Kos.

Canada's first and popular foray into 12-metre racing. The Bruce Kirby design went through to the semi-finals. Kos.

By late June, *Australia II* needed early rather than delayed action; the British needed all the time they could get; and the Americans were still very strategically placed whatever the time of the action, ready to reach peak in exactly mid-September. As the summer began to unfold, the programme most benefited the defenders in their system of trial races; they were always close and competitive, with the helmsman given clear directives by the selection committee; by contrast the six-nation challengers' event was a much less useful affair. At a very early stage it seemed that matching good challenging boats against bad was of doubtful advantage for anyone, and that the selection procedure suggested right at the start by the New Zealand sailmaker Tom Schnackenberg, attached to the Australian North loft – whereby the best contenders race against the best, and the less competitive against other less promising boats, but with a clever promotion scheme – would have suited the challengers best. The problem caused by having weak races, with good boats against bad, was that the contests were no test. Better, it seemed, for *Victory '83* to be beaten regularly by *Challenge 12* and *Australia* but to be learning from the hostilities, than to waste time and learn nothing in beating *Advance* and *Canada* easily. At least, that seemed the lesson after the first round of trials and when *Victory '83* established herself.

What it came down to after those first twelve races, all run despite some early difficulties with the weather – fog, calms and a day of strong winds – was that the top four boats were *Australia II*, *Challenge 12*, *Victory '83* and *Azzurra*. The latter was a fast improving boat with good speed and potential and better than expected crewing. *Azzurra* was likely to face protests over assistance and sails they were reportedly receiving from the Americans, if they progressed too far and too well as to be a threat to other challengers. Anglo-Italian relations had not been helped by some *Azzurra* protests and then the disqualification of *Victory '83*. This came after the first race between the two boats, on the third day of the elimination event, and after British pride had been partly restored with a win against *France III*, the old foe, following that stinging set-back against *Challenge 12*.

What happened was that the Italians had first hoisted a protest pennant in a race which failed to finish within the time limit over a half-size course and in which the British led, having overtaken the Italians, at the time that the contest was abandoned for the day. The protest was over the start. The very next day the Italians were protesting again at the re-start of the race the following day, and when there appeared to have been a faultless start. *Victory '83* went on to finish comfortably ahead by 1 minute 58 seconds, but a few hours later the yacht was disqualified under Rule 36 for a port-and-starboard incident. For a while it was an emotive issue, not least because it seemed that the jury was made up, to an extent at least, by the very same people who had sat to decide the fate of *Lionheart* and Lawrie Smith three years previously against *France III*. The facts of the incident were as follows: the protest was borderline on the water and the Italians themselves seemed to prove this by becoming the most frequent protestors of the first round, but gaining no success after that against *Victory '83*. Smith did not present the best of cases on the British side, though, it must be emphasized, he must be considered blameless in this respect because of *Victory*'s squad system. Sadly, the system let down Smith, *Victory '83* and the British cause very badly. It was only some fifteen minutes before the protest hearing that the Victory squad knew for certain that there was a protest; they found out only by chance and they did not know what the protest was in fact about until they entered the protest room.

An Italian witness acted as interpreter and a representative of the Italians' Yacht Club, Costa Smeralda, was allowed to give evidence. The Royal Burnham's Frank Kemball, however, was not – though the two gentlemen were standing side by side on the committee boat at the time of the said incident between the two yachts.

Peter de Savary was furious at being caught out, furious about the make-up of the jury – which, it must be said, seemed a little odd – and clearly furious that the syndicate or the challenging club, or both, had allowed a situation where an all-American jury would decide between the challengers. To say that an international jury made up solely of Americans would be impartial because they had no interest in the outcome of a protest between two challenge contenders was clearly nonsense.

This is not to imply that the Americans were not impartial, or that the jury which disqualified *Victory '83* was decided in any other way than as it was reported; the jury was formed before there was a protest, was standing by to hear whatever protest might first emerge from the challengers' event, and it was merely a coincidence that it happened to be a British boat. In American circles, certainly, the combination of the jury, based on members of the Ida Lewis Yacht Club, was considered to be one of the most proficient that there could be in the United States. Anyway, they found against the British and it was another defeat.

Starting techniques, the single most telling factor, it had seemed, as the British lost those opening rounds, were fast improving and, indeed, became so sharp as to lead neutral members of the committee boat to describe the start between Crebbin and Bertrand, when *Victory '83* and *Australia II* met for the second time, to have been 'the start of the century'. And that, apart from a win against *Challenge 12* when the two boats met for the second time, was the only real elimination series result of note from a British standpoint as winds generally continued light and as short, windward-leeward-windward leg events began more frequently to replace the half-size America's Cup course contests.

For the record, *Victory* beat *Advance* and *Canada* before overturning the result of the first race against *Challenge* with a win of around three-quarters of a minute. It was an intriguing contest, involving as it did the first real tacking duel of the series and from which *Victory '83* broke away, it seems, because of losing ground to the Australians on the tacks. Here was a concern: that *Victory '83* was suffering some of the problems of turning quickly that so limited *Lionheart*, by the same designer. It was for different reasons, of course: *Victory '83* was not a heavy boat like *Lionheart* and, indeed, her turning ability looked good except, perhaps, when compared to the likes of *Challenge 12* and *Australia II*. But it was early days to make a judgement. On the one hand the type of sails being used was blamed while, on the other, it was suggested that the hull was at fault. Anyway it was certain, before the defeat against *Australia II* which came after a second success against *France III*, that there was a long way to go yet. *Victory '83* finished that opening round of the elimination series with further wins over *Azzurra*, *Advance* and *Canada I* to stand squarely the third best boat of the seven challenge contenders so far as the points were concerned, but probably equal second with *Challenge 12* and behind *Australia II* when the results that mattered were considered.

The British crew during this first round continued to be changed. The afterguard was two chosen from Crebbin, Pattisson or Smith, with the odd man standing down. The crew for the first few races were Bill Bullard, Kelvin Rawlings, Alex Wadson, John and Jerry Thompson, Brian Bennett, Andy Burnell, Chris Mason and Derek Clark. Mark Preston, Richard Clampett and David Woolner were then brought in as replacements, followed by Mike Smith and Colin Edge, while, before the series ended, Michael Domican and David Powys were among others to be given a place. The crew had been worked very hard during the period from April, when they had begun preparations on *Victory '83* for her May launching, and right through to June 26 when the first trial ended. They were given a couple of days off – or, at least, most of them were, as the boat went back to Cove Haven for alterations and polish.

The extent of any modifications was something of a mystery to outsiders, who were told that the underbody was being trimmed to give more lift to the keel. That the boat would be given an extra burnish seemed perfectly acceptable. But as far as any changes to the keel or rudder went, it was not always certain that all of the syndicate knew exactly what was being done, that they remembered exactly what it was they were supposed to be saying that was being done, or that everyone could remember if any alterations were planned at all!

At the end of the round *Victory* was better tuned than *Advance*, *Canada*, *France* or *Azzurra*, and had some features to recommend her more than *Challenge*. The Victory team had the potential to better *Australia II*, if they would concentrate on matters that could be dealt with, like crewing, starting, sail-handling, and technology, but there were still many chiefs yet little real success on the water; so much planning, but no obvious progress.

On a normal race day there would be de Savary and Hobday in the Magnum; Peter Bateman and Rodney Pattisson and perhaps Robert Hopkins – 'Bo-Hop', a North 'expert' who later replaced Bateman (who returned to England) as a special adviser all in *Restless*, a Boston whaler; Alabaster on *Victorious*, a 44-ft motor yacht used for visitors; and others such as Melrose out watching sails in a runabout, Andy Cooper watching all sorts of things in an inflatable, and Pegler in *Charleston* and Winn still in *Revenge*, the official tender to *Victory*. Designer Howlett was also there when he was in Newport.

There were too many people and it was becoming a 'spectacle' which no longer impressed anyone and was beginning to offend, at sea anyway, British supporters and American observers. Certainly part of the trouble seemed to be that too many people were telling de Savary what he wanted to know and too few telling him what he ought to know. Or, if enough were telling him the 'truth', there were still too many others avoiding the obvious truth for the *Victory* boss apparently to get a clear, decisive picture on which to act.

There was no need for him to seek advice on the first-round results, which showed, as mentioned, *Victory '83* to be third of the seven yachts with 8 wins behind, respectively, *Australia II* and *Challenge 12* with 11 and 10 wins. For the seven yachts, this translated, by converting to the 20 per cent of points which carried into the second round, to:

Australia II	11 wins	2.2 points
Challenge 12	10 wins	2.0 points
Victory '83	8 wins	1.6 points
Azzurra	5 wins	1.0 points
Canada 1	4 wins	0.8 points
France III	4 wins	0.8 points
Advance	0 wins	0.0 points

The second-round programme was an exact copy of the schedule of the first, with *Victory* opening with the useful pointer of a match with *Challenge*, the yacht to which she had to consider herself superior in order to be considered likely to meet *Australia II* in the final. In the event, *Challenge* retired with a broken boom, proving nothing, and the British boat followed this with a walkover win over *France* which did not start her race.

Then came the biggest surprise, a success against *Australia II*, but against form and only because of enormous good fortune created by a period of flat calm which ended with *Victory* being wafted from astern to win by 3 minutes 56 seconds. No one, most of all the *Victory* crew, considered the success anything but good luck and so after three races the British had collected three totally bonus points which gave them the overall lead.

The position at the front was held even after defeat the same

day by *Azzurra* in further light and fluky conditions. The
reversal did not therefore seem specially significant at the time,
and it was not until later in the series, when *Victory* lost to other
less fancied boats, that it was seen that the defeat by the Italian
yacht marked the end of easy *Victory* successes and the unpalat-
able fact that some of the boats which had been easy conquests
were improving, while the British boat was not. *Victory* then
went on to beat *Advance* and there was a day of no racing and
then a lay day for *Victory* before the latest crew was named in
time for the meeting with *Canada I* on July 7. This was the crew
for the rest of round two: Bow – Bullard; Mast – Kelvin Rawlings; Pit – Alex Wadson; Grinders – John and Jerry Thompson;
Starboard Trimmer – Andy Burnell; Port Trimmer – David
Powys; Mainsheet – Chris Mason; Tactical Navigator – Derek
Clark; Skippers (rotated) – Phil Crebbin, Lawrie Smith and
Rodney Pattisson.

David Powys, an Australian, who had been with the syndicate
from the beginning and had helped build the first two 12-metres,
had been barred from possible selection until the New York
Yacht Club gave special written permission for him to be
allowed to be a member of the crew. Powys had been excluded
under the rule permitting only nationals of the country of the
challenge, but his length of association with Britain and the
12-metre campaign earned him a reprieve. And it seemed that
the enthusiasm, good humour and straightforwardness of the
Australian who stood up to 'PdS' would do nothing but good for
a boat with a crew which might, on first examination, have been
thought a little on the dour side, or studious rather than excitable – and anyway not immediately seen as humorous. But they
were an excellent, mature crew and there was nothing wrong
with that.

As the second half of the second round began with a further
meeting with *Challenge*, *Victory* was beaten when she was
forced to retire with a broken cap shroud before beating *France*,
but losing to *Australia* by 2 minutes 34 seconds in perhaps the
most disappointing of all the early *Victory* matches. The British,
after starting level with *Australia* and being considered to have
got on top in a long, opening port tack, failed to cover *Australia*,
and were crossed before the weather mark. There followed a
brief lift for the British camp as they beat *Azzurra* convincingly.
Then came deep gloom as *Victory* was beaten first by *Advance*

and then by *Canada*. So ended the second series for *Victory '83*, with a worse record than the first. Several boats, notably *Canada*, had markedly improved. The records of the second round read:

Australia	10 wins	4.8 points*
Challenge	7 wins	3.6 points
Victory	7 wins	3.4 points
Azzurra	7 wins	2.7 points
Canada	6 wins	2.7 points
France	2 wins	1.1 points
Advance	2 wins	0.8 points

* the 40 per cent totals of the second round that would carry into the third round.

Challenge had a better record than was shown because she had been cost a victory by disqualification; albeit a fate that had befallen *Victory '83* also in the first round, but the significance of which was far less than that attached to the *Challenge 12* penalty at that stage of the competition. Therefore *Challenge 12* had got no worse, while *Victory '83* had got no better. *Canada* was at last showing the improvement expected of her, with the stepping of a new mast, and the purchase and use of some new sails.

The second series came to an end on July 15, the day of the *Victory* Ball in one of Newport's amazing 'cottages', Beechwood, built for Mrs Caroline Astor at the turn of the century. Much heralded, much anticipated, here was an event with a certain outcome; that was the arrival of His Royal Highness Prince Andrew, which could not quite be rivalled by any other syndicate, whatever VIPs they might ask from their own countries. The band of the Irish Guards complete with pipers played, marched and countermarched and included in their selection 'Rule Britannia' (obviously) and 'A little bit of bloomin' luck' (inadequately?). American, Australian, Canadian and continental guests voted it the occasion of the season.

Twelve hours after the massive firework display by self-styled failed pyromaniac Michael Parker, and a breakfast which included North Sea kippers and Buck's Fizz, the Britain versus Commonwealth cricket match was in full swing with HRH bowling more than a few overs.

This intense social weekend contrasted with doings on *Vic-*

tory '83 as Derek Clark, surely one of the most valuable members of the British team, supervised her tow to Cove Haven for minor modifications and the customary haul out between rounds. How could the concentration and effort of the British not be preoccupied by the unprecedented show they were organizing on shore in front of senators, Rhode Island dignitaries, important members of the New York Club and competitors? However, the squad was numerically just large enough to contain some minds bent on pursuing the essential improvements to take *Victory '83* away from one of her low points of the campaign. One change, in rig position, meant that work on many of the carefully cut and tuned sails was rendered useless.

The day after the ball the New York Yacht Club began its observation trials with the three contenders for the defence: *Courageous*, steered by John Kolius, *Defender*, with Tom Blackaller and *Liberty*, with Dennis Conner.

X

And then there were four

Match racing is not the norm in yachting. Most yacht races have anything between half a dozen and a hundred or more yachts starting together. Only the peculiar conditions of the America's Cup with its single defender and corresponding challenger have kept match racing alive as a facet of the sport. Actually it is as old as amateur sailing, dating from the days when wealthy owners made wagers, which resulted in 'a match'.

So sailors experienced in the special needs of match race tactics are hard to find. An annual series in America, the Congressional Cup, is a match race regatta and it has spawned useful imitations in Australia, England and New Zealand. Such regattas are complex to organize in comparison with conventional yacht racing, and so are infrequent. Their entries are largely the few potential America's Cup helmsmen from the USA and the challenging nations.

These men have in the last decade developed match race tactics. Once on the course going to windward the leading boat has all the advantages: she must cover, stay always between the opponent and the weather. This may mean tacking again and again. But an eye must be kept on the compass as a windshift could give a sudden advantage to the yacht which detects it first.

On a reaching leg, there is little either yacht can do to alter her relative position, but on the running leg (see Figure 3), which is the fifth leg of the America's Cup course, the trailing yacht, if close enough, can try and take the wind of the leader. What follows is a gybing duel where a slip in handling the gybe could result in the boat astern getting through. The leader still covers, not allowing, for an instant, her opponent to gybe over on to one side of the course or other on her own.

It is the starts that in match racing appear quite different from other sailing. At the 10-minute signal the yachts approach from

the ends of the line to which they have previously been res-
tricted. The aim now is to tail the other yacht. This forces the
opponent away from the line, and under the rules prevents her
from tacking or gybing. This is the reason one sees two 12-
metres circling each other, each trying to sail just astern of the
other. This is the reason they shave past the committee and
spectator boats in an effort to throw each other off and break
clear for a clean, uncovered start.

Such tactics, of course, were to be seen not only in the
America's Cup challenge itself, but in every two-boat match in
round-robins one, two and three in the semi-final, in the challenger final and in the defender preliminary, observation and
final trials.

As the third round-robin was about to begin, *Victory '83*
looked increasingly unlikely to become the America's Cup
challenger in 1983 and qualifying as a semi-finalist would only
prolong the agony of the huge British band in Newport. Some
began to drift away of their own accord and there were few of
those left behind who would have swopped places to leave the
bright, compulsively appealing New England town which had
become the yachting centre of the world as it was set to become
the graveyard of yet another British challenge for the America's
Cup. Sadly, because it was now clear that so much had gone
wrong that it was more appropriate to ask what had gone right,
even the gold-and-blue rugby shirt uniforms of the crew and
supporters began to seem something of an affront to taste. These
were cute when the *Victory* cause was going well, but somewhat
too bold when going badly, compared to the 'innocent' white
colours of the Americans and the greens, blues and suchlike of
the other challenge squads.

This was the situation, then, during the third round of the
elimination series, the period from July 20 when *Victory '83*'s
fortunes were at an all-time low, to the beginning of August, by
which time they had begun to rise in terms of efforts on the
water, but had reached another nadir of unhappiness and embarrassment in relation to people and position.

Still to come were the intervention of the New York Yacht
Club in relation to the question about the validity of the radical
keel of *Australia II* – still worrying the holders, it seemed; the
revelation that *Defender* and *Courageous* of the defence candidates had decided to follow the lead set by *Liberty* and go for two

or three rating certificates so that the yachts could sail with
changed ballast, sails or booms to suit conditions daily; the
elimination of *Advance, Challenge* and *France* – not without
some late 'wriggling' and 'intrigue'; the strange fluctuations of
form in the series which finally involved 16 races, 6 over long
courses and 10 over short courses; the excessive demands on the
administration and race management team; the oppressive
atmosphere of Newport as the humidity increased almost with
the intrigue; and, above all, the various machinations of de
Savary and the Syndicate responsible for the safety of *Victory
'83*.

In the middle of the third series *Advance, France* and *Victory
'83* looked likely to be eliminated, for only four challengers were
allowed in the semi-final. The winner all along remained *Australia II* – which underlined the strength of the Royal Perth
Challenge with a total of 36 victories in 40 encounters. Not one
of those four lost races was a result of dominance by a rival; all of
Australia II's failures were to do with weather, equipment or,
once, an injured crewman. A defeat, in the first race of the third
round, of *Victory* by *Challenge* was disappointing but not
dangerous, and much according to form, as were the win over
the French by the British boat and then failure, expectedly,
against *Australia II*. There then came a good success against
Azzurra and a predictable success against *Advance* before the
British boat was again beaten by *Canada*, though this time on a
disqualification. The following day there was a slightly more
reassuring win against *Challenge*.

It had already begun to look as though *Victory* was as vulnerable as any of *Azzurra, Canada* or *Challenge* and that it would
be a grim struggle to remain in the top four. For though *Victory*
had been disqualified from the race against *Canada*, the truth
was that the British finished first only because the Canadians
had to complete the race with just a headsail. Until the halyard
broke, *Victory* had been the chasing boat. *Azzurra* then beat
Victory, in the twenty-eighth race of the series.

For the semi-final, de Savary at last decided on his skipper.
Judged by every other 12-metre in Newport, it was the eleventh
hour when he appointed Lawrie Smith, the man who had lost in
Lionheart in 1980. Alongside Smith was Rodney Pattisson, who
would take the downwind legs. Sadly this meant no place was
left for Phil Crebbin, who had been with the Victory syndicate

from the beginning, steering *Victory of Burnham* and then the Dubois *Victory*.

De Savary became convinced that the Smith–Pattisson team was the best one on July 31, after the important race against *Canada* which *Victory '83* had to win, and she did it by 3 minutes 5 seconds. What happened was that Smith lost the start, badly. He was covered by Terry McLaughlin, admittedly the best starting skipper among the challenge contenders, but in a match-race 'hold' so elementary that an American skipper visiting a British tender and known to be an especially astute student of match-race tactics, as well as a starter of some repute, could not credit that the British afterguard had learnt so little about the real life of match-racing.

However, by halfway up the weather leg *Victory* was ahead, according to Pattisson, because of brilliant tactics by Smith; but, according to the American expert, because of something of a lucky break by the British whose boat was, anyway, clearly going better than that of the Canadians in the conditions. However, this is not to impugn the reputation of Smith or Pattisson, but rather to throw light on how de Savary was operating at that time. Much was made of the success by de Savary but, surprising really in the context of what was about to happen, Pattisson did not sail again during the last few races of the third round of the eliminator which, after the defeat of *Canada*, reverted to short-course from long-course races. Subsequently *Victory* beat, in turn, *Challenge*, *Azzurra* and *Canada*, with a concluding defeat against *Australia*, to bow out of the event before the start of the semi-finals.

In that final race Bill Bullard, the experienced bow-man, misjudged the calling of the start against *Australia* to the extent of 2 seconds, and what might have been a brilliant British success ended as another defeat and hastened the departure of Crebbin. For the defeat against *Australia* had followed a lost start against *Canada*. In the *Canada* match, a windshift which left Crebbin on a slow broad reach against *Canada* was made worse by both yachts drifting over the finish line.

On Saturday August 6 de Savary told Phil Crebbin that his services were no longer required. Ironically, Crebbin had only the previous night, at a traditional New England clam bake in the grounds of Hammersmith Farm – the childhood home of Jackie Kennedy-Onassis – collected for the Victory group a prize given by Louis Vuitton, the sponsors of the challengers event. This was his only public recognition in the United States of his role as skipper, before he and his young wife Lyn were left to console one another as they prepared to leave Newport. It seemed the single most shocking incident of the de Savary campaign; more so than Cudmore, more a 'soldier of fortune', and who got out partly of his own volition and at a relatively early stage of the series; or of Law, who, though with a young family and having given up such a good job, only visited Newport for a matter of days. Crebbin, though, had devoted himself to the Victory syndicate since 1980 and for two years full-time.

Crebbin left Newport on August 7, bound for San Francisco for a week's paid holiday. As the Crebbins left, in surprisingly philosophical mood and without any attempt by Phil to explain himself or condemn the people who had replaced him, de Savary went off to sail *Victory* ('82) in a race around Jamestown Island. At that point he was left with only Kit Hobday of the group that had first been called together to announce the brave new British challenge on an earlier *Lisanola* three years previously just across Newport Harbour at the Goat Island Marina. Now Hobday and de Savary were frequently and openly in disagreement over tactics and policy. Crebbin's departure marked the end of the gentlemanly period of the campaign; even before Crebbin's shadow had left the Victory dock where he briefly said whatever he had to say to de Savary on his last morning, there was evidence of a less pleasant attitude. Now those members of the squad who had protected themselves by their political man-oeuvring and posturing were quick to show their colours with snide comments or catcalls. Crebbin, after all, had been the 'yachting intellectual' of the team and the obvious candidate round which any future campaign could have been built.

The third round-robin was designed to eliminate three of the challengers, leaving the best four to fight it out in the semi-finals. These four turned out to be *Australia II*, *Azzurra*, *Canada* and *Victory '83*. The passing from the Newport scene of *Advance*, *France* and *Challenge* was a sad but logical development; the French had become a real part of America's Cup lore over the years with Baron Bich, and the style of the French would be missed, even though M. Yves Rousset-Rouard had not brought with him the opulence of Bich. The Australians of the

Challenge and *Advance* groups were indistinguishable from their compatriots of the Bond team to the casual Newport passer-by, though they were really 'B' and 'C' squads.

Advance, the least successful of all the challenge contenders, had gone to Newport, it was said, only because the Royal Sydney Yacht Squadron who were backing her would have no representative on the water despite having the honour of being the Challenger of Record, if she did not compete. It was, however, considered a useful experience for another challenge for 1987. One cruel story ran that *Australia II* and *Challenge* were as pretty as a pair of dancing shoes, while *Advance* was like the box they came in. *Advance*, designed by Alan Payne, had gone to Newport as the most unusual 12-metre in hull design, at least since *Mariner* of 1974. The yacht had short overhangs, a steep straight stem and forefoot, hull fullness well forward, a thin, small delta keel, her ballast well up in the hull, a deep skeg/bustle, and a huge forward-raked rudder and high freeboard. This is the exact opposite, it might have been said, of the majority of the twelves built or modified for the 1983 series. But then Payne had waited for years for an opportunity to build a 'different' boat; his assessment of the best chance of winning the Cup against a better prepared defender. His thinking was that he would aim for his boat to be at her best in the frequent light airy days in August and September in Newport and hope that the weather would give the yacht a decisive edge on four of the seven race days. She was intended to be at her best in the sloppy seas and light winds so common off Newport. But, alas for her, it was never exactly sloppy – rather flat – and in any event the Royal Sydney ship did not shine, and indeed managed only two wins throughout the summer. Her experienced project director, Syd Fischer, said, 'We tried to re-invent the wheel and it came out square.'

Advance was never modified during the series, though skipper John Savage wanted to move the rudder forward during the elimination series. The Australian yacht may have won few races but she won many admirers for her valiant efforts; for instance, coming back to race after a dismasting.

The published *Advance* squad was:

Syndicate chairman	Sir William Pettingell
Project director	Syd Fischer

Designer	Alan Payne
Skipper	Iain Murray
Sail designer and co-ordinator	Peter Cole
Administration manager	Neil Wyld
Tactician	Martin Visser
Sailing team and reserves	Mark Andrews (physiologist), Tony Bellingham, David Brittain (administration assistant), Ian Baker (maintenance), Greg Cavill, Matthew Coleman, Andrew Crombie (maintenance), Ian Dodd, Bruce Edwards, Kevin Flower (sailmaker), Bruce Hollis (sailmaker), Peter Isaacs, Rick Magrath, Chris Messenger (rigger), Phillip Morgan (computer), Phillip Mulvey (maintenance co-ordinator), Peter Mounsey (tender skipper), Kim Sheridan, Paul Westlake, Andrew York.

As for the French, the second squad to fall at the first elimination hurdle, it is true to say that they began with plenty of confidence, despite a much lower budget, a stated $1.5 million compared with $4 million when Baron Bich was the chief backer in 1980. It was reported that the new team were banking on the philosophy that quality would do better for them than quantity. Bruno Troublé had much higher hopes of his sails than in 1980, when it was considered that they never did justice to the Johan Valentijn design, and although there were said to be only fifteen in number, largely from the Hood loft in Nice, they were considered by the skipper to be good. The keel was different from 1980, with an enlarged profile to compensate for the articulated trim tab the yacht was originally designed to include. Troublé maintained there would be a noticeable improvement in performance, especially in light air. In the event, the

French won a total of only eight races during the summer and were eliminated despite a late change of skipper.

The last real change had come towards the end of July, though, when the French altered the rigging, moving the mast forward, altering ballast and taking steps to counter the weather helm that had so hindered steering. It was to no avail. The French squad had originally been listed as:

Chairman	Yves Rousset-Rouard
General manager	Henri de Maublanc
Operation manager	Jean Castenet
Shore manager	Christian Bachelier
Administration	Jean Marie Leclabart, Virginie Leblond
Physical training	Pascal Blondelle
Skippers	Bruno Troublé, Patrick Haegeli
Architect	Jacques Fauroux
Crew	Jacques Caraes (lifts), Jacques Delorme (winches), Eric Desvaux (tender driver), Florian Foglietti, Yann Gouniot (hardware), Albert Jacobsoone (hardware), Gilles Jarnot (sails), Didier Kelly (winches), Bruno de Landevoisin (hydraulic system), Jerome Lesieur (electrician), Arnaud Lesur, Gilles Maillart, Gilles Martin Raget (mast), Christophe Mery (electronician), Charles Nissard (workshop), Philippe Peche (sails), Pascal Pellat-Finet (mast), Patrice Queyras (hydraulic system), Philippe Rinaldi (hydraulic system), Paul de Gaillant (electronician), Michel Tewelès (sails), Christophe

	Vanek (tender driver).
Cooks	Dominique Potez (chef),
	Yann Peron (assistant),
	Marina Tewelès (hand)

With respect to the Australians of the *Advance* crew and the *France III* syndicate, the demise of these two yachts was one thing, but the failure of *Challenge 12*, designed, like *Australia II*, by Lexcen, was quite another. Here was a yacht which arrived from Australia at the beginning of the America's Cup summer with the reputation of being almost as good as *Australia II*, and certainly showing the class at the start of the racing in the elimination event to join the other Lexcen yacht in the final of the elimination series. That she began to fade and then eventually to fall was perhaps the biggest upset of the challengers' early races.

That the yacht had potential was not only certain, but apparently reemphasized when she became the *Australia II* trial-horse. With some of the better sails from her more prosperous 'sister' and a crew reinforced with members from *Advance* and *Australia II* reserves, the Bond camp reported that she had again begun to beat the challengers' favourite. It was rather like the situation when the two yachts first arrived in Newport, with the Australians claiming that *Challenge* was every bit as fast as *Australia II*. This Royal Yacht Club of Victoria entry was regarded as the 'straight' boat of the three from Australia. Though a refinement of *Australia* (of 1980), she was considered light, long and reasonably conventional with the exception of a flat counter with vestigial chines and creases above her rudder. Her flattened stem became abruptly sharper with a 'bulb' or bump below the waterline measurement points. Her skipper, John Savage, was considered to have the fewest credentials of any of those in charge of 12-metres, defender or challenger. The crew work of *Challenge* was at first as good as any of the challengers, since they won all but one of their first five races and their only defeat was against *Australia II*. At that stage *Challenge* was considered the second favourite behind the Perth boat to be the challenger, and for some time rated the only real threat among the challengers to *Australia II*, which she did beat on one occasion. But then the trouble began – a broken boom and an easy win for her opponent, *Victory '83*, marked the beginning of the end. One of the interesting aspects of the challenger trials was that the form in the first round, with the exception of *Advance* and *France*, did not necessarily represent true potential. *Challenge* was the biggest surprise on form because of her earlier consistency, not least in lighter airs. With Richard Pratt – businessman, actor, politician and indeed a man of many parts – the chairman of the Challenge group joining the Bond camp with the yacht once she was eliminated, there was at least some Australian continuity apart from merely the Perth yacht.

The *Challenge 12* squad in Newport were listed as:

Chairman	Richard Pratt
Executive director	Rod Ledgar
Administrators	Jim Briers, Ian Fraser, Roger Lamb, Denis Wilkins, Barry Weston
Medical officer	George Clegg
Public relations	Christopher Forsyth
Coach	Mike Fletcher
Advisor	Lou Abrahams, Jock Sturrock
Skipper	John Stanley Savage
Tactician	Graeme Freeman
Crew	Col Anderson, Russel Evans, Damian Fewster, Julian Freeman, John Hall, Chris Harmsen, Peter Kane, Gary Simmons, Glenn Stone, Don Telford, Phil Thompson, Hugo van Kretschmar, Tom Walters, Stuart Will

There was, apart from the passing of the three casualties of the preliminary rounds, and the onset of the NYYC witch-hunt over the keel of *Australia II*, one other unfortunate accident in the first three rounds: it concerned Scott McAllister, the bowman of the Perth boat, who broke an arm during a race against *Canada* in the third round of the challengers' elimination event.

The accident occurred when McAllister, one of the veterans of previous Bond campaigns aboard *Australia II*, went aloft to try to sort out a mainsail problem. Unfortunately the head-boardcrane broke, the mainsail collapsed, and McAllister's arms were trapped beneath the wreckage at the top of the mast where, for a while, he hung unconscious. It was not until he regained consciousness and was able to free his arm that the *Australia* crew were able to hoist another man aloft to bring down his injured companion. He was taken ashore in *Lisanola* with the *Victory* medic Barrie Thomas in attendance, and then to Newport hospital. It marked the end of the America's Cup campaign for McAllister, whose place was taken by Damian Fewster, originally a member of the *Challenge* squad.

The third round, fortunately, did have its lighter moments, including the thirty-ninth birthday of de Savary – who received a number of impressive presents, including a signet ring with a wonderfully engraved motif of Winston the bulldog – and which came at about the time that he had been loaned three Aston-Martin cars. There was also the Canadian caper, the alleged attempt by two 'frogmen' to take underwater pictures of the keel of *Australia II*, and which resulted in the arrest of and two court appearances by James Johnston. Johnston had been charged with trespass after being caught in possession of a camera at the Australian dock by a security guard who swam in pursuit to apprehend him, but he was later dismissed when the Australian charge was dropped. The 'deal' was that in return for the film the Australians would not press charges.

And then, as the semi-finals were about to start, there was a visit to Newport from Vice-President Bush and his wife, who paid only brief visits to the various yachts. Just as well, perhaps, in view of the fact that exchanges over the alleged irregularities in *Australia II*'s keel were then at their height.

XI

'Such inequity requires correction'

*Every yacht entering a race shall hold such valid measurement
or rating certificate as may be required by the national authority or other duly authorized body, by her class rules, by the
notice of the race or regatta, or by the sailing instructions.*

— *Racing Rule 19 of the International Yacht Racing Union*

That the New York Yacht Club intended to query the validity of
the shape of the underbody of *Australia II* first came to the
attention of the press on July 31, when copies of a memorandum
dated July 24 from Robert W. McCullough, chairman of the
America's Cup committee, to Mark H. Vinbury, the American
member of the trio of measurers who granted the 12-metres
their rating certificates after measurement, were delivered to
representatives of the seven challenge syndicates. Almost immediately copies became available to members of the press,
though not from the NYYC, who had set off from Newport the
previous day on the start of their annual cruise. The uproar over
'the' keel was to continue unabated for days, though it was more
than a week before the NYYC were to make any comment on
the matter.

The first surprise was the timing of the New York Yacht
Club's question: after *Australia II* had won more than 30 races
and looked the yacht most likely to challenge for the America's
Cup in September. The outcry was amazing, not least because of
the number of Americans who, hearing an English or Australian
accent in the streets of Newport, would stop and apologize for
the action taken by the New York Club. By contrast there was
an absence of any public condemnation from the majority of
the newspapers on sale in the New England states at the time.
All sorts of words and phrases were used to describe the furore

caused by the NYYC's action, but few commentators in America at that time were ready to say that the New York Yacht Club had acted with anything other than sportsmanship. The communication from McCullough which started the uproar stated: 'This memorandum considers whether the yacht *Australia II* has been fairly rated under the rating rule and measurement instructions of the International Twelve Metre Class in view of the wing-like appendages which extend outward and downward from the bottom of her keel . . .', drawing attention to an attached diagram. The communication to Vinbury continued:

The question arises under Rule 27, which, in pertinent part provides:

'If from *any peculiarity* in the build of the yacht, *or other cause*, the measurer shall be of the opinion that the rule will not *rate the yacht fairly*, or that in any respect she does not comply with the requirements of these rules he shall report the circumstances to the National Authority, which, after due inquiry, shall award such certificate of rating as they may consider *equitable*, and the measurement shall be deemed incomplete until this has been done.' [Emphasis added by NYYC]

Also applicable is Measurement Instruction 7, which requires in 'doubtful cases' that:

'If from *any peculiarity* of build, construction, or fitting of any yacht, the National Authority, on the report of the measurer, *is in doubt* as to the application of the rules or instructions, *or the calculation of the rating*, it shall report the case to the IYRU, who after due inquiry shall award such certificate of rating as it may deem *equitable*: and the measurement shall be deemed incomplete (see Measurement Instruction 8) until this has been done.' [Emphasis added by NYYC]

At the outset, it must be recognized that it is not necessary under Rule 27 or Measurement Instruction 7 that there be a showing that the yacht fails to comply with the requirements of the rules. All that is required is some 'doubt' as to whether the yacht can be rated 'fairly' or how, in the light of the 'peculiarity', its rating is to be calculated. The manifest purpose of Rule 27 and Measurement In-

struction 7 is to assure that when a yacht has 'any peculiarity', which the rules do not contemplate, and which gives
the yacht a benefit or advantage that is not provided for in
the calculation of her rating, her rating must be recalcu-
lated so that she is rated 'fairly' and receives an 'equitable'
rating.

It is not necessary, therefore, in the case of *Australia II*'s
keel appendages, to find that they are prohibited by, or are
otherwise in violation of, any specific provisions of the
rules or measurement instructions. When, as is the case
here, three conditions exist, Rule 27 and Measurement
Instruction 7, then mandate the recalculation of her rating,
so as to make it equitable. The three conditions are:

1. The keel appendages are a 'peculiarity'.
2. They give the yacht a benefit or advantage.
3. That benefit or advantage is not contemplated by
   the rules or instruction and is therefore unrated.

It follows that *Australia II* is not fairly rated and does not
have an equitable certificate of rating.

There can be no question but that *Australia II*'s keel
appendages are a 'peculiarity', which, by dictionary definition, is the quality or state of being different from the usual
or normal. No 12-metre yacht, and probably no other
known yacht anywhere, has had such appendages on her
keel. Nothing within the four corners of the Rating Rule
and Measurement Instruction suggests that those who
drafted them had any inkling of such a 'peculiarity'. Indeed, Rule 27 and Measurement Instruction 7 would seem
to have been drafted to cover just such a situation as is
presented here. Finally, conclusive proof of the 'peculiarity' is afforded by the fact that the owners of *Australia II*
have gone to unusual, albeit questionable, lengths to
maintain complete secrecy as to the exact character and
dimensions of the appendages.

Stating that 'it is equally clear that the appendages give
Australia II a benefit and advantage she would not otherwise have,' the letter says that the yacht's draft, when
measured as the vertical distance from the lowest point of
the wingtips to the LWL plane, with the yacht in the
normal upright position, is 2.645 metres. However, when
the yacht is positioned at approximately 13 degrees of heel

the wingtips are immersed to a greater depth, thereby increasing her effective draft by .067 metre to 2.712 metres. The yacht's rating at that draft would become 12.476 metres.

It is not necessary, however, to delve into all the niceties of measuring the yacht while heeled. The fact remains, in any event, that when the yacht heels she gains unmeasured draft. The amount of the excess will vary with the degree of heel, but at all normal angles of heel the yacht *always* will have a deeper keel than she would have in the absence of the appendages. It goes without saying that the resulting increases in draft, lateral plane and stability are of material benefit and advantage to *Australia II*.

Once again, conclusive evidence of the advantage comes from the manner in which the designer and owners of *Australia II* assess it. The letter says that Ben Lexcen, the designer, claimed in an interview that the addition of the wings 'cuts down on leeway and increases stability'. And Alan Bond thinks the benefits of the appendages are so great as to warrant patenting them.

As noted before, neither the rules nor the measurement instructions contemplate appendages on the keel, which provide such unmeasured and unrated advantages. It would be argued that, because of the absence of punctuation, the words 'in any position' in Rule 6 apply equally to the 'hull' and 'movable appendage'. At the very least, it suggests that the framers of the rule were intent on prohibiting any devices for gaining unmeasured draft, and this is further emphasized by the severity of the penalty imposed for excess draft. These issues, as discussed above, need not be reached, for however they were resolved the inescapable conclusion would remain, namely that *Australia II* is unfairly rated. Their mention serves to emphasize that result.

The letter is signed by Robert W. McCullough, Chairman of the America's Cup Committee of the NYYC.

An initial reaction to the letter was that representatives of the seven challenge contenders met and the *Australia II* syndicate was assured by the other six that so long as the measurement committee responsible for such tasks in connection with the challengers' elimination event were satisfied that the measurement of the yacht was legal, they were happy to abide by that decision. There would not then be, as it had been thought might be the reaction to the NYYC's letter, a formal protest also from one of the challenge groups. If the NYYC had hoped to get their 'dirty work' done for them by an overseas team, they had been mistaken.

Next, the Americans got their lines of communication a little muddled, for their response to the inaction of the challengers was to get Vinbury to write to George Andreadis, acting chairman of the Keel Boat Committee (KBC) of the International Yacht Racing Union, asking for a ruling on the question of the validity of the keel of the yacht. Andreadis, a Greek yachtsman shortly to be confirmed as chairman, was only 'acting' at that stage because of the death, only a matter of weeks before the furore, of Sir Gordon Smith, the long-time and much respected chairman of the KBC.

Tony Watts, the Unions's Chief Measurer and head of the trio of measurers who had granted *Australia II* her rating certificate in Newport, made it clear that as head of the International Measurement Committee, who were the final arbiters of matters concerning measurement in the challengers' series, he did not have any doubts about the validity of the keel of *Australia II*. Nor did Jack Savage, the Australian member of the measurement committee. Vinbury, of course, was the third member. The NYYC made no headway either with the IYRU, for whom Nigel Hacking, the secretary-general, was quick to point out that the Union dealt with national authorities, not clubs. As a result another week went by in which Beppe Croce, a member of the *Azzurra* syndicate as well as the President of the IYRU, had gone to Newport for the announcement by the Italians that they would challenge for the trophy again, 'whenever and wherever it was next held'. In Newport Croce pointed out, first, that the keel question was one for the International Measurement Committee, not the Union's KBC, to resolve, though it might be involved in an appeal. Any communication to the IYRU should come from the United States Yacht Racing Union (USYRU), one of its members.

The matter had already been put to the Union, however, by James Michael, another member of the NYYC's America's Cup Committee and who delivered the communication to the Union's base in Los Angeles at the time of the 1983 pre-Olympic regatta at Long Beach. Michael, a court lawyer, had achieved notoriety in yachting circles in Europe in the 1970s, when he had campaigned against established rating rules for ocean racers.

The letter to Andreadis, dated August 3, stated:

> The America's Cup Committee of the New York Club requests a ruling from the Keel Boat Committee of IYRU to determine if the yacht, *Australia II*, has been 'fairly' rated in accordance with Rule 27 and Measurement Instruction 7 of the Rating Rule and Measurement Instructions of the International Twelve Metre Class (referred to herein as the 'Rating Rule'). It is further requested that your Committee 'award such certificate of rating as it may deem equitable' to *Australia II*, as required by said Rule 27 and Measurement Instruction 7.
>
> This request arises from the following circumstances. One of the three Measurers on the Measurement Committee appointed pursuant to the conditions governing the America's Cup Races this year, as well as the conditions governing the current trials being held to select the challenger and the defender, has questioned whether *Australia II* has been 'fairly and equitably' rated, and has urged that the matter be submitted to your Committee for a ruling.

The letter referred to another, from Vinbury to Watts, dated July 25 1983:

> Anticipating that the Measurement Committee will make such a submission to your Committee, we wish to join in that request and submit for your consideration, the results of our investigations of the matter.

Pointing out that *Australia II* had wing-like appendages that extended outward and downward from her keel as shown in attached diagrams, it was said, the letter did confess that the

> exact shape and configuration of the appendages may vary slightly from what is shown in the diagrams, but the dimensions are believed to be accurate for the purposes herein and can be confirmed by the Measurers.

The letter goes on:

> Preliminarily, it is to be noted that our inability to be more precise, as well as our inability to present this ques-

tion at an earlier time, stem from two circumstances. First, the *Australia II* Syndicate has gone to unusual (and, we submit, highly questionable measures) to maintain complete secrecy concerning her keel and its appendages. These measures have included: shrouding the underbody of the yacht when hauled from the water; using electrically charged screens surrounding her keel when berthed afloat; having the yacht measured in a closed shed to which access was barred by around-the-clock security guards; swearing the measurer to keep secret the shape and dimensions of the appendages and the like.

Secondly, the degree to which the yacht is not 'fairly rated' could not be conclusively demonstrated until she had sailed in a representative number of races. As this is being written *Australia II* has completed 36 races in the trials so far, and has won 33 of them, the three losses being primarily due to the luck of the winds rather than to boat speed. Even more important, however, are the following statistics: on the three windward legs in those races, over courses which, for the most part were shorter than the standard Cup course, she gained a total of one hour, one minute 56 seconds; on the reaching and downwind legs, she gained a total of two minutes, 54 seconds. When normal twelve metre yachts, sailing standard cup courses usually finish within a minute of each other, *Australia II*'s record is all the more demonstrative of the advantage she has.

Based on consultation with, and the opinions of naval architects experienced in the design of twelve metre yachts, as well as other practitioners and students of the Rating Rule, the America's Cup Committee submits that the following conclusions are inescapable:

1. The appendages to the keel of *Australia II* constitute a peculiarity within the meaning and intent of the terms 'any peculiarity' as used in Rule 27 and Measurement Instruction 7 of the Rating Rule;

2. The appendages give the yacht decided benefits and advantages, as witness her performance record;

3. The appendages are either illegal under the Rating Rule, or, at the very least, are not fairly rated thereunder;

4. And therefore, it is required that the Keel Boat

Committee award it such certificate of rating as is 'equitable'.

In support of these conclusions, the club offered various 'evidence and arguments' before adding:

There are several grounds upon which it can be ruled that the appendages are prohibited under the Rating Rule:

1. Rule 32 provides that 'Centreboards or similar contrivances are prohibited'. The conventional meaning of centreboard contemplates a movable device for increasing draft, particularly when the yacht is heeled sailing to windward. On the other hand, the term 'similar contrivances' is very broad and all-inclusive and clearly, it is submitted, bar the appendages of *Australia II*, for they effectively accomplish the same purpose as a centreboard within the keel, i.e. they extend the draft beyond the conventional keel when the yacht is heeled and sailing to windward.

2. There is precedent in the 5.5 metre class which is applicable here. Prior to the 1968 amendments to the 5.5 metre Rule, endplates and similar contrivances on keels were not considered permissible. The 1968 amendments permit them but subject to a specific restriction that the fixed surfaces be horizontal in cross section when the yacht is measured (Rule 10(viii) of the 5.5 Metre Rule). Unless, and until, a similar authorization is incorporated in the twelve metre Rating Rule, it can be argued that endplates, or similar contrivances on twelve metres, are prohibited. Also, *Australia II*'s appendages would not, in any event, meet the horizontal requirement.

3. In addition to these two grounds for prohibiting the appendages, Rule 6 of the Rating Rule, in the absence of any punctuation in the last sentence, clearly allows for measurement of draft in the heeled position. Until measured in that position, *Australia II* would have an invalid certificate. When so measured, her rating would increase to 12.476 metres, as demonstrated, argues the letter, in an enclosure. In that event, she would violate the aforementioned conditions of the America's Cup Races, and of the trials which provide that 'Yachts shall not rate over twelve metres'.

While any one or more of the above grounds is dis-
positive of the issues presented, if the Keel Boat Committee should interpret the Rating Rule in a different
manner, it will still have to face the question of awarding
Australia II 'such certificate of rating as it may deem
equitable'.

One further point is to be made. It is recognized that the
Rating Rule encourages development by innovation of
design. But it must also be recognized that the Rule clearly
seeks to protect yachts from 'any peculiarity' of design
which unfairly rates another yacht. The line between
acceptable design innovation and an unfair peculiarity,
may often be difficult to discern. But that is not the case
here, for if ever there is a 'pecularity' under the Rule, it is
the appendages of *Australia II*'s keel. The manifest unfair-
ness of her rating is the fact that it requires normal 12
metre yachts to race against her while she rates at least
somewhere between 12.5 and 12.8 metres. Such inequity
requires correction.

In closing, we respectfully urge your Committee to
expedite a resolution of this matter. With the selection
trials currently underway, and the America's Cup Races
themselves only a little over a month away, an early
decision is urgently needed. To postpone action by your
Committee until September 8, 1983, when, if *Australia II*
is the designated challenger, remeasurement would force a
ruling, in our judgment, would be the most unfortunate for
all concerned.

In the interests of time, we are sending complete copies
of this submission directly to all members of the Keel
Boat Committee. Copies are also being sent to all the challenger and defender syndicates, and to the Measurement
Committee.

The communication then included a number of letters, from
Vinbury, the original letter to Vinbury from McCullough, a long
memorandum to Michael from Halsey Herreshoff, navigator to
Conner on *Liberty*, a letter to McCullough from Paul Doppke, of
the Cove Haven shipyard, a telex message from Britton Chance
Jnr to Michael, and a memorandum from Bill Luders to
McCullough.

The Vinbury letter, to Watts, was interesting in that although not questioning the correct measuring of *Australia II* according to the rule, he went on: 'I am concerned, however, that the rule as it is currently written is not able to assess the unusual shape of this keel and thereby fairly rate the yacht.' He also suggested that the Measurement Committee of which he and Watts were members should request the KBC to give a ruling on the keel.

Herreshoff, in a seven-page memorandum, draws the conclusions that:

1. The NYYC and foreign contestants should promptly develop a position of protest in the matter of the *Australia II* keel.
2. The shroud should come off to enable competitors to fairly observe and assess that against which they are asked to race.
3. *Australia II* should be presented the following options:
   a) Withdraw from competition.
   b) Take a logical rating penalty for the keel wings.
   c) Remove or diminish the wings such that there is no increase in draft compared to a conventional keel at large heel angle.
4. The appropriate procedures and a hearing before measurers and the Keel Boat Committee should be conducted with alacrity.
5. The matter should be resolved before commencement of final foreign trials to select a challenger.

In his introduction to his memorandum, Herreshoff states:

If the closely guarded peculiar keel design of *Australia II* is allowed to remain in competition or is allowed to continue to be rated without penalty, the yacht will likely win the foreign trials and will likely win the America's Cup in September 1983.

The America's Cup has traditionally been an open, but carefully controlled, competition combining yacht design, construction, with development of sails and gear and especially in recent years emphasizes the tactical as well as speed considerations of yacht racing. While a few times over the years there have been bitter controversies involving allegations about design and yacht flotation, the competition has traditionally been conducted on a high plane of openness, fairness and honesty. While in addition to sailing skill, the design and development of boats has mattered, offbeat elements outside the provisions and intent of the rule have not been allowed to enter.

Thus, over the 132 year history of the Cup there is no precedent for anything like the loophole oddness of an *Australia II* keel. Also, there is no precedent for the shrouded, clandestine attitude of the Australian syndicate shutting out competitors from their rightful knowledge of that against which they are competing under known, strict rules.

The New York Yacht Club and foreign challenge candidates should immediately face this issue which threatens unfairly to control the 1983 competition and which threatens a new dimension and approach that could ruin America's Cup competition for all time. For us to do nothing would be to slack (sic) our duty in protecting the most magnificent competition in sports.

Astonishingly, acknowledging that his deductions are 'based on limited observations aided by press and rumor reports', he nonetheless speculatively constructs 'the characteristics and implications of the *Australia II* design'. He states:

She is evidently a relatively short L, relatively light hull of quite unusual underbody design. There is a depth of forward profile and fullness of volume forward exceeding that of conventional 12-metre boats. The conventional aft 'bussle' is largely absent giving less than usual aft displacement. The keel is extremely short and of most unusual profile, particularly in the absence of a long sloping keel transition forward. There are double axled trim tabs (not a new development). The keel bottom has a full bulb for reasons of weight and possible tip effect. One of the principal benefits of the elimination of the 'bussle' and of large keel platform is a drastic reduction of wetted surface which serves to cut frictional drag – the principal component of drag at the slower speeds. All of the above would seem to be innovative but legal and proper choices for a designer to make in seeking a winning design.

In a totally different category, is the employment of large, principally horizontal wings at the bottom of the

Australia II keel. There is no precedent before 1983 for such in serious competitive yacht racing. There is obviously no intent in the framing of the 12-metre rating rule to provide for such. Thus, for *Australia II* to be allowed to race, her keel wings should be removed or the yacht should not be fairly rated to provide penalty for this feature.

Essentially, the remainder of the Herreshoff memorandum argues technically how the wings on the keel of *Australia II* defeat drag and cheat the 12-metre rule, thus his conclusions.

The letter from Chance suggests that a precedent had been set in the 5.5-metre class to penalize the 'peculiarities' of *Australia II*, while the memorandum from Luders suggests how the necessary rating adjustment could be made concerning the Australian 12-metre. The letter to McCullough from Doppke merely sets out how the Cove Haven Corporation were asked to provide a shed with no other boats in it for the purpose, originally, of measuring *Australia II*. Thus far, really, the NYYC intention had clearly been to raise as many doubts as possible about the keel of the Lexcen design and suggest proof of a conspiracy to defeat or beat the 12-metre rule.

Now came the turn of the US contenders to have their ratings questioned. It became known that there was a practice of using more than one rating certificate for *Liberty*. First revealed by a member of the opposing *Defender* camp, it had become public knowledge that *Liberty*'s backers had found a way to race at different times with three certificates, though this was really one certificate with amendments. The giveaway was that there were three measurer's marks at each measurement point on the sheer, fore and aft. The arrangement, made with what measurer or measurers it was not known, meant that the *Liberty* crew could remove or add ballast daily before any one race, repaint their flotation marks, have it checked by a measurer and use bigger or smaller booms and more or less sail as the conditions desired. It seems that the NYYC had been told and had given permission for the practice to be started, but had not required that anyone else be told. Not only did the revelation about the *Liberty* system surprise the challenge groups, it clearly upset even more the rival defender syndicates who had been caught out. Though an attempt was made to blow this up into a row equivalent to the Lexcen keel, it was a minor procedural matter

and the defending yacht would undoubtedly have a single rating
in good time for the Cup races.

One amusing detail, which rather attested to the fact that the
Americans had not got their act together, was that at precisely
the time that Conner was essentially denying that any such
thing had happened, the NYYC's America's Cup Committee
chairman McCullough was admitting that it had. His statement
about the NYYC/USYRU approach to the IYRU included these
words:

> In sport, the fairness of competition is paramount and
> should be free from question. With this in view, we also
> have asked the KBC for a ruling on another matter. The
> Challenger of Record, the Royal Sydney Yacht Squadron,
> has questioned whether it would be correct for the defen-
> der to compete in the actual Cup Races with the opportun-
> ity to change rating certificates from race to race. *Liberty*
> has done this in our selection trials, with the permission of
> the measurers, for the purpose of enabling her to determine
> her best trim.

But, lest anyone should suddenly forget what the NYYC
considered the more important issue, the McCullough statement added immediately:

> However, in the case of *Australia II*, our primary con-
> cern is that the America's Cup is won or lost in yachts that
> are truly 12-Metres. Only the KBC has the authority to
> determine this. If *Australia II* rates too high, she then
> could conceivably be modified to measure within the rule.
> But for Australia to compete with a yacht that could well
> be greater than a Twelve would make the competition
> meaningless.

NYYC was unfortunately the butt of the most abusive comment from what might be described as ordinary, ill-informed
man-in-the-street Americans. Some of the jokier comments
about the NYYC at this time included: 'They are too arrogant to
be embarrassed'; and, more cutting still: 'The shortest book in
the world is the New York Yacht Club's book of ethics.' The
NYYC began to consider that the matter was getting out of hand
because they sought a private meeting with *Australia II* syndicate chief Bond and Warren Jones, the excellent and efficient

executive director of the Perth operation. It took place at Bond's home in Newport on August 7 and involved on the one side Bond and Jones, and on the other Bob Stone, Commodore of the NYYC, McCullough and Emil 'Bus' Mosbacher.

There was never an official statement about the meeting, though Jones was ultimately to acknowledge publicly that it did take place, and the comments which were made described it as having been rather like 'two brick walls sitting and facing one another for a couple of hours'. That nothing in the way of a conciliation was achieved seemed to be confirmed by the continuing pressure put on by the NYYC, despite a calming influence at a 12-metre class meeting in Newport on August 8 by Olin Stephens, designer of 12-metres since 1938 and one of the greatest authorities in the world on yacht racing rules.

Stephens publicly congratulated Lexcen on the design. ('It was rather like being blessed by God', was Lexcen's comment later), and proclaimed for all to know that *Australia II* was a proper 12-metre and there was no question but that her measurement was correct. Further, Stephens, like the meeting which also approved a first 12-metre regatta for the Costa Smeralda the following summer, deplored any multiple rating practice. It had by this time become clear that the *Defender/Courageous* camp were to try a similar system.

Boiling point on the keel issue was about to be reached, the final heat being generated so far as the NYYC/USYRU were concerned by a brief message from Tony Watts, chairman of the International Measurement Committee. Transmitted so that the challengers' semi-finals could start on time, and sought by the organizers in Newport, it read:

> To: Bill Fesq and Jock Smith [chairmen of the Challenger of Record and 'Race' Committees respectively]:
> The Measurement Committee unanimously reaffirms that the keel of *Australia II* is legal. By a majority, the Measurement Committee agrees that Rating Rule 27 is not applicable in this case.

Obviously the 'majority' were Watts and Savage, the dissenter clearly being the American Vinbury. The note brought a rapid response from Jones, reportedly 'delighted' at the reaffirmation of the legality of the keel:

Obviously we have never had any doubts about the legality as we have, in our possession, a measurement certificate to prove it.

Let's hope that this whole affair is now behind us and that we can now all play by the referee's decision.

We are looking forward to the subject of our keel being discussed in November at the proper forum – the annual meeting of the Keel Boat Committee.

The past week has been a bit of a problem for us. We should have been concentrating on the important task of winning the semi-final series.

He added the last sentence in reference to the resumption of the challengers' elimination event the following day, August 11.

In the event the resumption, considering the importance of the contest, was disappointing and perhaps the most feeble day's racing of the entire summer. It was the race in which *Canada* retired from her race with headsail problems on the final weather leg of the full, 24.4-nautical mile America's Cup-type course, giving *Australia II* an easy win, while *Victory '83* began with an even easier point against *Azzurra* which retired with a broken jumper strut on the opening beat. Two days of inactivity in the semi-finals followed, racing being impossible in strong northerly winds which whipped up big seas in Rhode Island Sound where the Race Committee did require the yachts to be, before finally abandoning competition on the second of the two days. On the first day of the gales, the yachts did not even leave harbour.

But if there was no action afloat there most certainly was plenty ashore, where the USYRU showed their hand with a long communication to Hacking at the IYRU after receiving a message which had doubted, clearly, whether it was the task of the Union to act on the American request over the Australian keel. It did also mark the entry into the squabble of Tom Ehman, Executive Director of the USYRU, and to whom the Hacking message was addressed. Referring to a letter from Michael, supplementing his original of August 3 to the KBC, it read:

This letter does not appear to ask for an interpretation of the rating rule but for the IYRU to determine if *Australia II* has been fairly rated and to award a certificate . . . as it may seem equitable.

The IYRU does not issue rating certificates except under

measurement instruction 7. For USYRU to ask IYRU to interpret a rule would seem to be in order but before doing so we would need to know the reasons why the IYRU should intervene in this challenge event in view of condition for selecting a challenging yacht clause 20 and America's Cup conditions clause 22. And we would need to be satisfied that the IYRU was not usurping the functions of the measurement committee.

Clearly, if the NYYC/USYRU had thought they would find the IYRU a willing ally, they were very much mistaken.

After this the tone of the American requests for action from the IYRU were becoming more frantic and, frankly, wild and inaccurate. For example, in the Michael letter of August 10 he weighed in with characteristic overemphasis, pointing out that his letter was a supplement to that of August 3 requesting a ruling on the *Australia II* appendage:

> We wish to make two additional points.
>
> First, we understand that the Chief Measurer of IYRU has expressed the view that the questions raised regarding *Australia II*'s keel appendage are for the exclusive determination by the three man measurement committee (which he heads) established by the conditions governing America's Cup trials and match. While we would agree that the conditions do leave questions of interpretation to the measurement committee, we submit the questions presented here do not fall within that proscription.
>
> Please note that the conditions also provide that the Measurement Rule of the International Twelve Metre Class shall govern the trials and the match. Not only that the yachts must comply with that rule, but also must the measurers. The measurement committee cannot ignore *any* provision of the rule, and that means they have no right not to comply fully with Rule 27 and Measurement Instruction 7.
>
> Least of all can the measurement committee refuse to seek and obtain a ruling from the KBC when there exists a 'peculiarity' of the magnitude presented here. The only body which the rule recognizes for purposes of awarding the yacht 'such certificate of rating as it may deem equitable' is the KBC. The measurers, of course, routinely make

decisions interpreting the rule, but when it comes to a question whether a yacht with 'any peculiarity' can be fairly rated under the rule, they are bound by the rule itself to seek a ruling from the KBC.

There are now in place all the circumstances which *require* a ruling by the KBC to-wit:

1. Mark Vinbury, a duly certified measurer, measured *Australia II*.
2. He recognized the 'peculiarity' of her keel appendages, and reported his doubts as to whether the yacht could be fairly rated.
3. Based on that report, the USYRU, as the national authority, has now placed the case before the IYRU.
4. Faced with these circumstances, and having met all the requirements of Rule 27 and Measurement Instruction 7, it is now *obligatory* upon the KBC 'after due enquiry' to 'award such certificate of rating as it may deem equitable'.
5. Finally, by the specific and unequivocal requirements of Rule 27 and Measurement Instruction 7, *until* the KBC takes such action, *the measurement of* Australia II *'shall be deemed incomplete'.*

None of the above facts, and none of the required actions which flow from them, is, in any way, changed or affected by the conditions governing the trials and the match. They all arise and stand on their own feet independently under the rating rule.

The fact that *Australia II*'s measurement is incomplete (from which it necessarily follows that she has no valid certificate of rating), until the KBC issues her such certificate as it deems equitable, underscores the urgent need for immediate action by the committee.

Secondly, we enclose a copy of a letter from the USYRU to the IYRU formally requesting, under IYRU Regulation 7, an interpretation of the Twelve Metre Rating Rule per our submission of August 3, 1983, copies of which already are on file with the Secretariat of IYRU, as well as all members of the KBC.

This independent action by the USYRU requires the issue to be considered and passed upon by the KBC wholly apart from the conditions governing the America's Cup trials and match, and irrespective of any actions taken thereunder by the measurement committee.

The questions presented are of the utmost importance, and involve 'a matter of principle' requiring an immediate and definitive ruling on the substantive issues. Specifically, the KBC must decide:

1. Are the keel appendages of *Australia II* permitted, or prohibited, under the Twelve Metre Rating Rule and Measurement Instructions?

2. If permitted, are such appendages 'fairly' rated by the Rating Rule and Measurement Instructions?

3. If not fairly rated, what 'equitable' certificate or rating should be awarded to the yacht?

The resolution of these matters is of great concern to all who are involved with the America's Cup, in this year. For that reason, the apparent efforts of the Chief Measurer to side-step a ruling by the KBC should be unavailing. One of the more important purposes for which the IYRU exists is to provide the proper forum in which such questions may be resolved. For the IYRU to shirk its responsibilities in this instance would result in a disservice to the sport of yachting for major proportions.

Copies of this letter are being sent to the IYRU Secretariat, and all members of the KBC.

The letter was high-handed, complete with its American legal jargon; and, since they had taken it upon themselves to send copies of it to the members of the KBC after accusing Watts of attempting to side-step a ruling by the IYRU, it was considered rude and impertinent. But if the Michael letter was impertinent, the communication which followed on August 12 from Ehman was downright insulting, and seen as such by the Australian camp at least. It read:

Replying to your August 11, 1983, telex; the questions which require the interpretation of and a ruling by the KBC are listed on page 3 of Jim Michael's supplemental letter of August 10, 1983, copy of which was sent to you. Without waiving our request for a clarification and interpretation under IYRU Regulation 7, and in order to meet your requirements for issuance of a rating certificate, USYRU hereby submits the August 3, 1983 letter of the America's

Cup committee and August 10, 1983, supplement thereto as the report of this national authority to IYRU persuant to Measurement Instruction 7 and requests the earliest possible ruling by the full KBC. All of the conditions required for such a ruling have been met as outlined on pages 2 and 3 of said August 10, 1983, supplemental letter.

Neither the action of USYRU, nor the action which we submit is now required of IYRU, is in conflict with the America's Cup conditions. Neither usurps the functions of the measurement committee. There are several reasons for these conclusions:

First: The requests of USYRU under Regulation 7 and now under Measurement Instruction 7 are made independently of and are not in any way governed or affected by the America's Cup conditions. As a national authority, USYRU is entirely within its own rights in invoking the requested action of IYRU irrespective of what actions the measurement committee may take under the conditions.

Second: While the measurement committee is authorized to decide questions of interpretation arising under the measurement rule the conditions do not give it the power to determine what rating will be equitable under Rule 27 and Measurement Instruction 7. Only the KBC is qualified to do that. The measurement committee cannot ignore those provisions of the rule.

Third: With all due respect to him, the chairman of the measurement committee is apparently unwilling to follow the obviously proper courses and obtain a ruling from the full KBC and this notwithstanding the doubts which have surrounded *Australia II*'s keel appendages from the outset.

Indeed, the following unusual background circumstances, we submit, make it incumbent on USYRU and IYRU, to act. When *Australia II* was measured in Australia the measurer evidently had doubts about the peculiarity of her keel appendages and in accordance with Rule 27 reported it to the Australian Yachting Federation. That Federation convened a special committee to advise it, which committee included Jack Savage, now one of three members of the America's Cup Measurement Committee. The special committee evidently unanimously recommended that the designer of *Australia II* seek a ruling on the keel appendages from the KBC and that the Australian Yachting Federation report the case to the IYRU pursuant to Measurement Instruction 7. The designer declined to follow the recommendation, and the Australian Yachting Federation was persuaded not to make the report.

Ever since, the keel and its appendages have been shrouded in the utmost secrecy. From these circumstances, it is manifest that every measurer who has been involved with *Australia II*, including two of the measurers on the measurement committee, and excluding only its chairman, have recognized the need for a definitive ruling from the KBC. In the best interests of the sport USYRU and IYRU must act, and promptly.

The replies were succinct and to the point and need no comment. Savage wrote to Watts on August 13:

The facts as stated in the third conclusion in the telex from USYRU to IYRU on August 12 are incorrect and the inference is more so. I did, at a Sydney meeting, recommend reference to the IYRU. Reason being to pre-empt anticipated action as is at present taking place if the boat proved successful. This is to confirm that as of then I am still firmly of the opinion that *Australia II* is a development within the 12-metre rule and rates as a 12-metre.

John Fitzhardinge, Commodore of the Royal Perth Yacht Club, the appointed representative of the club during the challengers' trials, said on the same day that the Club had reviewed all the data relating to the measurement and rating of *Australia II*. They had no doubt whatsoever about the legality of *Australia II*'s rating, or that the decision of the International Measurement Committee was final.

The suggestion by the USYRU that the Australian measurer or the AYF had erred was totally unfounded, he commented in a statement, which added that unfortunately, it now appeared that statements were being issued by authorities without them checking the accuracy of the information. 'We join with the *Australia II* syndicate in saying let's get on with the racing,' Commodore Fitzhardinge concluded.

Then came the biggest bombshell to that period of the America's Cup summer, and, indeed, one of the most significant developments, it seemed at the time, in the recent history of the trophy. The 'bombshell' was an announcement at a press conference on August 13 – the second day on which it had not been possible to continue the challengers' series because of the weather. The statement by Warren Jones, the *Australia II* executive director, was released to the press in the following, well-prepared form:

'In view of the further announcements by the NYYC during this week and the statements of the USYRU regarding the rating of *Australia II*, the syndicate felt that it should correct certain errors contained in the releases.'

Regarding the correctness of procedure outlined by the NYYC, Jones released a letter he had sent to the president of the IYRU on August 10, 1983, which he said clearly established that the International Measurement Committee is responsible for the final decision regarding the correct rating of *Australia II*.

'As our letter indicates, no entity and certainly not the NYYC or the USYRU has any right to request that the IYRU re-rate or comment on the rating of our boat at this time according to clear IYRU rules.'

Jones said that after the NYYC had finally determined that they were not an authority recognized by the IYRU, they then turned to the USYRU for support. 'In fact,' said Jones, 'even though the USYRU is *a* national authority, they are not *the* national authority to which measurement instruction 7 refers, in this case.'

As *Australia II* is an Australian yacht and was measured by an Australian measurer, it is the AYF that would be obliged to refer to the IYRU if they saw fit, not the USYRU.

'We find objectionable the inferences contained in the '*Third*' point of Mr Ehman Jnr's telex to Nigel Hacking of the IYRU; firstly, those relating to the chairman of the measurement committee and, secondly, that an official measurer of the AYF could, in any way, be influenced regarding the correctness of procedures they should follow.

Australia II was originally measured by Mr Ken McAlpine, the official measurer of the IYRU responsible for measuring *Australia II*, who reconfirmed this morning that he had no doubts in signing *Australia II*'s measurement certificate stating that *Australia II* was fairly and equitably rated within the 12-metre Class Rule.

McAlpine said that the statement by the USYRU saying there had been a special committee meeting convened by the AYF was totally incorrect and that any thought that either he or the AYF was influenced in their decisions was a gross distortion of the fact.

As is normal procedure the rating certificate was signed by the AYF, which apparently also had no difficulty in completing the certificate.

Jones said: 'Since *Australia II* first demonstrated her worthiness as a serious challenger for the America's Cup, we have been consistently and improperly badgered by false accusations concerning *Australia II*'s keel design and rating.'

It was most pleasing when, at the International 12-metre Association meeting this week, the most respected authority on 12-metre yachts in the United States and possibly the world, Mr Olin Stephens, said that, in his opinion, *Australia II* was correctly rated and that her designer, Ben Lexcen, should be congratulated for the innovative concepts he had employed. Stephens added that he would hate to see *Australia II* removed from competition merely because she was fast.

Notwithstanding the practice of the NYYC and now the USYRU in making public its rhetoric relating to the *Australia II* keel, it had been our intention not to issue publicly copies of correspondence relating to this matter.

'We now feel compelled however, to make sure that people are aware of the extent to which some Americans have been prepared to go to hold the Cup. We now reveal that only a few weeks ago one of the American syndicates attempted to purchase plans for a keel identical to that of *Australia II* from the Netherlands Ship Model Basin, which did the tank-testing for the *Australia II* keel.

'The American efforts to buy and install the Australian-designed keel on an American yacht in time for the Cup finals appear to be in direct contravention of the NYYC's own 1980 resolution governing the America's Cup, which

requires each competitor's boat to be designed by nationals
of that country.

'More significantly, it appears curious to us that the
syndicate backing the leading yacht in the defenders' trials
has tried to purchase our keel design while the NYYC and
now the USYRU is attempting to have the design re-rated
by incurring a penalty.

'Moreover, the NYYC has stated that it had only recently become aware of the details of the *Australia II* keel.

'We would like to know where these details were
obtained, since it is common knowledge that we keep all
details of our boat secret, aside from divulging full details
in strictest confidence to authorities such as the measurement committee, whom we trust implicitly.

'If the NYYC is in receipt of specific information it can
only be through improper means and we have a right to
know who passed it to them and under what conditions.

'We had hoped,' said Jones, 'that the re-confirmed unanimous decision of the measurement committee, which is
the final authority on this matter, would have put an end to
this subject, which is absorbing so much of everyone's
valuable time.

'The America's Cup is recognized as the most prestig-
ious yachting competition in the world. It is extremely
unfortunate that the NYYC and its supporters, as well as
the USYRU, has chosen not to accept the measurement
committee's decision as final because they are detracting
from the image of this event by attempting to refuse to
abide by their own rules and the final decisions of the
measurement committee.'

Attached to the Jones letter was also one from him to the
President of the IYRU, dated August 10. It read:

Dear Sir,
    We are writing to protest the actions of the NYYC
which has sought, in a letter to Mr George Andreadis
(chairman KBC) of the IYRU dated August 3, 1983, to
circumvent the agreed upon rules for America's Cup 1983
by asking the IYRU to reconsider the rating of the yacht
Australia II. We respectfully submit that the NYYC's
attempt to change the rules in the midst of the competi-

tion not only violates the binding conditions of the America's Cup competition and the rating rules of the IYRU, but violates fundamental principles of equity and fair play as well. We respectfully submit further that the IYRU's rules prohibit any change in or new interpretation of its rating rules, or certificate of rating of any challenger, at this time, regardless of the requesting entity.

Australia II was designed and constructed in Australia for the express purpose of competing for the America's Cup in 1983. Rule 12 of the Conditions Governing the Rules for America's Cup 1983, to which the NYYC agreed to be bound on January 10, 1983 (the 'Race Agreement', a copy of which is annexed to this letter), provides that

'The Measurement Rule of the International 12-Metre Class as established by the IYRU effective March 1976, amended November, 1977 and November 1979, shall govern this Match.'

Thus, the race agreement expressly provides for certainty of application of the rules in existence for at least 1½ years before the America's Cup. This consistency of rule application is obviously essential, where the participants in the Cup races, as we did, spent months if not years designing and re-designing their yachts in an effort to gain technical superiority *within* the framework and requirements of the existing Rules. It is clear that Rule 12 of the race agreement is intended to prevent a change in the rules and interpretations at the eleventh hour which would effect ratings which were valid when issued.

In pursuit of our goal, an extraordinary amount of time, money and technical expertise has been devoted to developing a yacht which, we believed, would be faster than the competition. Significantly, our design efforts were based strictly on the Ratings Rules and Measurement Instructions for 12-metre Class yachts of the IYRU which were to govern the 1983 races. *Australia II*'s designer, Mr Ben Lexcen, relied on the terms of those rules in developing a yacht which, we all hoped, could challenge successfully for the America's Cup.

Now that the competition is underway, and it appears that an Australian yacht has a chance to finally succeed in its attempts to win the Cup, the NYYC seeks to retroac-

tively change the rules and disqualify *Australia II* simply
because it fears she is indeed faster than the competition.
All the NYYC's technical arguments amount to no more
than repetition of the unsupportable contention that
Australia II should not be rated at 12-metres because she is
faster than other 12-metre yachts.

There is no question that *Australia II* is properly rated at
12-metres. She consistently has received a 12-metre rating, first from the AYF on March 4, 1983, and again by the
unanimous determination of the measurement committee for the America's Cup competition, on June 16, 1983.
Mr Mark Vinbury, the NYYC appointee to the measurement committee, recently confirmed that there is 'no
question that our committee measured *Australia II*'s keel
according to the rule.'

The NYYC's request, therefore, is nothing more than an
attempt to change retroactively the IYRU rating rule to
nullify a valid design innovation developed in accordance
with, and in reliance on, the established rating regulations
and procedures of the IYRU.

The 12-metre Class is a developmental class and, as the
NYYC explicitly recognizes, such design innovations are
'encouraged' by the rating rules, not prohibited. Possibly
without exception, in prior America's Cup challenges,
there were design innovations in the American yachts
which gave them benefits and advantages relative to the
competition. Within the three prior challenges in which
we were involved, we did not seek to protest or prohibit
such innovation, but accepted it as an aspect of the competition, and increased our own efforts to develop a successful challenger.

The NYYC, however, seems unwilling to accept such
design competition, particularly from non-Americans, and
has chosen instead to pursue these spurious charges over
Australia II's rating.

The timing of the NYYC's request, coming on the eve of
the semi-final challenge rounds, underscores the inequity
of its position. When the *Australia II* was initially presented to the measurement committee and rated at 12
metres, no doubt was expressed about any aspect of its
design or structure. Each of the three members of that

Committee expressed to me their view at the time that the design of *Australia II* created no problems for them in terms of rating.

The NYYC states that it is only *Australia II*'s *performance* in a 'representative number of races' which led it to conclude she was not fairly rated. Under the NYYC's self-serving argument, no challenger for the America's Cup can ever be certain of its rating until it has completed a substantial number of qualifying races and, perversely, the more successful it is in those preliminaries, the more likely the NYYC is to decide it is rated 'unfairly'. Such an argument obviously has no basis.

The NYYC's request for reconsideration of the 12-metre rating of *Australia II* is clearly improper under the IYRU rules and the rules of the race agreement. *First*, there is no IYRU rule of which we are aware that would permit the NYYC (or any other entity) to challenge the duly issued IYRU Certificate of Rating or to request an IYRU re-rating of *Australia II* at this time.

Certainly Rating Rule 27 and Measurement Instruction Rule 7 speak to doubts expressed *only* by the Official Measurer, or the National Authority, during the course and at the time of awarding a yacht's rating. There were no such doubts expressed in this case. There is no IYRU provision authorizing the KBC, or any other officer of the IYRU, to usurp the role or second-guess the decisions of either the Official Measurer or the National Authority insofar as their Certificate of Rating is concerned.

Second, the NYYC and all other participants agreed to Rule 20 of the Race Agreement which provides that

'The decision of the (Measurement) Committee on questions of interpretation of the Measurement Rule of the International Twelve Meter Class shall be final.'

The NYYC's request to the IYRU for a new substantive interpretation of its Rule at this time is in clear violation of the express letter and spirit of the Race Agreement. The IYRU should neither indulge this transgression by the NYYC, nor permit such interference with the role of the Measurement Committee, which has already interpreted and applied the IYRU's Rules in issuing a 12.0 metre Certificate of Rating to *Australia II*.

This morning we were delighted to receive a copy of the following telex:

'To: Bill Fesq and Jock Smith

The Measurement Committee unanimously reaffirms that the keel of *Australia II* is legal.

By a majority, the Measurement Committee agrees that Rating Rule 27 is not applicable in this case.

Tony Watts

Chairman

Measurement Committee'

Third, we submit that IYRU's Rating Rule 1 also squarely is intended to prevent the precise effort being made by the NYYC here. Rule 1 provides that

'no rule change shall take effect within 18 months of the America's Cup Races.'

It is apparent that any re-rating of *Australia II* at this time must be based upon a substantive change to the Rating Rule. As Mr Vinbury concedes, the Rule 'as it is currently written' has produced consistent 12.0 metre ratings for *Australia II*. There is simply no reason to doubt or reconsider that Rating at this juncture.

In sum, *Australia II* unquestionably has been designed and rated as a 12.0 metre yacht pursuant to the current IYRU Rules, by both the IYRU Measurer and National Authority, and the America's Cup Measurement Committee. On the strength of these ratings, *Australia II* has sailed in over 40 races, taken a place in the semi-finals of the challenger's trials, and may receive the challenger's designation for the match races next month.

Finally, evidence has appeared which raises serious questions as to the NYYC's good faith in mounting this request for reconsideration of *Australia II*'s rating. It appears from the attached telexes that members of a United States defenders' team associated with the NYYC actually has sought to *purchase* the design of a keel for installation in their yacht similar to the keel they now claim should disqualify *Australia II* from competition.

It seems that only after the American syndicate was unsuccessful in obtaining such a keel design did the NYYC decide to take the position that *Australia II*'s keel design was improper. These telexes are all the more curious because they also establish that the Americans sought to purchase a non-American, Australian keel design, in clear violation of the 1980 Resolution of the Board of Trustees of the NYYC. The NYYC, whose defenders' team has tried to purchase the same keel design for this year's races, simply should not be heard now to complain about our rating.

In short, the request by the NYYC to your committee is grossly inequitable, unauthorized by any rule of the IYRU or the America's Cup Competition and apparently motivated by nothing more than the desire to win at all costs.

It would grievously injure the sponsors of *Australia II*, who have to date expended millions of dollars in reliance on the rating rule of the IYRU and the terms and conditions of the agreement governing the America's Cup. We submit that such a request should be rejected out of hand.

There had to be considerable sympathy for the IYRU at this time for the amount of correspondence they had to deal with, but at least the documents from the *Australia II* syndicate were well argued, well reasoned and reasonable when compared with the wild, inaccurate and muddled facts put by the American authorities. While overseas syndicates were worried by the muddle of American officialdom, the American syndicates must have been nonplussed by the real revelation of the Australian press conference – namely, the details of the attempt by the United States to secure a keel similar to that of *Australia II*. Again, it was a copy of a telex message which was released and it read, in its entirety:

1983-07-21
ATTN.: DR P. VAN OOSSANEN, VISITING
FROM: NSMB. A. KOOPS
WE RECEIVED FOLLOWING TLX FROM OGDEN MARINE, NEW
YORK:
QUOTE
TO: NETHERLANDS SHIP MODEL BASIN
    WAGENINGEN NETHERLANDS
    FROM: EDWARD DU MOULIN
    ATTN.: DR VAN OOSSANEN

UNDERSTAND THAT YOU AND YOUR TEAM ARE RESPONS-
IBLE FOR DEVELOPMENT AND DESIGN OF SPECIAL KEEL FOR
AUSTRALIA II.
WE ARE FINALLY CONVINCED OF HER POTENTIAL AND
WOULD THEREFORE LIKE TO BUILD SAME DESIGN UNDER
ONE OF OUR BOATS.
WE WILL KEEP THIS CONFIDENTIAL AS NOT TO JEOPAR-
DIZE YOUR AGREEMENT WITH ALAN BOND. HOWEVER
DUE TO COMPLEXITY OF PROBLEMS, NEED YOUR MAX-
IMUM INPUT AND EXPERIENCE.
WE CAN START NEXT WEEK AND BE READY BY AUGUST 25.
PLEASE TELEX US YOUR DESIGN AND CONSULTANCY FEES
AND ANY OTHER CONDITION WHICH MIGHT APPLY.
AN IMMEDIATE REPLY IS OF UTMOST IMPORTANCE. USE
TELEX NBRS 620148, 224060, 420418 OGMAR, NEW
YORK.
KIND REGARDS, EDWARD DU MOULIN
MANAGER, FREEDOM CAMPAIGN.

Never before in the long and devious history of the America's
Cup can a document so damning of the NYYC come into the
hands of the opposition so easily. And the answer to the telex
was just as priceless. It read, in its entirety:

1983-07-26
ATTN: DR P. VAN OOSSANEN, VISITING
WE HAVE ANSWERED OGDEN MARINE FOLLOWING:
QUOTE
1983-07-22
TO: OGDEN MARINE NEW YORK
ATTN.: MR EDWARD DU MOULIN, MANAGER FREEDOM
CAMPAIGN
FROM: NSMB, DR VAN OOSSANEN
YOUR TELEX EDM/JO OMI 391 OF 1983-07-20
WE HAVE RECEIVED YOUR TELEX ADDRESSED TO ATTEN-
TION TO OUR DR VAN OOSSANEN AND WOULD ASK YOU
TO NOTE FIRSTLY THAT WE WERE ASSOCIATED WITH THE
AUSTRALIA II CAMPAIGN BY WAY OF A TANK TESTING
CONTRACT. THEIR DESIGNER MR BEN LEXCEN RESIDED AT
WAGENINGEN FOR FOUR MONTHS WHILST HE COM-
PLETED THE DESIGNS FOR BOTH AUSTRALIA II AND CHAL-
LENGE 12.

AS WE ARE CONTRACTED TO THEM NOT TO TEST 12 M
MODELS FOR ANY OTHER 12 METRE SYNDICATE UNTIL
THE COMPLETION OF THE 1983 CAMPAIGN WE HAVE
TODAY ADVISED THEM OF YOUR QUERY AND REQUESTED
THEIR PERMISSION TO UNDERTAKE WORK FOR YOU. BUT
UNFORTUNATELY THEY HAVE ADVISED US THAT THEY ARE
NOT PREPARED TO ALLOW SUCH DISPENSATION.
WE THANK YOU FOR YOUR ENQUIRY AND WOULD BE ONLY
TOO DELIGHTED TO DISCUSS WORK FOR YOU RELATED TO
ANY CAMPAIGN IN 1986.
THIS REPLY IS ALSO ON BEHALF OF THE NLR AEROSPACE
LABORATORY.
REGARDS.
UNQUOTE

In anyone's terms, save, it seemed, the most reactionary of
American press – and some of their comments were even more
asinine than their reporting of the events was behind the times,
some seven to ten days behind the rest of the world – it was
'Game, set and match' to the Australians. The Americans had
been caught with their hands in the till. It was clear that they
had tried to get the keel declared illegal *only* after they failed to
get a similar one for themselves.

With the NYYC's trials to decide the twenty-fifth defender
due to begin on August 16 there was no shortage of their
members in Newport to comment on the developments and
there was a statement from the *Freedom* syndicate. This read, in
full:

As part of its program of being fully prepared to defend
the America's Cup, the *Freedom* campaign has studied
carefully the results of the foreign challenger trials. It has
become increasingly apparent that *Australia II* is the most
likely challenger. Because of the extraordinary measures
being employed by the *Australia II* syndicate to keep its
unique design secret, it has been difficult for any potential
defender to prepare to compete against her.

It appears that there is a need to use racing tactics
entirely different from those of traditional match-racing
competition. To have made *Magic* fully competitive
would have required need of major rebuilding and substantial funds. Neither the time nor funds were available but

most important it would have been illegal to copy a foreign design.

In an effort to acquire an appropriate trial-horse, the *Freedom* campaign considered the possibility of modifying its retired 12-metre *Magic*. Accordingly on July 20 1983, Ed du Moulin, general manager of the *Freedom* campaign sent a telex to NSMB in Wageningen, Holland.

The purpose was to ascertain whether or not, within the restraints of the contract with Mr Alan Bond, the NSMB could help with the principle of employing a bulb-wing configuration on keels. Since the performance characteristics of *Magic* are known, an assessment of the sailing characteristics of this unique configuration could be ascertained.

Contrary to certain allegations by the *Australia II* syndicate, it was never our intention to enter an American yacht with a winged keel in competition. The date of August 25 in the du Moulin telex was the last practical date for such a program to be of any use as a trial-horse for *Liberty*. Regardless of other issues, there was no way that *Magic* could have been modified and designated as the *Freedom* campaign entry in the August selection trials by August 15.

Ed du Moulin, general manager of the *Freedom* campaign, emphasized that all his group is interested in is the prompt resolution of all outstanding issues in getting on with racing on a fair and equitable basis.

The surprising thing, above all, at the time of all the wrangling over the keel and about which, incidentally, the *Australia II* syndicate sought but failed to secure a second meeting with the NYYC trio of Stone, McCullough and Mosbacher before realizing their 'evidence', was why, really, the Americans were going to such lengths.

They must have realized that in appealing to the IYRU, a most unwieldy and mercurially unstable body outside of the secretariat, they were dealing with an organization that was also ponderously slow in making decisions. The IYRU simply did not have the means and conditions for making snap decisions on the whim of a national member and the US, its biggest subscribers and provider of members, should have known that only too well. More of them, nearly all NYYC members, had sat through more of the interminably long and excruciatingly dull meetings in London each November than almost anyone. It simply was not a body to come up with the sort of answer the Americans seemed to be looking for. So if the NYYC did not want an IYRU decision, why were they diverting attention thus? Was it simply a matter of providing plenty of excuses if they should lose the Cup, or of generating sufficient steam when they could not protest officially to cover the embarrassment of doing so once the America's Cup got under way, and probably against *Australia II*?

Or was it simply a way of causing confusion and concern in the *Australia II* camp? It did achieve some of that.

As the Americans began their final trials to decide the defender, it became clear that the NYYC would not get the IYRU rushing to its aid. Said Hacking as the US trials began with *Defender* first beating *Courageous* by 10 seconds and then being beaten by her stable-mate by 1 minute 9 seconds: 'We are to have a meeting of the officers of the IYRU.' He did not know when, but not before the beginning of September, it seemed. In the end it was set for August 30. The officers were Beppe Croce (Italy), Harry Anderson (US), Paul Henderson (Canada), Jonathan Jansen (UK), Andrei Kislov (USSR) and Peter Talberg (Finland). George Andreadis (Greece), the new KBC chairman, 'would be in attendance', it was said. The IYRU secretary-general added also that he had 'heard from the AYF', but would not comment at that stage on the matter.

What was all the fuss about? When *Australia II* first arrived in America, she was one among several boats; Bond was criticized by the Americans for having sold his trial-horse *Australia* to the British and it was logically maintained also that breakthroughs in 12-metre design were unlikely, as radical boats had shown themselves to be more liable to failure than success. No, at that early stage of the summer there were American voices which suggested that there was less reason in 1983 for the NYYC to be alarmed than there had been three years previously. This reasoning, of course, is all per the conventional America's Cup 12-metre folklore, legend or ballyhoo. But it has always been safer to assume in the America's Cup world that nothing of any great importance will happen anywhere but in the United States camps and so such confident reasoning as prevailed in Newport at the start of the '83 campaign was perfectly reasonable and justifiable.

When *Australia II* was observed to have her keel concealed at all times, the *America's Cup Report*, a popular and reliable weekly record and barometer run from Newport by Jeff Spranger and Barbara Lloyd, mused: 'As with many Australian tactics, it is difficult to know whether the hydrodynamic efficiency or the psychological effect is more important.'

For a few days, *Victory '83* joined in the argument over the rule validity of horizontal fins on a 12-metre keel. Remember, Ian Howlett had been back in England on re-design work. At a joint Australian–British press conference, exchanges between Howlett and the IYRU were released. During the conference Alan Bond asked the American designer Gary Mull, a member of the KBC, to leave after asking a loaded question: de Savary maintained that the latest KBC rulings meant that the argument was dead.

The brief release was as follows:

LETTER FROM IAN HOWLETT TO THE IYRU
DATED 28TH JULY 1982 [the previous year]
'TWELVE METRE RULE INTERPRETATION – IN CONFIDENCE'
AS DISCUSSED TODAY, I ENCLOSE THE POINTS ON WHICH I WOULD APPRECIATE RULE DEFINITION.
YOUR EARLIEST REPLY WOULD BE MUCH APPRECIATED.
YOURS SINCERELY,
IAN HOWLETT.

FROM KEEL BOAT COMMITTEE – IYRU TO IAN HOWLETT
TWELVE METRE RULE INTERPRETATION
NON-PLANAR LIFTING SURFACES – SIMILAR TO END PLATES

QUESTION	ANSWER
1. Are Winglets permitted on the keel?	Tip wings are permitted so long as the static draft is not exceeded.
2. May these be adjusted in trim?	Adjustment of the angle of incidence is not allowed.
3. May they be retracted?	Winglets may not be retracted.

CONCLUSION

IT IS OUR OPINION THAT THESE INTERPRETATIONS OF THE 12-METRE RULE ARE RELEVANT, WHEN CONSIDERING THE KEEL OF AUSTRALIA II. THE WINGED KEEL WOULD APPEAR TO US THEREFORE TO BE LEGAL.

So far, so good. Difficulties arose the next day when the *Victory* group asked Vinbury, 'out of courtesy' and to 'avoid any trouble', to check that the British boat was not illegal because of the fitting of the 'winglets' as they called them. According to de Savary, Vinbury had assured the British, after carrying out the task, that there was no need to re-measure the yacht, that the rating certificate was still valid and that 'there was no need to talk to anyone else about the matter'. But, within 45 minutes of their measurement being done, that matter had become 'public knowledge' and within 1¼ hours the Victory group had been handed a copy of a letter Vinbury had allegedly written to the USYRU and the race committee stating that in his opinion the yacht violated Rule 27 regarding peculiarities and had thus invalidated herself.

'To say I am upset is an understatement', de Savary commented at the time. 'I am extremely angry with what I call the lowest level of poor sportsmanship by the Americans. Now I am really on the warpath', he added. 'We have been put in a very compromising position. Mr Vinbury should have told us he had changed his mind. We would have taken the wings off. They have won the first round. But that is it. I am now on the warpath. All out. I have no objection to the view of Mr Vinbury. But I object most strenuously to the way he has acted.' The Victory team had decided to go ahead with the alterations only because they had been approved all along by the IYRU. Indeed, it was after this that the full correspondence with the IYRU relating to the 'winglets' was released.

A British statement read as follows:

The Victory syndicate have been experimenting with the addition of fins on the bottom of the 12-metre keel since January 1982. Ian Howlett, the designer of *Victory '83*, indicated that he felt that the performance of 12-metre yachts could be improved by the addition of fins to the keel and that he proposed carrying out a series of wind tunnel tests to investigate the effect of the fins on model keels.

The tests were performed at Southampton University and the results were encouraging so a ruling was sought from the keel-boat committee of the IYRU, in order to establish whether or not it was worth going ahead with the project.

Then the question and answer exchange, above, was quoted.

This interpretation was given in confidence in 1982 under IYRU Regulation 7.4.4., to Ian Howlett and would not normally be made known to the public until November 1983 when it would have been confirmed. The International 12-metre Class is a development class, interpretations of the rating rule are kept confidentially, if so requested, until after the next America's Cup Match and such interpretations, when given by the IYRU, are in force for the America's Cup Races following the date they are made, which means for example that winglets are allowed on *Victory '83* in the America's Cup Match this year. This is exactly the same procedure as used in 1979 to confirm the legality of *Lionheart*'s bendy rig for the 1980 trials.

When *Victory '83* was built her keel was designed and built to allow for the addition of fins at some convenient time during her trials. When she was measured in England on her completion, and again before the trials in America, these wings were brought to the attention of the measurers. At the pre-trial measurement, Mark Vinbury, the New York Yacht Club nomination for the America's Cup Independent Measurement Committee, Jack Savage, the Royal Sydney Yacht Squadron's appointed representative and Tony Watts, the jointly appointed representative agreed with Ian Howlett that the addition of wings would not affect *Victory*'s rating. It was however agreed that a re-measurement may be required if they in any way affected her draft or her flotation.

Full scale trials of the keel fins have taken place all summer long in Newport on the trial horse yacht *Australia*, in an effort to confirm the wind tunnel and tank tests of 1982. Any improvement in performance has been very marginal and difficult to quantify, however, it was decided on Sunday evening, 21st August, 1983, that the fins would be fitted to the keel of *Victory '83* overnight in time for the final race of the semi-finals against *Australia II*.

Mark Vinbury was informed of a change to *Victory '83* and was asked to report to the dock Monday morning about 8:00 a.m., to check the rating of the yacht and to decide whether or not the changes would require a re-measurement. He arrived at about 7:50 a.m., and having inspected them agreed that the fins were neutrally buoyant, and thus that they would not affect the yacht's flotation, neither did they increase the yacht's rated draft, and therefore, her Certificate of Rating would remain unchanged and no re-measurement was required. This meeting was held in confidence.

If Mark Vinbury as a member of the Official Measurement Committee was in any doubt about the rating or if any objection had been made to the fins, they would have been removed from the yacht before she raced. There were no such doubts so the boat was put in the water and left the dock at about 9:30 a.m., for the race course.

Very shortly afterwards the attached copy letters were hand delivered by Mark Vinbury himself, the first being a letter Mr Mark Vinbury wrote to the USYRU, immediately he left the yacht thus breaking a confidence without first informing Mr de Savary or Mr Howlett, and the second a reply in the form of a letter to Mr de Savary with copies to IYRU, and Race Committee. Again a copy to Race Committee without prior approval is a breach of confidentiality.

It is the Victory Syndicate's view that *Victory '83* rates 12-metres with or without fins on the keel and that in any case the USYRU has no authority whatsoever to issue any instructions with regard to this yacht. The Victory syndicate resents pressure of this sort from such an authority and considers the existing interpretation of this matter by the IYRU as final.

Every effort has been made to keep the rating authority fully informed throughout this campaign and at this time the Victory Syndicate is undecided whether to fit the fins for the finals or not.

Attached to this statement were copies of letters from the

USYRU to de Savary and that from Vinbury to the USYRU. The letter, referring to *Victory '83*, reported, baldly:

> The owner of the above 12-meter Class yacht has installed two horizontal foils which attach to either side of the keel of the yacht.
>
> The installation of these foils does not increase the yacht's rated draft nor does it invalidate the certificate of rating under the contingencies of Rating Rule 29.
>
> I am of the opinion that these foils constitute a peculiarity in the build of the yacht and believe that the rule will not rate the yacht fairly while they are attached. I am therefore reporting the circumstances to USYRU as required by Rating Rule 27.

The letter from the USYRU to de Savary said:

> The USYRU has received from the measurer Mark Vinbury the attached advice that under International Twelve Metre Class Rating rule 27, Certificate of Rating, it is his opinion, after personal inspection, that the recently installed wings on the keel of *Victory '83* are a 'peculiarity' and that 'the rule will not rate the yacht fairly. . . .'
>
> Since Mr Vinbury has reported this circumstance to the National Authority (USYRU), it would appear that until the due inquiry required by rule 27 is complete that the measurement of *Victory '83* in the wing-keel configuration must be '. . . deemed incomplete . . .'
>
> In accord with Twelve Metre Class Measurement Instruction 7, Doubtful Cases, we are, by copy of this and Mr Vinbury's correspondence, reporting this case to the International Yacht Racing Union (IYRU) because of our doubt in the calculation of the rating.
>
> We are also reporting the matter to the Race Committee as prescribed by Yacht Racing Rule 70.4.

It was signed by Kenneth B. Weller, Offshore Director of the USYRU, and indicated that copies had been sent to the IYRU and the Challengers' Race Committee.

The next development was a letter to the USYRU from Bill Ritchie, President of the Royal Burnham YC. Copies went to the Measurement Committee, the IYRU, the Victory syndicate and the Challengers' Race Committee. It read:

We have received a copy of your letter of 22 August addressed direct to our Challenger, *Victory '83*. We regret that we must raise the strongest possible objection to Mr Vinbury breaking his confidentiality as a measurer appointed under the conditions of the America's Cup Elimination Series and Match and to the action taken arising out of his letter to you. In particular, we refer to the following matters:—

1. Rating Rule 27 refers to the issue of a certificate of rating and does not apply to a re-checking that a yacht still complies with the certificate originally issued as in this case.

2. The owner of *Victory* has complied with Rating Rule 29 as the Measurement Committee has certified and Mr Vinbury's letter to you confirms. Therefore, no further referral is permissible under that rule.

3. In any event, both the defenders and challengers for the 1983 America's Cup have by mutual agreement set out all the conditions both for the Match and Elimination Series. Those conditions make it clear that the decisions of the Measurement Committee on questions of interpretation of the measurement rule shall be final. Both that Committee, and the IYRU have ruled on the question of the foils and confirmed their legality and, again, no further referral is permissible.

4. Racing Rule 70.4, even if it were applicable in this case, is subject to Condition 9 of the Conditions of the Elimination Series and Condition 10 of the Match, which makes it clear that in the event of any inconsistency the Conditions of the Series and Match shall prevail. In this case the measurer must proceed in accordance with Condition 20 of the Elimination Series and Condition 22 of the Match. Once again the Committee has ruled and that is final.

May we respectfully suggest to you that the USYRU has no standing or authority to take the action that it has; further, that in any event, since the conditions of the America's Cup, which constitute a binding contract between all the Clubs concerned, make it clear that the decision of the Measurement Committee is final, that is an end of the matter.

The NYYC seemed unlikely to settle for the interpretation done for the Victory syndicate because it did not really apply itself to Rule 27 as they wanted and, for another, Vinbury and the USYRU had clearly ignored the interpretation when responding to de Savary and had again referred to Rule 27. This became, in a way, even more of a lifeline, since another line of investigation that had been going on in Holland seemed unlikely to pay dividends.

This was a New York Yacht Club delegation which had set out quite clearly to prove that the design of *Australia II* was not done entirely by Lexcen. Details of the investigation were brought to the attention of the Australia II syndicate in Newport by Dr Peter van Oossanen, in charge of the Ship Model Basin at Waneningen and who, it transpired, had spent several years of his life in Australia and who had, indeed, qualified as a naval architect at the University of New South Wales. It was Dr Oossanen and a Dr J. Sloof, in charge of computer design at the Dutch Aerospace Institute outside Amsterdam, who were questioned most closely about their involvement in the design of *Australia II*. In both instances they insisted that they had merely provided assistance and that the design input had been the work wholly and solely of Lexcen. Dr Oossanen described what was happening in one telex message thus:

YESTERDAY, AUGUST 24, WE RECEIVED YET ANOTHER VISIT FROM A DELEGATION REPRESENTING THE INTERESTS OF THE NEW YORK YACHT CLUB. I THINK YOU SHOULD KNOW WHAT TRANSPIRED AT THAT MEETING.

MR RICHARD S. LATHAM, AN OFFICER OF THE NYYC SERVING ON THE AMERICA'S CUP SELECTION COMMITTEE, AND MR WILL VALENTIJN, WHO PRESENTED HIMSELF AS A RELATIVE OF JOHAN VALENTIJN, THE DESIGNER FOR THE US *LIBERTY/FREE-DOM* SYNDICATE REQUESTED THAT I SIGN A TWO PAGE 'AFFI-DAVIT' THEY HAD PREPARED CONCERNING THE WORK WHICH THE NETHERLANDS SHIP MODEL BASIN AND NLR AEROSPACE LABORATORY DID FOR MR BEN LEXCEN AND THE *AUSTRALIA II*'S SYNDICATE.

THIS AFFIDAVIT CONTAINED MANY INCORRECT STATEMENTS WHICH ATTEMPTED TO SUGGEST THAT BEN LEXCEN WAS NOT SOLEY RESPONSIBLE FOR THE DESIGN OF *AUSTRALIA II*.

I REFUSED TO SIGN THE DOCUMENT, AS THE CONTENTS WERE INCORRECT. WHAT IS MORE DISTURBING TO ME IS THAT THE NYYC REPRESENTATIVES ASKED ME TO SIGN THIS AFFIDAVIT KNOWING THAT THE CONTENTS WERE INCORRECT, BECAUSE THEY WERE TOLD SO BY ME ONCE BEFORE.

IN MY TELEX TO MR EDWARD DU MOULIN OF THE *LIBERTY/ FREEDOM* SYNDICATE, DATED 26 JULY, 1983, FOR WHICH MR VALENTIJN IS THE DESIGNER, I STATED CLEARLY THAT MR LEXCEN HIMSELF DESIGNED *AUSTRALIA II* AND THAT THE NATIONAL AEROSPACE LABORATORY AND NSMB PROVIDED ASSISTANCE SOLELY PURSUANT TO A TANK TESTING CON- TRACT. AS YOU WILL RECALL, MY TELEX WAS IN RESPONSE TO THE *LIBERTY* SYNDICATE'S EXPRESSED INTEREST IN PURCHAS- ING THE DESIGN OF *AUSTRALIA II*'S KEEL.

FURTHER, ON AUGUST 9 AND 10, MR WILL VALENTIJN AND ANOTHER GENTLEMAN VISITED ME TO INQUIRE ABOUT THE DESIGN OF *AUSTRALIA II*. THEY TOLD ME THEY WOULD BE MAKING A FULL REPORT OF THEIR VISIT TO THE NYYC. I INFORMED THEM AGAIN THAT MR LEXCEN WAS SOLELY RE- SPONSIBLE FOR THE DESIGN OF *AUSTRALIA II*, AND EXPLAINED FULLY THE NATURE OF THE TESTING WORK WHICH WE PRO- VIDED TO MR LEXCEN. MR LATHAM YESTERDAY ACKNOW- LEDGED THAT HE HAD RECEIVED THIS REPORT, BUT NEVER- THELESS ASKED ME TO SIGN THIS AFFIDAVIT.

MR LATHAM FURTHER INFORMED ME THAT THE NYYC WAS CONSIDERING CHALLENGING THE DESIGN OF *AUSTRALIA II* BASED ON WORK DONE WITH THE NSMB AND NLR AERO- SPACE LABORATORY. I INFORMED HIM THAT, BASED ON THE WORK DONE BY MR LEXCEN HERE, THERE WOULD BE ABSO- LUTELY NO TRUTH TO A CLAIM THAT *AUSTRALIA II* WAS DESIGNED TO ANY EXTENT BY ANYONE OTHER THAN MR LEXCEN.

I TOLD HIM THAT WE ACTED SOLELY PURSUANT TO MR LEXCEN'S DIRECTIONS AT ALL TIMES. I FURTHER INFORMED MR LATHAM THAT THE COMPUTER SUPPORT WORK PROVIDED BY NLR AEROSPACE LABORATORY AND TANK TESTING BY NSMB FOR MR LEXCEN IS SIMILAR TO THE COMPUTER SUP- PORT WORK AND TANK TESTING PROVIDED BY THE DELFT

UNIVERSITY OF TECHNOLOGY HERE TO THE DESIGNER OF
MAGIC AND *LIBERTY* IN 1981.

I FIND THE NYYC'S POSITION AND EFFORTS ON THIS MATTER
TO BE DEEPLY DISTURBING AND OFFENSIVE. I HOPE THEY WILL
HAVE THE GOOD SENSE TO DESIST FROM FURTHER UNTRUE
CHARGES ATTRIBUTING THE DESIGN OF *AUSTRALIA II* TO
ANYONE OTHER THAN BEN LEXCEN. IN THIS REGARD, I AM
PREPARED TO HAVE MY COMMENTS ON THIS MATTER MADE
PUBLIC.

Before the NYYC had time to reply to this outspoken message
or the IYRU interpretation, Warren Jones had another word to
say on the matter. First he released the copy of a letter from
Victor A. Romagna, secretary of the NYYC's America's Cup
committee (the full membership of which, incidentally, was
McCullough, Harry Anderson, Bob Bavier, Briggs Cunningham,
Stanley Livingston Jnr, James Michael, Emil 'Bus' Mosbascher
Jnr, and A. E. Luders). The letter stated:

> Officially your tank tests in the Netherlands Ship Model
> Basin are entirely within the rules if:
> 1. They were under the sole supervision of Australian
>   nationals.
> 2. The designs were from the drawing board of Austra-
>   lian nationals.
> 3. Results are used in the design of that Australian
>   challenger only.

Jones said that he was shocked and angered by this latest
attempt of the NYYC to avoid racing *Australia II* by manufac-
turing false issues regarding the Australian yacht's right to
compete. 'Since the NYYC's efforts to protest *Australia II*'s
rating as a 12-metre yacht have thus far proved fruitless,' he said,
'the NYYC now appears desperately to be looking for some
other basis to seek to avoid honest competition on the water
against *Australia II*.' Jones went on:

> It is unfortunate that the NYYC America's Cup com-
> mittee which is an arm of the prestigious NYYC has
> chosen to conduct this reprehensible campaign of harass-
> ment and false claims stemming from statements or

claims from unknown persons or perhaps just dockside scuttle.

It has now been necessary for Ben Lexcen to seek legal advice on his position which he does with our agreement, as statements made are defaming his reputation.

Jones also noted that the NYYC had failed to provide information as to where it obtained specific details about *Australia II*'s keel, which had never been released and which had been strenuously protected by shrouding the keel. Jones reiterated that the NYYC could only have obtained such detail through persons who gained the information illegally.

There was uproar now, with even the more partisan American press being forced to face up to some of the less appetizing facts of life. Yet the USYRU did have time for one last snide swipe – at the Royal Burnham, low-key and obviously happy about it for the main part as a riposte to the surveillance issue of the previous summer. The letter to them was signed by Kenneth B. Weller, who is actually the offshore director of the USYRU, on behalf of USYRU in the absence of Tom Ehman.

Thank you for your letter of August 23 in which you put forward the views of the Royal Burnham Yacht Club America's Cup Committee regarding recent matters relating to the keel of *Victory '83*. We appreciate your deep concern in this matter and the points you have raised, which we would like to address in the same sequence:

First, concerning your allegation that Mark Vinbury broke his 'confidentiality as a measurer appointed under the Conditions of the America's Cup . . .', we are obliged to inform you that only 'information contained in the Certificates shall be regarded as confidential . . .' (see Conditions) and Mr Vinbury has not divulged to us one iota of information contained in the 12-Metre rule certificate of any yacht. There is no statement in the Conditions that the qualitative appearance of a yacht is confidential.

Second, it is self-evident that Rule 27 is an integral step in rating the yacht and must always be considered following modifications to the yacht. To hold otherwise is to suggest that the Rule can be circumvented by withholding questionable design or construction features until the yacht has been once rated. Thereafter, any measurer must work with his blinders fitted. With such an interpretation, Rule 27 would be absolutely useless in the Rule.

Third, an International 12-Metre is subject at all times to the entire Rule, not simply the items brought to the owner's attention in Rule 29, which pertains to owner obligations.

In this connection, we note that Rule 31 states that 'Every owner sailing under these rules shall permit all reasonable inspection by or on behalf of the National Authority . . . in regard to measurements, marks, fittings *and such other matters as fall within the scope of a measurer's duty.'* [emphasis added].

Fourth, Mark Vinbury is a certified USYRU Measurer, he is a qualified 12-Metre measurer, and at the request of the owner he has taken measurements, made inspection, and applied judgement in accord with the International 12-Metre rule for the purpose of rating *Victory '83* a 12-Metre yacht.

The authority for the International 12-Metre Class rule is the IYRU and by definition a yacht is an International 12-Metre only if so rated by the application of these pre-scriptions and procedure unaltered. The application of altered procedures may produce a 'rating' acceptable to the event sponsors who prescribed the alterations, but may not produce an International 12-Metre rating.

As action by the National Authority is prescribed by the 12-Metre rule, the USYRU has attempted to fulfill its obligations thereunder. Local event conditions can have no bearing on our obligations as a National Authority under an International Class rule. Nor can interpretations by a local event committee.

The IYRU interpretation to which you allude applies to the legality of 'winglets' and not to the rating thereof. The USYRU has reported to the IYRU its doubt regarding the calculation of rating for *Victory '83* with her winged keel. This is not only a right, it is a requirement of the 12-Metre rule and the USYRU is entitled to an answer.

Whether the proper discharge of our obligations has any effect on a local event is ultimately up to the event spon-sors as set forth in the conditions or sailing instructions.

Fifth, there is nothing stated in either the Challenge

Conditions or the Match Conditions abrogating the measurer's responsibility to report circumstances to the National Authority as may be required by 12-Metre rule 27. If the report is made, the rule states 'the measurement shall be deemed incomplete . . .'. It is obviously proper to report this to the Race Committee under 70.4 of the Yacht Racing Rules.

Finally, we have discussed above the status of the USYRU as a National Authority under the 12-Metre rule and in relationship to the measurer. We further observe that the measurement is being conducted in the United States and the America's Cup Match is conducted according to conditions agreed by, and with the Race Committee of, a USYRU constituent member. The jurisdiction of the USYRU is territorial. The USYRU is the National Authority in the United States as defined in Article 6.2 and identified in Article 8.4 of the IYRU Constitution.

What next? For surely both sides had covered paper enough to equate with the sail area of a 12-metre. Possibly a protest would appear at the Cup races themselves, throwing the necessity of a decision in the lap of the appointed race jury. Or would the NYYC refuse a challenge for reasons it had already stated?

In the event the controversy ended in a whimper. At 2 p.m. on August 26 the NYYC let it be known that it would not take any of its objections any further. In front of the press and many others appeared Commodores Robert W. McCullough and Robert G. Stone. Their statement was this:

> The New York Yacht Club is pleased to announce that questions relating to the keels of *Australia II* and *Victory '83* and the design thereof have been resolved.
>
> We have now received verification from the IYRU that an interpretative ruling respecting the design of the British keel was issued in August of 1982. That ruling under the IYRU regulations is controlling for the 1983 match and the NYYC accepts it as such. We are also advised that the same ruling applied to the keel of *Australia II*.
>
> For reasons unknown to us neither the British challengers nor the IYRU saw fit to advise the USYRU or us of this fact and regrettably this omission has resulted in unnecessary controversy.

The NYYC, through the USYRU, intends to pursue the submission heretofore made requesting clarification and interpretation by the Keel Boat Committee as to how to rate peculiarities of design such as appear on *Australia II* and *Victory '83*. These submissions will be made to insure the fairest possible ratings for future matches but, as noted above, such ultimate rules will not be applicable to the upcoming match commencing September 13.

On the second issue concerning the design of *Australia II*, and the extent of participation therein by Dutch organizations, the question arose from reports and newspaper articles in the Dutch Press intimating that the keel design was the product, if not the invention of Dutch experts. Having been put on notice, the NYYC was obliged to investigate the matter and for this purpose interviewed such Dutch experts regarding their participation in the testing and development of the keel. As trustee under the America's Cup Deed of Gift, it is obligated to be satisfied that the terms of the trust are fully complied with by all participants. Having completed such investigation as we felt necessary and proper we have concluded that the evidence available to us to date is insufficient to press the matter further at this time.

The statement ended:

With these matters resolved we now can all focus on the match itself to be settled on the water and may the better yacht win.

They indicated that they had asked for the special meeting of the IYRU, then only four days away in London, to be called off; that nothing was being done at that time by the American syndicates to imitate the Australian keel; and that they still thought they would win the America's Cup.

As for the longer-term future, the New York Yacht Club had announced earlier that the next challenges would be accepted for 1987. This extended the three-year cycle to one of four years, to cope better with the intensity of multiple challenges and the response needed to meet them.

John Bertrand makes **Australia II** *go. Note the Kevlar-Dacron vertical genoa. Kos.*

Around they go. Starting tactics between Azzura, *sailed by Mauro Pelaschier, and* Australia II. Kos.

Liberty *moves fast when close-hauled.* Kos.

Liberty. *Her sails and deck look exactly right.* Black.

Defender *in Newport sunshine tries to live up to her name.* Black.

The old lady who kept the Cup in 1974 and 1977, the much refitted Courageous, *so well sailed by John Kolius.* Black.

A typical match race start. Both boats with genoas backed, near the committee boat. Note bow men. Black.

The not uncommon Newport fog. Two 12s try and cope with it. Black.

The wing keel of Australia II, *cause of heated exchanges during the trials in July and August.* A.P.

Azzura *to windward of* Australia II. *The curved masts and almost standard 12-metre sail plans are conspicuous.* A.P.

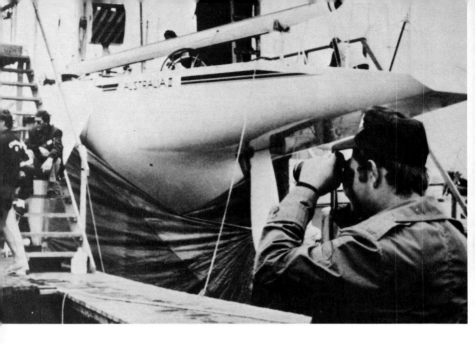

Above. *Every night the keel of* Australia II *was shrouded and guards kept watch.* A.P.

Left. *Ben Lexcen, a man with 12-metre design experience second to none.* A.P.

Below. *John Kolius showed that old boats when refitted can be fast boats.* Ulmer.

John Bertrand and his wife Ros on the night of his unique feat. A.P.

The 'unthinkable' takes place. The America's Cup is brought to Newport and relinquished by the New York Yacht Club. Alan Bond has achieved his daring ambition. A.P.

Up spinnaker on Courageous *as* Liberty *closes the weather mark.* A.P.

XII

Semi-final

Press liaison had always been a weak feature of the British campaign. De Savary obviously believed that, in having Hobday, a PR man, as his vice-chairman, he was getting the best advice. He may have been in so far as projecting a tycoon image of himself, but when it came to the niceties of proper press liaison, the Victory group were at a loss. They did not ever produce proper press releases. There were invitations or vague statements, but proper, regular releases on day-to-day matters such as the names of the crew, the choice of sails – non-sensitive stuff, of course – was always absent. If a pressman were to telephone the dock press office in Newport he would not get a fully trained press officer; he would get a pleasant enough answer to his question but with no real understanding of the difference between the requirements of a weekly magazine or a daily newspaper. Now that the semi-final loomed, in which all but two challengers would be eliminated, detail became more important than ever.

Victory raced *Australia II* in the first pairing, and after leading for four legs of the course she was beaten convincingly by 1 minute 54 seconds. British optimism turned to disappointment first, as the breeze which freshened and died and shifted all day played its part, and then Australian brilliance took over. The race began in a 12-knot north-north-westerly, continued in a light north-easterly, and the southerly course to the finish should have been south-westerly as the wind continued to veer. But, with essentially a 9-mile beat to the finish as the final run became a weather leg, the conditions were exactly those in which the Australian yacht had excelled and the crew turned a deficit of 17 seconds at the fourth mark into an advantage of 1 minute 10 seconds beginning the final leg.

Admittedly benefiting from an Australian error at the start of the contest, the British had still done everything right up to the start of the final two legs to the finish, but by which time the *Victory '83* lead had been whittled down to about 20 seconds. As the breeze filled in and tactics told, though, *Australia II* surged ahead to lead by 1 minute 10 seconds at the beginning of the last leg. The problem was, first, the failure of the British to cover, *Victory '83* splitting tacks with *Australia II* at what should have been the weather mark but what had become the end of a downwind leg, and, second, the shifting breeze.

Clearly still believing that they were incapable of matching *Australia II* in a tacking duel – the stated situation by the *Victory '83* afterguard on more than one occasion in defending the lay-line tactics – the British yacht went off on port while *Australia* tacked on to starboard up the left-hand side of the course to what had been the leeward mark, but had become the weather mark and the side that was to pay handsome dividends.

Victory '83 had begun with the amazing bonus of a 45-second advantage over *Australia II*, the margin being the sum of the Royal Perth yacht's folly of being over the line and having to re-start. The pre-start manoeuvres had gone as much the way of the British boat as that of the Australians, too, Smith having no problems in answering the tricks of Bertrand, but who, one suspected, was already adopting the policy of taking no chances.

The Bond boat had come too far, and obviously felt the important races were still ahead, to risk damage without real cause. After all, *Australia II* had been beaten only once by the British in the three previous series, and that after being becalmed in the wrong place, and was not much concerned by the threat of *Victory '83* which had still to confirm any major improvement in boat speed.

True, the Australians may have misjudged the capabilities of the British yacht, but the Bond crew had still to discover that because the two boats had broken off hostilities some 1¼ minutes before the start. It had seemed that *Australia* would start at the committee boat-end of the line, and *Victory '83* at the other. But *Australia II* came back on starboard and crossed early, while *Victory '83*, 13 seconds behind the gun, briefly covered her retreating opponent.

Early on, with *Victory '83* offering only token cover, it seemed that *Australia II* was gaining, but the British held onto their advantage and led by 38 seconds at the first weather mark. At the gybe mark she led by 32 seconds and the crew made a neat spinnaker change as the northerly died from about 12 knots at the start to some 6 knots beginning the second reach. The crew work on *Victory '83* was becoming especially good, and seemed the more so as there followed a succession of sail changes which ended with the British about 1¾ minutes up beginning the crucial second beat and with the breeze down to 4–5 knots. Notably, *Victory '83* was now flying a protest pennant.

The question was, whether *Victory '83* could hold her illustrious rival in conditions which previously had helped *Australia II*, generally unstoppable upwind, more than the British. But within half a mile there had been a further shift which made the leg a near dead run, and the luck had again swung Britain's way. They had the edge downwind, which was where Pattisson was now steering. *Victory '83* arrived some 20 seconds earlier at the second weather mark than *Australia II*, though both yachts were under spinnaker – and ahead also of *Azzurra* and *Canada*, which had started 15 minutes earlier in their semi-final heat. But such were the conditions that it was not surprising, as the two boats began what should have been the run, that they split tacks into a freshening southerly breeze. This was '*Australia* weather', and *Victory* was wary of a tacking duel with the Bond boat. That, anyway, was essentially the end of the race and, more important, the end of a chance for a famous British victory. The protest pennant had been broken out because of the use by *Australia II* of a spinnaker from *Challenge 12*, and still with her sail number, 10, on it. But the Australians had written to the race committee to get permission to use the sail, which had, of course, been properly measured. So the protest was withdrawn.

The following day *Victory '83* won against *Azzurra* in one of the closest skirmishes so far seen that summer off Newport. Ahead for more than the first half of her fourth semi-final race, she was then overtaken by *Azzurra* and faced a 7-second deficit beginning the last leg. It had been an absorbing race throughout, with the failure by *Victory '83* to cover her opponent – the fundamental cause of her mid-race problems, it had seemed – before the crew reported the luff zipper failure.

From the start, the two yachts went off on a long port tack, with *Victory '83* up to weather of the Italian 12-metre. It was 14 minutes before they tacked on to starboard and, although they had built a useful lead, the British boat was soon out of phase

with *Azzurra*, which was first to tack and which issued the
'challenge' to duel. When *Victory '83* had completed the opening weather leg into the southerly breeze of around 10–12 knots,
she was just 11 seconds ahead of the Italian yacht, and it was
clear that the British were unlikely to win as easily as in their
first semi-final race against the yacht, and when *Azzurra* was
forced to retire.

Victory '83 had increased her lead to 13 seconds at the second
mark and was 19 seconds ahead at the halfway stage of what had
become a close and impressive contest. As the yachts began the
second windward leg, into a breeze now inducing the 'growth' of
some white caps to the slight chop, there was further 'warfare' as
the Italians again engaged the British in a tacking duel. Surprisingly, considering the setbacks they had encountered against
Australia II the day before – and, indeed, seen *Canada* suffer
similarly against *Azzurra* – the British covered only briefly at
first and gave it up altogether halfway up the beat. The result:
three-quarters of the way up the leg the Italians were ahead. So
much for lay-line tactics, it seemed, as *Azzurra* earned a useful
lead at the second weather turn.

The Italians were only 7 seconds ahead beginning the beat to
the finish and they must have felt very insecure, especially as
they had a broken backstay which inhibited them from engaging
in a proper tacking duel to cover the British. The result: *Victory
'83* got back ahead to win by about half a minute. The success
gave *Victory '83* a winning record of 3–1 which, with Canada the
opponents the following day, seemed likely to ensure that it
would quickly become 4–1 and that a place in the final would be
in sight.

The British crew obviously felt very pleased with themselves,
and well they might after the shocks and setbacks of the earlier
rounds and when their credibility was rather stretched. But
some of them lost sight very quickly of the reality of the
situation – that their three wins had been partly the result of an
element of luck. This is not to say that they had not sailed well
or that there was any reason for them to have believed other
than that they were equal to the task ahead, but in making an
objective assessment of the situation and to weigh their prospects it was impossible to overlook that element of luck. Of
course their durability and morale were important considerations and it could not be denied that the crew seemed to have

settled into a happy and efficient group after the changes that had been wrought so late in the game. It is impossible to give high odds on a boat that has merely completed the course, any more than on a steeplechaser which has won against fields which had always had a great number of fallers. *Victory '83* still had no more than pedigree and staying power. She had not shown any ability to 'sprint finish', to battle against the odds, and to meet aggression with aggression. That the crew chose – to continue the equine simile – to be blinkered, was not only sad but a discredit to themselves. There was a nasty-looking incident at the start of the subsequent race, which ended with *Canada* on starboard and *Victory '83* on port. *Canada* hoisted her protest flag, but the protest was later dismissed as there had been no contact and the starboard tack yacht was not obstructed. A video film taken from the de Savary helicopter hovering overhead was to show at the subsequent protest hearing – where the advocacy of Bryan Willis was again to carry the day and for which he got the use of the squad Rolls Royce for two days – that no infringement had occurred. It was in the last 1½ minutes of manoeuvring before the start that *Victory '83* and her rival were involved in the incident on the starboard quarter of *Mirage*, the race committee boat. After that, Smith broke off and headed for the pin end of the line. The result was that *Canada* started with a 6-second advantage up to weather of *Victory* and in the middle of the line, covering the British yacht for the first 5 minutes on starboard tack.

The British tactics were perfectly understandable; they knew they had better boat speed than the Canadians in the condition of 10–12 knots, and that time lost at the start could be more than made up during the race. The worry was, though, that *Victory '83* would be allowed no such latitude against *Australia* in the final, if they both reached it, as seemed likely – indeed, had been predicted before the preliminary series began in June – or, further, against an American yacht if they managed to reach the challenge round proper. It was true, of course, that the British crew may have been as concerned as the Australians to avoid damage to craft or prospects, but while the Australians had demonstrated their mettle in combat, the British had still to show theirs. After a further 20 minute port tack *Canada* went on to starboard and it was clear that she was astern of her rival, trailing by 39 seconds at the first turn.

Canada gained slightly on the first reach to be 34 seconds astern at the second mark, but *Victory '83* pulled away again to be 1 minute 16 seconds up beginning the second beat and well in command. The conditions, the breeze having backed slightly and freshened, and the sun having obliterated the fog which threatened the start, did no harm either as *Victory '83* increased her lead to more than 2 minutes beginning the run. With the breeze, which freshened to perhaps 15 knots at the finish, and *Victory '83* showing good boat speed, there was no relief for the Canadians, beaten by 1 minute 58 seconds. The British yacht was beginning to look more like a finalist, except that while the yachts and the crew seemed to be getting better all the time, tactics were still too suspect for comfort for the sterner battles ahead.

The British semi-final record of four wins in five races seemed likely to remain unchanged after the succeeding race against *Australia II*, but – surprise, surprise – the match was to end in the most notable success for the British all summer. It had seemed that *Australia* was going less spectacularly well after a less than full-blooded start by Bertrand, who claimed after the defeat that he had made the mistake of testing a new mainsail unsuitable for the prevailing conditions. The British crew thought differently, that *Australia II*, the crewing aboard which had been more upset than may have been evident to outsiders by the loss of McAllister from the bow, had not made several headsail changes for fun and that the unusual shouts from the Australian yacht seemed to suggest that they were finding the defeat far from their liking. It did seem that *Victory '83* was going very well, unhindered by any nasty, tough tacking duels or aggressive starting tactics. However *Australia II* was not only going less well but there seemed to be less than a full-hearted attempt to make amends in the usual aggressive Australian way.

Conner commented to the press that Bertrand was 'sandbag-ging' (American for holding back), though the statement was retracted for him the following day by McCullough and an apology made to the Australian camp. It was not enough, though, for the *Victory '83* crew – or the more excitable of them, at least – who seemed to have been set to lynch anyone who had the temerity to question the completeness of the success. Sadly, a few of the more immature loud-mouths in the squad – egged on by those who had more intelligence and should have known better – were out for blood; de Savary himself intervened, where one might have expected a distinguished afterguard to have acted.

As for the race, both Bertrand and Smith had spurned aggression at the start, perhaps preferring to keep their powder dry for the challengers' final in which they seemed destined to meet. After six, wide, clockwise circles, the two yachts broke off and hovered just short of the line for 4 minutes before *Victory '83* broke for the pin end and *Australia II* for the committee boat end of the line. *Australia II* then 'swung' under the committee boat stern and, on starboard, crossed the line. *Victory '83*, which started on port towards the committee boat, remained on port for 6 minutes. She then tacked and crossed the Australian yacht. Going very well, the Royal Burnham boat then covered the Royal Perth yacht for the remainder of the first weather leg, beginning the first reach with an advantage of 16 seconds. *Victory* then led on all legs of the course and by the end had carved a convincing lead of 2 minutes 50 seconds. *Victory* got a rousing reception from a good collection of spectator vessels at the finish, and the celebrations were continued with most of the crew and dockside supporters being thrown into the water when they got back to the Newport Yachting Centre.

The premature celebrations were not to continue for long. The next day fog meant a long wait for nothing at sea, followed by, the day after, a defeat by *Azzurra*. Here was a setback and a ready reminder of the actual level of *Victory '83*. While *Australia II* made sure of her place in the final by roundly beating *Canada* by 1 minute 11 seconds, despite suffering a broken jumper strut, *Victory '83* was beaten just as roundly, by 50 seconds. So the British were kept waiting for another day to secure their second place, expectedly against the luckless Canadians who had still to win a semi-final race. That was how it was, *Victory '83* beating *Canada* by 2 minutes 26 seconds on Sunday, August 21 after leading throughout except for a period on the first beat, when the two yachts were at first becalmed and then there was the threat of an upset before the British grabbed the new breeze first and took their second place in the semi-final alongside *Australia* – which had notched a further unnecessary win over *Azzurra* by 1 minute 39 seconds.

So it was farewell to two further friends, *Azzurra*, which had earned untold numbers of friends by her crew's friendly, low-key but remarkable efforts, and the Canadians, who had the sympathy of most for the continual shortage of funds with which to campaign a yacht. *Azzurra*, a modification of *Enterprise* which the Italians bought before the series – and a very shrewd move it turned out to be – arrived in Newport with a reputation of being fast, and it was a reputation which was to be confirmed as it was shown that, with a higher stern, but shorter, more angular keel than her American 'cousin', she could probably tack faster than *Enterprise*. What was so pleasant about the Italians and their team manager, Cino Ricci, who pointed to the inexperience of his crew at match-racing as a main reason why they did not expect to last very long in the elimination series, was that they denigrated their own efforts, never boasted about their exploits, and yet had much to be proud of as they made such excellent progress. Some others could well have followed such an example of discreet behaviour and maturity.

Questions were posed at times about the authenticity of some of their equipment being Italian, but then there were few syndicates among the foreigners in Newport in 1983 who could have stood all of the tests of 'neutrality'. Certainly *Azzurra* was in the top three challengers. The syndicate members were:

	His Highness Aga Khan (President, Yacht Club Costa Smeralda)
	Cmdr Gianfranco Alberini (President, Italian challenge)
	Riccardo Bonadeo, Beppe Croce, Andrea Vallicelli, Gianni Agnelli, Franco Carraro, Carlo Rolandi, Enrico Cecchi, Luca Cordero di Montezemolo, Bruno Mentasti Granelli
Designer's assistant	N. Sironi
Sail designer	G. Cavalazzi
Crew	F. Apollonio, G. Ballanti, E. Buonomo, G. Devoto, A. de Marinis, D. Gabrielli, A. Giorgetti, E. I. Emburg, M.

Lugaresi, G. Maletto, L.
Mazza, D. Mosca, T. Nava,
M. Piani, N. Reggio, S.
Roberti, P. Rocca, F. Scala,
M. Valentini, F. Zamorani,
G. Zolezzi, L. Cordelle, M.
Pellaschier (helmsman),
Cino Ricci (skipper)

Canada 1, the design of Bruce Kirby, and of which so many spoke so highly when she first went to Newport and which was considered potentially so good because of the advantage of having the former American 12-metre *Clipper* as a trial-horse, was, in the end, perhaps the most disappointing craft of the lot. She had trouble at the beginning in Newport when she broke a mast, and she had trouble continually at the end when she failed to finish two of the semi-final heats because of damage of one sort or another.

She did though, have perhaps the fewest of all changes made to her during the series, being lightened by only 1,000 pounds towards the end of the event. Otherwise, everything stayed pretty much as it had been at the beginning when the boat was late to be launched and then made only a short series of trials during the winter off Miami with the French. She had a minimum of shoreside support. Her record is summarized more easily than that of any of the challengers: she began badly, got quite excitingly good and then went badly again. It probably all had to do with money and the shortage of equipment, and it would seem very likely, as with *Azzurra*, that more would be seen of her in a better light in the future. The Canadians were also very much on their own in terms of accommodation. They had the same berth on the Point as *Lionheart* in the 1980 challenge series, and consequently less close company like the Australians, French and Italians at Newport Offshore, with the defender syndicate entries.

Administration	Douglas Keary, Kevin Singleton, Hugh Drake, Robert Whitehouse, Bruce Kirby
12-metre Crew	Sandy Andrews, Jeffrey Boyd, Don Campbell, Tom

Cumming, Brent Foxall,
Philip Gow, Edward Gyles,
Paul Hansen, Eric Jespersen,
Robert Kidd, Fernando
Larrey, Jay McKinnell, Alan
Megarry, John Millen,
Robert Muru, Daniel
Palardy, Paul Parsons, Fred
Schueddekopp, David Shaw,
Robert Vaughan-Jones,
Robert Webb, Peter Wilson,
Robin Wynne-Edwards,
Terry McLaughlin.

Support   Bill Beebe, Tom Corness,
Kevin Curran, Steve Fleck,
Fran Ford, Brook Hamilton,
Shepherd Higley, Mark
Hillman, Micaela Jeltes, Jim
Johnston, Denise Larue,
Kent Luxton, Jim Lyons,
Mark Millen, Sharon
Mooney, Brian Pearson, Paul
Phillips, William Powell,
Jennifer Scott, Gordon
Smeaton, Julius Szabo, Dale
Webb, Peter Wilson.

For the last day of the semi-final round, though the series had effectively been decided by the eight races, the contestants went ahead with the ninth *Azzurra* v *Canada*, which resulted in a narrow win for the Italians after the Canadians had led for half of the course; and a convincing win for *Australia II* against *Victory '83*, which that day only had been fitted, as an experiment, with the winglets.

XIII

Challenger and Defender

Things are calmer this time. We are cognizant of the foreigners, but in the end it comes down to you against the other guy. You take it one day at a time

– Dennis Conner, 1983

Readers of magazines and newspapers in Australia and England might think that with all the doings of the challenging syndicates ashore and afloat, the American defenders were inactive. They would not have been more wrong. The US syndicates with their customary single-mindedness were intent on one object only: to defend the cup in mid-September. The New York Yacht Club had no need to run long series of races in accordance with rules agreed by several countries: it had instead to determine the best yacht for racing against a challenger. The challenging managers themselves were the first to admit that this more precise task of the defenders gave the latter an advantage that was not possible to counter.

The three US contenders, *Courageous*, *Defender* and *Liberty*, came to the final trials after an immense amount of preparation and with crews of high experience.

From the beginning Dennis Conner of the Freedom Campaign 83 of Fort Schuyler was the favourite to be selected, and in the event he was. He started from a position of enormous strength as skipper of the winning *Freedom* from the 1980 Cup. During 1981 he was able to try two further new 12s, *Magic* and *Spirit*, and had the luxury of rejecting both, arriving in Newport in the spring with *Freedom* and the new Johan Valentijn design, *Liberty*. For a time it seemed that even *Liberty* might not have a margin on the wonderful *Freedom*, but by June Conner had decided: *Liberty*, US 40, would be the Fort Schuyler contender against *Courageous* and *Defender*. So not only was there a boat improved in hard racing from 1981 to early 1983, but the crew contained such persons as John Marshall of North Sails, with four Cup campaigns to his credit, and Jack Sutphen who had been sailing 12-metres since the late 1960s. As for Conner himself, not only was he winning skipper of the 1980 America's Cup, but he was starting helmsman on the successful *Courageous* in 1974, and since he was also twice winner of the Congressional Cup (see Chapter 10) he was the world's most accomplished match race skipper. Like Bertrand, he was an Olympic bronze medallist, but in the Tempest class; he was twice winner of the Star world championship, twice winner of the Southern Ocean Racing Conference, and twice skipper in American Admiral's Cup boats.

Against this talent were pitted the two boats of the syndicate known as the Defender–Courageous group. Unlike the British, with crews revolving among the boats owned by a syndicate, *Defender* and *Courageous* each had an appointed skipper and chosen crew (among whom over the months individuals were changed from time to time). *Defender* was the new boat, designed by David Pedrick, who was used to creating large yachts and had worked on 12s with Sparkman & Stephens. Her skipper, Tom Blackaller, distanced himself from Connor, though, like him, had twice been Star world champion, and was a Californian. His tactician and closest adviser was Gary Jobson, who had helped Ted Turner to victory in 1974.

As will be seen, Blackaller was to take third place to the old *Courageous*, winner of the America's Cup in 1974 and 1977, which made her the oldest serious contender for the defence since 1958, when the pre-war *Vim* made such a mark. John Kolius of Ulmer Sails in Houston, Texas, and J-24 champion, was skipper of the much revamped hull with its entirely new rig and of course excellent new sails from North as well as from Ulmer. She was designed and subsequently modified by Sparkman & Stephens under the supervision of Bill Langen. S & S were the firm that designed every Cup winner except one from 1958 until 1977. In the 1960s and 1970s their ocean racing designs led the world. Then came the retirement of Olin Stephens, after fifty years of sailing and designing racing yachts, while younger designers who had served their time with his

New York firm set up on their own. Stephens is still consulted on many aspects of yacht racing, as we have seen in the keel argument.

The New York Yacht Club trials to find a defender were simply stated.

June 18 to 25 preliminary races

July 16 to 27 observation races

August 16 to September 8 final selection races.

Before the first preliminary race, the crew and support group for *Liberty* were announced:

Bow	Scott Vogel, Adam Ostenfeld
Mast	Robert Campbell, Robert LaBanca
Pit	Thomas Rich, William Trenkle, Thomas Chiginsky
Grinders	Kyle Smith, John Hufnagel, James Nicholas, Tod Raynor
Tailers	Jon Wright, Edward Trevelyan, John MacGowan, Matthew Flood, Graham Kelly Jnr
Mainsheet	John Marshall, William Rogers, Ian McKechnie
Navigators	Halsey Herreshoff, Christy Steinman
Tactician	Thomas Whidden
Helmsman	Dennis Conner, Jack Sutphen, Malin Burnham.

The announcement added: 'We anticipate several different combinations to be used throughout the summer, but it is expected that the following will sail in the first race: Robert Campbell, Halsey Herreshoff, John Hufnagel, John Marshall, Thomas Rich, Kyle Smith, Edward Trevelyan, Scott Vogel, Thomas Whidden, Jon Wright, Dennis Conner.'

The support group consisted of the following: Mr and Mrs Fritz Jewett; Mr and Mrs Edward du Moulin; Mr and Mrs Dennis Conner; Mr and Mrs Jack Sutphen; Mr and Mrs Richard Chesebrough; Mr and Mrs John Marshall; Mr and Mrs Tom Whidden; Mr and Mrs Johan Valentijn; Mr and Mrs Malin

Burnham; Dr and Mrs Fred Frye; Mr and Mrs Robin Fuger; Mr
and Mrs Bob Conner; Vic Tyson, Jon Wright, Kyle Smith, David
Chatham, Bill Ruh, Tom Rich, Scott Vogel, John MacGowan,
John Hufnagel, Ian MacKechnie, Bill Rogers, Bill Trenkle, Tom
Chiginsky, Bob Campbell, Adam Ostenfeld, Bob LaBanca, Matt
Flood, Graham Kelly, Tod Raynor, Ed Trevelyan, Jim Nicholas,
Christy Steinman, Jean Blanco, Ann Whiteman, Antoinette
Stockenberg, David Hirsch, Sam Harris, John Chase, Don
Wyatt, Sheila Hill, Liz Rooney, Linda Packer, Ken Donnelly,
Richie Comer, Laurent Esquier, Halsey Herreshoff, and Mr and
Mrs Jake Farrell.

Conner had also signed on Robin Fuger, one of the earliest of
de Savary's appointees, and one of the first to go in 1982. De
Savary's loss was very much *Freedom*'s gain.

The linking of *Courageous* and *Defender* was the third successive time that two yachts and crews had joined forces osten-
sibly as equal contenders, but under the same management.
First it had been *Courageous* and *Independence*, in 1977, and
then *Courageous* and *Clipper* in 1980. *Courageous* was considered merely a veteran and there was little hope at first that she
would prove much more than a useful trial-horse.

The full, listed *Defender/Courageous* line-up was given
as:

Management	
Syndicate chairman	Chuck Kirsch
Project director	Chuck Wilson
Team house and shoreside activities	Jim Mattingly
Operations manager	Marty O'Meara
Public relations	Jim Ford
PR	Mrs Sanderson H. Carney
Vice-chairman, Defender/Courageous group	David Vietor
Designer	David Pedrick
Crew	*Defender*
	Tom Blackaller (skipper), Gary Jobson (tactician), Peter Stalkus (navigator), Rod David (mainsheet trimmer), Jim Flagenhoef

(grinder), Bruce Epke
(grinder), John Mulderig
(below decks), Ken Keefe
(mastman), Dana Timmer
(bowman), Mike Toppa
(tailer), Paul Cayard (tailer)
Courageous
John Kolius (skipper), John
Bertrand (tactician), Bill
Campbell (navigator), John
Gluek (mainsheet trimmer),
Courtenay Jenkins (grinder),
Mike Sullivan (grinder),
Hank Stuart (below decks),
Jim Whitmore (mastman),
Robbie Young (bowman),
Glen Darden (tailer), Curt
Oetking (tailer)

The preliminary defence trials began with a fine start by *Courageous*, and she was distinctly better in the light airs in which she had previously done less well. Her first success was 2 wins against *Liberty*, subsequently going down twice to *Defender*. When the preliminary series ended, *Courageous* had the best record: 6 wins and 5 defeats. *Defender*'s score was 5–6 and *Liberty*'s 5–5. Gary Jobson, the tactician on *Defender*, was quoted as saying 'the Cup is winnable', while Conner was reported as having said it was not *Courageous* that worried him, but 'the trick keel on *Australia II* scares the hell out of me'.

Liberty had got better as the series progressed, during which it was discovered that, due to a measurement error, *Defender* had been racing with a boom that was shorter by 9 inches than necessary, and therefore a smaller mainsail than required. It was said to have had 20–30 square feet area less than it might have had. The *Courageous* excuse for not doing even better was that their rudder bearing had been dislodged at the beginning of the trials, and no one realized it until it was inspected by Olin Stephens. The yacht went to Cove Haven for refairing and replacement rudder bearings. *Defender* was having the 9 inches reinstated to the boom and it was planned also by

Pedrick to do something to the girth measurement while the mast and rudder were to remain as they were. *Liberty* was not having any work done on her at this stage, since Conner had resumed his 'leapfrog' policy of improving one boat while racing the other, and so it was *Freedom* that was to be worked on. He considered that *Liberty* could have 1,000 pounds taken out of her to improve her light air performance.

In the event it was *Defender* which had the most spectacular surgery up to that time: a wedge-shape cut from the top of the keel, up over the topsides, across the deck and down the other side. At deck level the width was said to be merely three-eighths of an inch, yet the job was done by chainsaw. What else? It was reported that the task was 'relatively easy' and had taken only three hours. The object of the exercise was to raise the ends of the boat that were sagging. The deck was welded back together and the yacht given an extra 40 square feet or so in sail area. The job was said also to have reduced girth, yet increased draft by lowering the centre of the yacht. *Freedom*, meanwhile, had had 2,000 pounds of lead taken from her keel as the American syndicate decided to make their boats lighter to meet an Australian challenge.

When the observation trials got back into motion in July it was to be *Liberty* which ended with the best second-round score – 13 wins and 5 defeats for an overall score of 18–10 in the two series, while *Defender* with an 8–5 second-round score and a total of 13–11 also passed *Courageous*, which faded badly to 2–13 for an overall 8–18. This was a complete turnabout.

When the series got going after the break for alterations no contender seemed to have a major boat speed advantage over any other. Tactics thus played a more important part in a series which did not do much to impress the selectors. It was not until the second half of the observation series that *Liberty* was to emerge as the outstanding contender. Blackaller was allowed to have the series programme altered so that *Defender* could be taken out of the water to be altered. Her after-end was narrowed, her skeg deepened slightly, and her rudder moved farther aft. The belief was that she might tack slower but would track faster. It was at this stage of the trials that the word was to get out that *Liberty* had been racing with an option of more than one rating certificate, thus experimenting with different combinations of freeboard, sail area and so on. As a result of adverse publicity the NYYC wisely decided that ratings must be allotted precisely before the selection. A change then, if needed, would entail permission to have a proper measurement: there would be no switch at the skipper's option.

The final defence trials began with two successes by *Liberty* against *Defender*, though in the event the main talking point in mid-August was to be the revival of the fortunes of *Courageous*, no longer discussed now as a veteran craft but as quite a different yacht from the one which won two Cup series. Kolius, too, was now considered very hot property, while – surprise, surprise – Conner, it was being suggested, could be on his way out. In the event, though, it was Blackaller and *Defender* who went out first, on Saturday, August 27, after two defeats against *Liberty* and after the NYYC selection committee had clearly decided that the yacht was a threat only in lighter airs. At the time she still had a slightly better win–loss record than *Courageous* for the summer, but had slipped badly to third place in the selection series. So it was between *Courageous* and *Liberty*, apparently having lost some of its shine and with the question whether Conner had chosen the wrong rating. It was certain, though, that the defence trials were by no means over yet, even though the selectors decided a lay-day when the two-boat challengers' final was scheduled to begin.

Yet ten days later *Liberty* stood at six wins and her opponent *Courageous* at two. So on Friday, September 2, the NYYC selection committee thanked Kolius and *Courageous* and invited Conner and *Liberty* to defend the America's Cup. Dennis Conner thus became only the fourth skipper in America's Cup history to defend the trophy for a second time. It had been expected all summer that the burgundy-coloured *Liberty* would become the chosen yacht, and her trials record of some 34 wins and 17 losses to a tally for *Courageous* of 19 wins and 32 defeats seemed to support that conjecture. A further piece of good news for the NYYC selection committee was the announcement from the *Defender/Courageous* syndicate that they would be back in 1987, and with Kolius as their skipper. Kolius said that he hoped to have most of the crew back, too.

The challenger trials under the flag of the Royal Sydney Yacht Squadron started on August 28, so the American result came in the middle of them. The New York Yacht Club had already been at it for sixteen days when they called a halt with the announcement of *Liberty* to defend. The challenge final was, as we have seen, quite a different affair: the defender would select herself once she won 4 (out of 7) races.

Before the final the British crew were flown down to New York and received warmly in the New York Yacht Club. There they gazed at the Victorian pitcher in its own octagonal shaped room and saw model after model of winners and losers of the Cup, as well as the hundreds of models of hulls owned by members of the club since its foundation in 1844. The day before the beginning of the finals the British crew returned to preparing *Victory '83*. It was noticeable that the *Australia II* squad did not go away, but worked on the yacht, giving her further outings under sail. After his 1974 Cup success with *Courageous*, Ted Hood had remarked that he believed that one of the biggest of the Bond mistakes at that time was his decision to take the crew on sightseeing trips. The only thing to do, maintained Hood, was to stay and sail and work on the boat. There could be no time away for America's Cup crews.

It was interesting also, in 1983, that Warren Jones had a comment to make about the similarity of the de Savary outfit in its first Cup campaign to that of the Australian effort in 1974 with *Southern Cross*. Said Jones: 'That is one way to do it. If you are trying to gather a large amount of knowledge in a short time you really need quite a big machine. The second time around you start to get smaller and it is only with experience that you learn how to cut corners.' On the eve of the best-of-seven race final series, Jones commented that he did not think the Australians were 'big-headed in saying we can beat *Victory*; merely because our summer's record indicates to us that in a best-of-seven series we should be able to beat them'. He went on: 'But we are budgeting to beat them in four straight; merely because we are here to try to win the America's Cup and we would like as much time as we could between the challengers' series and the America's Cup series to do a lot more testing of our sails.'

The Executive Director acknowledged *Victory* 'to be the most improved boat here' and felt that the 'big foundation work' of the British was 'much misplaced – which happens in first-time campaigns – but with the miles under the keel has meant that two years of work has paid off for them'. Discussing the Australian campaign, Jones maintained that they were a tight-knit group, all living in one house, obeying strict house rules which included clearly defined guidelines for guests.

'The crew house is a continual source of inspiration to all of us,' he said. 'Everyone trains together, everyone has breakfast together and we have our crew meetings every morning at breakfast. No single outsider is allowed in and there are no secrets between crew and management. I have never observed any pressure on the crew over the keel. We treat each other as equals. If we can't win this time, I don't think we can do any better. This is our best shot. Someone else will have to take over from where we have got. We don't have any problems, everything happens properly. That is the result of experience. If we have only the same boat speed as them we will be incredibly lucky to beat them. To beat them we must be even faster,' he commented in his typically open, matter-of-fact way.

A large armada of spectator craft, including the NYYC selection committee, turned out to see this famous turn of speed on the first day of the final, an overcast day with some early morning thunder and heavy showers and with visibility poor under light southerlies. It seemed from the beginning that there would be a late start to the contest, if there was a start at all, with perhaps the only hope a breaking of the clouds to let the sun through and encourage a sea breeze. The race committee were not prepared to wait, sending the boats home at 1.50, some 1 hour 50 minutes after the race should have started but when there was no wind at all.

The attraction was the performance of *Australia II*, seen as the first likely threat in many a year to the invincibility of a NYYC defending yacht. Though the anticipated clash did not come that day and seemed threatened again early on the following day, which dawned grey and windless like its immediate predecessor, there was the short 'side-show' of a race between the Aga Khan's *Shabaz*, the Don Shead-designed, high-powered motor yacht with twin gas-turbines, against de Savary's sleek, diesel-powered Magnum *Lisanola*. *Shabaz* won – a 'crock of gold race' repeat in a way, when Bond's *Apollo* was beating de Savary's *Victory of Burnham* at Cowes in 1981 – and the significance of which seemed to be that the de Savary circus would be in Porto Cervo for the planned first regatta for 12-metres.

It seemed more unlikely that the first race would get under

way on the second day than the first. With fog out on the course early on and with the same threat of thunder, rain and light winds as on the previous day, the race committee decided to hold the boats in harbour. The NYYC did the same with the defence contenders. The NYYC were quick to change their minds and to order their boats to sea and it was only shortly afterwards, as a southerly breeze piped up, that the challengers were on the same trek out to Rhode Island Sound. Indeed, so hopeful were the signs that it seemed, as the start approached, that the *Victory* crew might at least have a decent blow, conditions they had for so long craved, in which to tackle the Australian opposition.

The breeze was quickly to die and when the start came, only some 40 minutes behind schedule into a south-easterly, it was down to 10 knows and still dying. After that it was really *Australia II* all the way, building a 3 minutes 46 seconds lead at the first weather mark and increasing that to 4 minutes 55 seconds at the gybe and 3 minutes 58 seconds at the leeward turn. By that stage, with *Victory* showing some of her downwind advantage, it became apparent that there was already a danger that the race would not end within the time limit. The boats needed to be back at the second weather turn before 4.30 to beat the 3 hours 50 minutes time limit for the first four legs and, in the event, *Australia II* managed it with only about 15 minutes to spare but with a lead of 6 minutes 11 seconds. It might have been more, but for a windshift making the final cables to the weather mark a fetch, from which the British boat was most to benefit.

On the succeeding downwind leg, as it became more certain than ever that there was only a remote chance that the race would finish within the time limit, the breeze died and as the two yachts gybed this way and that, *Victory* closed the gap to 2 and a half minutes at the beginning of the final beat. *Australia II* had now to complete the final 4.5 mile weather leg at an average speed of around 9 knots, an impossibility in most weather. The Australians widened the gap again to an estimated 6 minutes before the race committee abandoned racing as the 5 hour 15 minute time limit expired. Both yachts acknowledged that they were willing to race again the following day.

It was another sad start to what should have been a proud event. The grey skies, rain and lack of wind made for anything but the backcloth that was necessary for the pageant unfolding before a smaller grandstand than the previous day, but one which was well aware of the history that was in the making. Here was a yacht which could well worry the Americans. It must have been all the more annoying to the Australians that they had not got a race under their belts when it was discovered later that day that the Americans were experimenting with 'wings'.

The understanding was that *Defender* had gone to Cove Haven to have wings fitted as part of an experiment that would result, if successful, with the appendages being transferred to *Courageous*. Then, when the weather prevented racing again the following day – again too little wind – the sight that faced the challengers when they returned to harbour was of *Freedom*, having sprouted wings! Valentijn and Halsey Herreshoff had done the design work with the assistance, it seemed, of experts at the Boeing Aircraft Corporation at Seattle and at the Massachusetts Institute of Technology. If successful, the wings could be transferred to *Liberty*.

All the more frustrating, therefore for the Australians that there was no racing on Tuesday. There was on Wednesday (August 31) though, and the Australians had more cause to be upset at that; they lost by 13 seconds to *Victory* in a contest which was almost a total reversal of form of the race in which they had led so convincingly. *Victory '83* was now in total command throughout and *Australia II* in arrears all the way and never really looking all that threatening after a start which Bertrand lost by 14 seconds. When the course signals had been hoisted at 1150 for a start at 1210, it was a cold, grey day, with big, confused seas and a south-westerly of around 20 knots. Things began tolerably well for *Victory '83*, with Smith indulging in a series of six, wide, lazy clockwise circles before breaking off the action and heading downwind towards the spectator fleet, which he reached and made clear he intended to circle as the 5-minute gun went. There were shouts from the British yacht to spectator boats to stay still and the hair-raising spectacle then of the two 12-metres passing either side of a vessel but with not more than 15 yards or so on either side because of the presence of other vessels. Smith then circled another vessel and it was at this stage, the Australians complained later, that they lost command of the situation and the result was that *Victory*

'83 came out of the manoeuvre up to weather of the Australian craft and with perhaps less than a minute and a half before the starting gun. *Victory '83* hovered slightly, bore off down the line but with *Australia II* under and to leeward and managed a start which she won by 14 seconds. It was the best and most aggressive British start of the summer. Smith piled on the agony for *Australia II* by covering assiduously all the way up the first weather leg to lead by some 12 seconds at the first mark.

It had been spectacular stuff, with *Victory '83* clearly preferring the right-hand side of the course and keeping *Australia II* off on the left. It was close and exciting match-racing and with *Victory '83* certainly looking the better sailed boat at that stage. On the two reaches *Victory '83* made a slight gain, beginning the second beat – by which stage the wind had moderated to around perhaps 12 knots – with an advantage of 19 seconds. Not enough to hold the Australian craft at her best on a good weather leg, it seemed. But again *Victory '83* held on admirably and was some three-quarters of a minute ahead beginning the run at which time came an *Australian II* protest over a port and starboard incident which had taken place as *Victory '83* rounded the mark and bore down on their rival who was to allege that she was forced to alter course.

Approaching the leeward mark for the second time, with the wind still lighter, there came another incident which briefly seemed likely to be a bigger problem for *Victory '83*; Bullard, on the bow releasing the spinnaker for the rounding of the leeward mark, went over the side and into the water, grabbing as he did the spinnaker pole. It seemed that he had lost his grip. In fact, the topping lift had let go and the luckless bowman had no way of saving himself. But he was hoisted back aboard almost immediately and *Victory '83* rounded the mark with an advantage of some 44 seconds. It did not look good for *Australia II*, even though the wind and sea had moderated to more like the conditions in which she had previously performed so well. At the finish the British crossed the line with an advantage of 13 seconds.

There were, however, three immediate questions; the protest and counter protest, the worry whether it was *Victory* doing well in the conditions or *Australia II* doing badly. Only time, it seemed, would tell, for the first clue, the subsequent press conference, gave no real answers. Bond maintained that the

shifts had favoured *Victory* and that the Australians had chosen
the wrong genoa and perhaps the wrong mainsail and that,
anyway, both were being used for the first time in a race. *Victory
'83* had very little to say; or, to be precise, in the absence of de
Savary and with the afterguard not appearing at the press office
it was Alabaster, who admitted that he had not been afloat
because of a shore crisis among the *Victory* staff – Suzy Pearce
had had to go to hospital with appendicitis – and had not got all
of the answers from the crew. It was just as well they had no
more to say in a way because it had long seemed that the best
thing was for *Victory* and her crew to prove themselves on the
water. If that was what they were beginning to do then there
were a great number of their supporters who would be much
relieved and pleased that after the various manoeuvres of the
summer there was still a chance that honour would be more
than satisfied. Both skippers indicated that they would be
prepared to race the following day, when the fifth race would
have been starting had the boats been able to race every day
since the final had opened on August 28.

And when Thursday dawned, bright and more like summer
again but with light winds, *Victory*'s crew knew that they were
leading 1–0 – the Australian protest of the previous day having
been dismissed after a three-hour meeting. So, this was a surprise and Britain would begin with a success which few outside
of the *Victory '83* camp had expected. Euphoria was short-lived,
however, as the light-air race, officially given as 7–8 knots and
210 degrees at the start and finish, was won by the Australians
with a margin of 4 minutes 53 seconds; this was very much
more than the previous day. The start had been tame by comparison with that of the first race and the margins were big from
the first mark after which the race was like a procession. The
two skippers broke off manoeuvring a series of wide, anti-
clockwise circles some three minutes before the start, and two
minutes from the gun *Victory '83* went for the pin end and
Australia II the committee boat end of the line. Bertrand was to
tack on to starboard and crossed in the middle of the line,
perhaps 200 yards to weather of Smith and by the weather mark
the difference was 1 minute 45 seconds to the Perth boat. The
margins thereafter were 1 minute 42 seconds at the gybe mark, 1
minute 38 seconds at the end of the triangle, a staggering 3
minutes 10 seconds at the end of the second weather leg.

Australia II started the final weather leg with an advantage of 2 minutes 54 seconds.

The Victory syndicate asked that the next day should be their one lay day. The British meteorologist, part of the team all summer, was predicting light air. In the event the defence boats were out and it was 15 to 17 knots of wind. The British, who, it had seemed, had decided to fit the 'fins' for the third encounter, must have been regretting that as much as the light weather which followed their breezy lay day.

The *Australia II* camp was not only astonished at the British tactics but delighted also. They still had a lay day available for gear failure, which the Victory syndicate did not, but the halt had given them time also to re-cut the heavy-weather main which they held most responsible for the defeat they had suffered. The next race really did demonstrate something of an immaturity in the British camp. The start was after a further attempt by the *Victory* team to get rid of *Australia* in a chase through the spectator fleet. It did not work. Bertrand started as he wished on starboard tack while *Victory*, though probably intending to go to the 'favoured' starboard-hand side of the course and not minding passing below her rival to start on port, was, within a minute, covered by the Perth boat which tacked on top of her. That, effectively, was the end of another processional race – though helped even more on this occasion by a particularly unruly spectator fleet which was well out of control even on the first leg.

Having manufactured a seven-second lead at the start, Bertrand rounded the first mark 1 minute 41 seconds up on Smith, who was forced by the spectator boats to give up hope of benefiting from a windshift on the right and instead had to slog up the middle at the mercy of his opponent. The time at the gybe mark was 1 minute 49 seconds to *Australia II*; it was 4 minutes 55 seconds at the leeward turn where *Victory* (it was thought at the time, perhaps flying a protest flag because of interference by the following boats) faced almost certain 'slaughter'. It was with a gap of 5 minutes 49 seconds that the British began the run – proportions not dissimilar to the days in September 1967 of *Constellation* and *Sovereign* – and then went on down to 3 minutes 40 seconds at the beginning of the beat to the finish because of a favourable 15 degree windshift and a series of helpful gybes to generate boat-speed: the winning margin was 3

minutes 7 seconds. A windshift on the final leg, a slight freshening of the breeze and perhaps even a certain prudence by Bertrand in not getting completely out of the *Victory* section of the
Sound may also have played its part. The question was whether
the British would proceed with and make capital from their
protest and whether they would concede help or hinderance
from the fins? They chose not to take up the protest and the
official reaction to the fins was the same as before the race: 'No
comment'. Rather than protest, de Savary had written to the
race committee asking for more coastguard vessels, more patrol
boats – which he would supply and provide with flags – and for
stricter discipline on the course at the start. He wanted spectator vessels to remain behind the racing yachts until five minutes
or more after the start.

For the fourth race the start itself had been fairly tame with
just a few manoeuvres which did not really bring the boats close
together and which were followed by Smith taking *Victory '83*
just round *Lisanola*, of the now well-policed spectator fleet, to
wipe off *Australia II* which then made a safe leeward start
towards the pin end while *Victory '83* started on the opposite –
port – tack towards the committee boat end of the line. It was
obviously what both skippers wanted and it meant that the
British had got the generally more favoured starboard side of the
course, from which they were first to benefit from the shifts.
After two tacks *Victory '83* crossed ahead. Smith kept her on the
same tack for some 17 minutes, but *Australia II* climbed above
them to weather and led them on the first reach by 1 minute 10
seconds with what had been an 8-knot south-westerly at the
start and which had begun to die a little. There was nothing
Victory '83 could do against Ben Lexcen's close-winded yacht.
Victory pulled back some six seconds on the first reach and a
further six on the second reach. It was not enough, though, as
Australia II demonstrated by moving 2 minutes 12 seconds
ahead on the second weather leg and actually increasing her lead
on the run for the first time in the final by some four seconds.
Her advantage was increased by a further 4 seconds on the final
beat when the wind freshened to 12 knots.

Monday was Labor Day, dawning with a sombre, funeral-like
shroud of New England fog, which, for once, seemed appropriate. It was, too, an ominous sign, allied perhaps to the belief
among the *Victory '83* squad that it would be another light-

weather race as they prepared for the 1210 start with a light to moderate-weather mainsail set as on the previous day. The decision was that the course should be south-westerly in a wind of around 10–12 knots. The start was more thoughtful, the yachts avoiding direct circling manoeuvres and preferring instead large sweeps which brought them side by side on a series of occasions before *Victory '83* finally set off as in the past, towards what Smith presumably hoped would be the sanctuary of the spectator fleet. This time, though, there was just one rounding of the committee boat by *Victory '83* before she, in turn, was 'wiped off' by *Australia II* heading for the line at the committee boat end well up to weather of *Victory '83*. The latter, within eight minutes, had been crossed by *Australia II*. If that was not the end of the race, then a series of three quick tacks which cost *Victory '83* valuable ground in the 12th and 13th minutes was. It showed again that *Victory '83* could not live with *Australia II* in a tacking duel. It did seem that she may have a touch of the same problem that had afflicted the only other Howlett 12-metre to be built, *Lionheart*. The latter was notorious for her lack of turning ability.

After that, with the breeze freshening a little here and dying a little there, *Australia II* tramped on to lead by 1 minute 15 seconds at the first mark, 1 minute 11 seconds at the second and 1 minute 14 seconds at the halfway stage. *Victory '83* fell to 2 minutes 42 seconds behind on the second weather leg, was 2 minutes 18 seconds down beginning the final weather leg and finished 3 minutes 19 seconds in arrears.

There was a cacophony of horns, sirens and firecrackers for the victors – and magnums of champagne from de Savary for the *Australia II* crew – and in Newport Harbour a welcome the likes of which few observers could recall. Hundreds of yachts and tens of thousands of spectators lined the docksides or milled around the boat which had won the challenge series. There was no doubt now who were the Americans' favourite 'cousins'. The Australians had become such a regular part of Newport life that Newporters and the yachting fraternity generally had come to see them as the natural challengers.

It was at the same moment the end for the present of *Victory '83*. It had been a gallant attempt and a noble failure. Though the ingredients might have been right, the mix was not. People would point to the lack of good sails, the bad luck of all but one of the races taking place in light breezes, or the choice of the wrong afterguard or something seriously amiss with the yacht. All or none may have been true. As we have seen in these pages it was a much longer story than that.

XIV

There was no second

'*Wake up the wife, wake up the children, wake up the dog! Get them up to celebrate the greatest day in the history of Australian sport.*'
  — *John Raedler, radio reporter in Newport, broadcasting live to Sydney, September 22 1983*

Wind north-east, 5 knots or less. Temperature cooler than for several weeks at 75 degrees. The ocean off Rhode Island, slight. The day, Tuesday September 13, fixed two years before as the opening race of the best of seven 1983 America's Cup matches. The start, as on every day to follow, was intended for 12.10 p.m. If the weather did not meet the rules to enable a start by 2.10 p.m. there would be no start that day.

The previous night Alan Bond received a long letter from the Committee of the New York Yacht Club. It requested that he sign a statement that everything in respect of his yacht *Australia II*, sailing under the flag of the Royal Perth Yacht Club, was in accord with the requirements of the deed of gift of the America's Cup. Now he headed for the America's Cup buoy watching the two masts, *Liberty* and his own boat, being towed across the smooth, blue, sunlit water. The headquarters vessel of the Australian challenge, *Black Swan*, was difficult to pick out among more than one thousand other craft, but for her Australian ensign and coastguard priority spectator flag. There were tall ships, imitation tall ships, ocean passenger vessels, warships, sailing yachts from 30 to 130 feet, power boats by the score, dinghies which should never have been so far off shore and the controlling fleet of US coastguard cutters. From Newport and other New England havens they came to watch the race.

In the north-east air the start was to seaward of the race

course. Thus the spectator fleet streamed across the planned course causing the answering pennant – the international postponement signal – to be broken out at 12.08. The answering pennant stayed aloft on the committee boat, the international signal of boredom, for the light air gyrated by more than 30 degrees. The weather mark boat radioed that the wind there bore no resemblance to the direction near the start line. At 2 p.m. no further gun had been fired and racing was, under the rules, abandoned for the day.

First race

Wind north-east 16 to 18 knots. Air temperature distinctly cold and rain forecast. The race began on time. It was, as former America's Cup helmsman Bill Ficker, who conducted the daily Press conferences, was later to remark, rather like two people meeting at a blind date. And, he added, they knew what each other looked like at the end of the race.

Liberty had been allocated, on the toss of a coin, the committee boat (starboard) end of the line. Thereafter the yachts swapped ends each race. When the committee vessel, *Black Knight*, fired the 10-minute gun, both yachts approached each other. There was a feint by *Liberty*, as though she was about to indulge in a clock-wise circling manoeuvre with *Australia II*, but which ended, after another feint one minute later, with *Liberty* to leeward of her opponent.

The protagonists then sailed slowly along the starting line and then crossed it before *Liberty* turned to face *Australia II* and to wipe her off her transom on the pin end of the line. But on the 5-minute gun, *Australia II* was again on *Liberty*'s transom as, for a whole minute, the two yachts headed towards the spectator fleet on the starboard side and towards the stern of the committee vessel. But while Bertrand had been in charge initially, it was Conner who came out on top some 3 minutes before the start; up to weather and slightly astern of *Australia II*.

When the start came, both yachts were briefly on starboard: *Australia II* still to leeward but slightly ahead, while Conner was where he wanted to be. He was to state later that he considered the start even. After a port tack and then another starboard one, after 8 minutes it was *Australia II* which was marginally ahead. Conner got ahead on the first beat, on the fourth tack and after 34 minutes, though Australia was back

ahead 4 minutes later as the wind continued to shift between 5
and 10 degrees. The Australian advantage was 10 seconds at the
first weather mark.

The Australian lead was again 10 seconds at the gybe mark
but then came what Bertrand was later to acknowledge was
a mistake. He let *Liberty* through to weather and then 9
minutes after rounding the weather mark Conner gybed and got
between *Australia II* and the leeward mark. The initiative had
passed to *Liberty* which, but for an acknowledged mistake by
Conner, was to hold it in the main until the finish. *Liberty*,
though, was quickly shown not to favour the idea of a close
tacking duel with *Australia II* on the second beat during which
the 25 tacks were in the form of loose cover. They earned
Conner an advantage of 28 seconds at the second weather mark
compared to the 16 seconds by which *Liberty* had led at the
leeward mark.

It was right after rounding the weather mark that Conner
made what was arguably his one mistake and which, in truth,
became so only because the wind continued to shift between 5
and 10 degrees. Conner gybed onto port as soon as he rounded
the weather mark insisting afterwards that at the time that he
carried out the manoeuvre it was the right side to be. But by
two-thirds of the way down the run it was *Australia II* which
had got back on level terms – if not actually ahead – and it was
only a sudden gybe towards *Australia II* which appeared to catch
Bertrand unawares which gave *Liberty* back her advantage. As
Liberty bore down, *Australia II* gybed astern of her and then
broached and, it was to be discovered later, broke a bracket
holding a sheave which operated the rudder. From that point
until some 10 minutes up the following weather leg Bertrand
had to steer with trim tab only. It gave Conner all the latitude he
needed to go from 35 seconds ahead at the second leeward turn
to 1 minute 10 seconds ahead at the finish. It was a bitterly
disappointing outcome for the Australians, but the various
incidents appeared to show what had been feared by her
supporters all summer – that *Australia II* had not had quite the
same vital preparation of tough competition in the challengers'
event that she would need in the challenge round. Bertrand
confessed as much after the contest, stating that the race against
Liberty had been the closest and toughest of the summer.
Conner was ready to admit that *Australia* was not so slow in a

breeze as had been suggested; nor as slow downwind as the Americans had been led to believe that she might be. He was, he said, 'generally impressed' and thought that the '*Australia* crew looked awfully good to us today and did a very nice job'.

Second race

The second race of the America's Cup started in a 17-knot north-easterly wind which had faded to perhaps 10 knots by the finish. *Liberty* demonstrated an ability in lighter airs, though the race did not turn out to be a drifting match in flat calm. It was light enough to show that *Liberty* was very much an all-round boat: while she had seemed less impressive in light winds in the defender trials, it was because at that stage *Defender* and *Courageous* had been even better.

Liberty set a heavy-weather main sail because of three conflicting weather reports received before the start. So the Americans were up to now the better prepared in this as in other departments. In the choppier seas and stronger winds which had prevailed only occasionally during the early part of the summer, and against a yacht and crew which had come through a much harsher baptsim, *Australia II* again proved vulnerable. The trouble was that the car which carries the headboard of the mainsail to the top of the mast broke as she was manoeuvering for the start. The sail came away from the headboard car and was kept at the top of the mast only by a 1 inch strip of Kevlar. The damage meant that from then on it was impossible for *Australia II* to hoist the mainsail to the top of the mast; the top of the sail was 18 inches short of the top and though the mast was raked forward and the boom lowered, the Australians were unable to get the maximum power from the sail. This applied especially when the wind went light halfway through the course. Incredibly on the first leg of the race, even though the main was loose and flogging, *Australia II* still footed faster than *Liberty* and, indeed, rounded the first weather mark with a lead of 45 seconds after a late, 10-minute tacking duel by Conner of some 16 tacks. Then, Australian joy at the turn of speed shown by their yacht – clearly faster on the day and in the conditions than *Liberty* – and the superior tactics demonstrated, was to turn to frustration as the American yacht got ahead on the second beat and began the dead run with an advantage of 48 seconds.

On the second beat there occurred an incident: the tacking of *Liberty* on top of her opponent, which was to lead to a protest by *Australia II* but which was not to be heard by the International Jury – increased from three to five in strength to avoid any possible appeals through the USYRU – until the following day which was also a lay-day. As early as the first reach Colin Beashel made his first 11-minute trip to the top of the mast to secure the headboard in order to prevent further trouble. *Australia II* rounded the gybe mark 31 seconds ahead and then Bertrand, good as his word of the previous night, assiduously nudged up to weather in order to prevent *Liberty* from slipping by on this second reaching leg as she had done in the race before. *Liberty* gained but she was still 21 seconds adrift at the leeward mark after Beashel had been at the top of *Australia's* mast for a further 9 minutes.

Now came the critical second windward leg. At first Bertrand appeared to have made a clever, windshift-hunting move, but it proved tactically incorrect and allowed Conner to steal back the vital inches and to take the lead on the 18th tack. Australian cover had been light also. According to both camps the breeze, shifty throughout and varying – according to rival estimates – from 5 to 50 degrees, also went light. Bond maintained afterwards that in the lighter airs it had been impossible for *Australia II* to get involved in a tacking duel because of the mainsail problem and it was because of this – not a tactical error – that Bertrand had had to seek out the windshifts. *Liberty*, with her 49-second advantage at the second weather mark, was 31 seconds ahead after the dead run and gained on the leg to the finish as the wind shifted this way and that and came stronger in puffs and streaks. Australian tactics seemed haphazard as Bertrand chose widely divergent courses at times from those of Conner. *Liberty* crossed the finishing line 1 minute 33 seconds ahead of her rival, wearing the red 'B' protest.

Australia II also signalled for a lay-day, but according to Bond at the Press Conference the Americans had signalled first. He was to threaten further protest action if the lay-day was not accorded to *Liberty* – which had requested it 'four or five seconds ahead of *Australia II*'. The race committee said that it was *Australia II* that had signalled her request for a lay-day by flying code flag N for negative, at 16 hours 58 minutes 14 seconds – the actual time of the expiration of the time allowed in which to seek a lay-day. They stated that *Liberty*'s signal had been hoisted at 16 hours 58 minutes 15 seconds, one second outside of the expiration of time. No lay-day would have been allowed had *Australia II* not requested one.

The protest over the incident on the second weather leg was not heard until the following morning. It began at 9 a.m. and the official announcement by Judge Livius Sherwood, chairman of the five-man International Jury, that the Australian protest had been dismissed, came more than 6½ hours later. It was a bad blow for Bond and Bertrand and the Australian crew and meant that they faced the enormous uphill task of having to win four out of the remaining five races to win the Cup. True, in 1970, *Gretel II*, the second Australian challenger from the Royal Sydney Yacht Squadron, skippered by Jim Hardy, came back to win the third race after falling 2-0 behind, but, and here was the crunch, no other yacht in the history of the event had ever managed it. Any hope of reversing the result on the water disappeared in the protest room with the decision of the International Jury, consisting, incidentally, of Livius Sherwood, the chairman from Canada, Kirkland Cooper from Bermuda, Goran Petersson from Sweden, Ken Ryan from Ireland and Robert Sloane from Mexico. The release from the jury read as follows:

Facts Found

On the second windward leg of the second race for the 1983 America's Cup, *Australia II* on port tack and *Liberty* on starboard tack converged. *Australia II* was moving marginally slower than *Liberty* as a result of having just tacked onto port tack, and she was sailing about 15 degrees below close hauled. When *Australia II* was about 1 boat length from *Liberty*, her course was pointing at the helmsman of *Liberty*. *Australia II* would have passed astern of *Liberty* had *Australia II* maintained this course.

Liberty luffed to commence a covering tack ahead and slightly to windward of *Australia II*. Until *Liberty* reached head to wind, the course sailed by *Australia II* was clearing *Liberty*'s stern. As *Liberty* was luffing toward head to wind, *Australia II* put her helm hard over to port in the locked position, luffed and tacked very rapidly onto starboard tack, clearing the stern of *Liberty* as *Liberty* was completing her tack onto port tack. When *Australia*

II's bow and *Liberty*'s stern swung toward each other, they cleared by about 4 feet at their closest point.

Decision and Grounds for Decision
Protest is disallowed. *Australia II* could have kept clear of *Liberty* either by maintaining her course or by tacking as she did to avoid *Liberty*'s covering tack. *Liberty* has satisfied the jury that she completed her tack in accordance with rule 41.

Later the same day the International Jury were to decide also that the lay-day had been requested first by *Australia II*.

After the lay-day, the next race failed to finish owing to lack of wind. The Australians not only won the start – an 11-second lead and the favoured, committee-boat berth – but led at every mark and were 10 minutes or more ahead when the race was abandoned 1.7 miles from the completion of the final weather leg in a freshening breeze. Had the wind filled in 20 minutes or so earlier, *Australia II* would have been certain to win easily and the score for the following day would have been just 2-1 to *Liberty*. But this is yacht racing; every-day yacht racing. And the facts of the race which failed to finish are just as simple. From an 11-second advantage at the start in a south-south-easterly of around 10 knots, but shifty and suspect, the Australians built a lead of 1 minute 15 seconds at the first weather mark.

It was a convincing lead and one which became 2 minutes at the gybe mark and 1 minute 58 seconds at the leeward turn as the breeze began to die, but not sufficiently to cause too much concern. Towards the end of the second weather leg, which *Australia II* completed with the margin 1 minute 46 seconds, the breeze had gone so light that doubts were cast on the race finishing within the time limit of 5 hours 15 minutes.

In the end it had taken *Australia II* 1 hour 24 minutes to complete the second weather leg compared to 56 minutes on the first beat and this gave just about 2 hours to complete the remaining two legs. In the event, there were 62 seconds remaining when the challenger began the final leg and hopes were by then doomed. There just was not enough wind.

Third race

The start came at 2 p.m. precisely, after the first attempt of the day at 12.10 had been abandoned because of an insufficient wind at the warning gun. The pre-start manoeuvering was again fairly passive early on, with Conner generally running away from Bertrand, but with *Liberty* being manoeuvered to weather and slightly ahead of *Australia II* at the vital time of about three minutes before the start. Conner got the position he wanted, nearer the committee boat and on the right-hand side of the course where it was thought likely the windshifts would come from, changing, fairly soon after the start, into a 7-knot but bonny south-westerly. But then, with the suggestion by some Rhode Island Sound 'freaks' that a breeze as young as this which had enabled the NYYC to get the race started would bring shifts from the left side of the course first, Conner lost the edge. He tacked away to start on port and was so slow rounding the bow of the committee boat that the 8-second advantage with which he was credited by the race committee was lost as it was gained. *Australia II*, pointing higher and also on port shortly after the start, was between 5 and 6 boat lengths ahead after 22 minutes and the first major tack of the first weather leg.

It was then that Conner, having misjudged the start, made his second and probably crucial mistake of the race, engaging *Australia II* in a short-tacking duel which cost him perhaps another 5 to 6 boat lengths, and after 13 tacks, the Australians led by 1 minute 14 seconds at the first weather leg. *Liberty* pulled back a little to be 52 seconds astern at the second mark and she had pulled up to within 42 seconds of her adversary at the leeward mark. Then, with the breeze freshening slightly to around 10 knots at times and then dying to around 4 or 5 knots, there was concern that the conditions might again cheat the Australians of the victory they deserved and which they seemed certain to get when they arrived at the weather mark for the second time with a lead of 1 minute 15 seconds.

However, *Australia II* increased her lead to 2 minutes 47 seconds at the start of the final leg to the finish and she went capably on, crew and skipper making not a suggestion of a slip to notch a famous victory. It had been hard fought for and long deserved.

Connor, who had outwitted Bertrand on the question of the lay-day was able to save his first lay-day until after the fourth race, if there were to be more than 4 races. In the event, he chose it the day after he lost the third race. It was the widest margin by which a defender had been beaten by a challenger since 1871 when *Livonia*, the first challenger and 106ft overall, beat

Columbia in the third race of the series by 15 minutes 10 seconds. The time by which *Australia II* beat *Liberty* was 3 minutes 14 seconds; better even than the 2 minutes 26 seconds by *Shamrock IV* against *Resolute* in 1920 and better also than the 2 minutes 9 seconds by which Sir T.O.M. Sopwith's *Endeavour* beat Harold Vanderbilt's *Rainbow* in 1934. Conner when afterwards asked about the calling of the lay-day and what conditions he would like for the resumption on the Tuesday, said: '40 knots.' He made no excuses for the race and said that the *Liberty* crew had 'tried everything we could think of today', acknowledging that *Australia II* 'looked very good to us ... awfully good downwind'. He was even better at humour than usual and, when asked if he thought that *Australia II* might have been 'sand-bagging all summer', replied: 'I learnt a month ago that sandbagging is something that you do at the beach.' He was referring to the 'sandbagging' (not trying) remark he had made about *Australia II* earlier in the challenge series which had got him into trouble reportedly with his syndicate.

Australia II, which had so convincingly shown in the first two races and the first attempt at running the third that she had the speed to beat *Liberty*, had now done so by the sort of margin her more ardent supporters had claimed she would. The victory on that memorable night of September 18 – the sun setting on a silver Rhode Island Sound after a magnificent race by *Australia II* in generally around 7-10 knot winds and on a flat sea – had sent shivers up the spines of the New York Yacht Club members. Here was a yacht demonstrably capable of winning the America's Cup.

After each race Bill Ficker, helmsman of the 1970 defender, ran scrupulously fair Press conferences and was at pains to praise the performance of *Australia II* which, he maintained, had provided racing on Rhode Island Sound the likes of which had never before been witnessed. He clearly realized that there, indeed, was a yacht which could part the NYYC and the Americans from their famous trophy. Yet surely Conner, his crew, the NYYC and their experts would be prepared for just such an eventuality with some late and telling answer. That the NYYC always let Conner go alone to the Press conferences while Bertrand was always accompanied seemed as though the former was being left to take full responsibility for any failure. But, it was the NYYC that had selected him and his yacht and it was unthinkable that they would not have something to say about the matter. Their very absence from the after-the-race analysis by the skippers was somehow chilling in blistering Newport.

With temperatures soaring in New England to unseasonable highs of 85 and 95 degrees on the Monday, Conner could be seen to have made the right decision to seek a lay-day that day, when the forecast for the Tuesday was of southerly winds of between 15 and 25 knots – nearer to *Liberty* weather. What else would happen in the intervening period, one wondered? What would the Americans do? Would they remain as submissive as they had been since their acceptance of the keel situation or would they come up with something more worthy of their notorious reputation.

Fourth race

The following day was sunny, with more record high temperatures but winds of around 10-17 knots. The race began with a really major error of judgement by Bertrand. He mistimed his run at the starting line, allowing *Liberty* to tack across his bow and gain a 6-second advantage on which Conner built throughout the race. *Liberty*, starting from the pin end in the south-westerly which, as was correctly forecast, was to freshen during the race, became involved in a series of clockwise circling manoeuvres with *Australia II* from just 1 minute into the starting sequence. This continued until the 5-minute gun before the two yachts ended up, head to wind and hovering for some 2½ minutes before *Australia II* bore away on port. *Liberty* then moved off on starboard and it was not until a minute before the start that both turned and approached one another, *Liberty* on port and *Australia II* on starboard. It was then clear that Bertrand had made a mistake, arriving too late at the line and allowing Conner to cross the *Australia II* bow and gain the 6-second advantage. Conner began the race on a port tack and *Australia II* on starboard. *Australia II* was first to tack after some 2 minutes and she was crossed by her opponent some 3 minutes 41 seconds into the first weather leg.

Conner then demonstrated that he intended to make it a 'drag' race, ignoring the tacks of *Australia II* and just windshift hunting as he took only 5 tacks, one fewer than Bertrand, on that first 4.5-mile leg. Conner did, though, make a headsail change as the breeze freshened and seemed to be favouring the American craft. On the second reach, there was a spinnaker change on *Australia II* and there was a further headsail change on *Liberty* on the second beat when the Americans took 10 tacks and the Australians 2 more. Conner was putting only a loose cover, though, on *Australia II*, which also made a headsail change after having followed earlier the *Liberty* example of setting a staysail on the 2 reaching legs.

Australia II had made her usual gain on the dead downwind leg, but even with that and 13 tacks, the same number as *Liberty*, she was unable to get back into the race sufficiently to trouble Conner and his crew. Conner had sailed a masterly, tactical race and his lead at each mark was respectively 36 seconds, 48, 48 again, 46, 35 and 43 at the finish. It was Conner and *Liberty* all the way, resulting in a 3-1 lead for the USA.

Afterwards Conner denied that there had been any changes to *Liberty* other than the use of a different mainsail, denying that there had been any alternations of ballast and, by implication, that the mast had been raked as had been suggested. However, whatever had, or had not been done to *Liberty*, there was no doubt that she was a different boat in that fourth race than in the third which she lost. Conner was in jocular mood, saying that though they won the start they were not, on *Liberty*, having any 'champagne celebrations' because they had started with just a boat-length advantage. But that, clearly, was the end of the beginning for *Australia II*. Though she briefly threatened on the first weather leg and came back on the run to offer a bigger threat on the final beat to the finish, there was no budging Conner. Now the defenders needed only one more win to keep the cup. Had not *Gretel, Gretel II* and *Australia* all been beaten 4-1 in previous Australian challenges?

The Australians were still optimistic, saying they would fight as their compatriots had fought in Gallipoli, though Bond did reaffirm that he would not be back in Newport again, win or lose the cup.

Fifth race

Now fortunes changed. On a beautiful sailing morning, with a fresh breeze, sunshine and steepish seas, it was noticed that *Liberty* was in trouble. She had two men up the mast at work on what, it was discovered, was a broken port jumper strut, and there were hasty radio messages seeking hacksaws and blades and a request, rejected, for a US Coastguard helicopter to be used to bring a spare part from shore. There began a frenzied race against time to strip the mast of the offending strut and replace it, when it arrived after a high-speed chase by one of *Liberty*'s smaller tenders with 470 hp engines. The new jumper strut took until after the course signals had been hoisted on *Black Knight* to be fitted. The work aloft was done by Tom Rich and Scott Vogel, and they came down to deck from their labours just 2 minutes before the 10-minute gun.

It had all been a most impressive operation, calmly directed by radio by Halsey Herreshoff, who showed no panic in his voice and who had time even to take a coded weather report from 'Charlie' at the weather mark just as the crew were getting to work to hoist their headsail. Then, more trouble came for *Liberty* as her headsail tore and it was necessary, now into the starting sequence, to lower it and hoist a replacement. By this time, the Americans were being harried by *Australia II* which was later seen to be wearing a protest flag as the yachts approached the line to start. Whether the incident came early or late about which the Australians were to protest was not then known. *Liberty* completed the hoisting of the replacement sail some 3 minutes 3 seconds into the starting sequence and shortly before Conner was to choose to round the US Coastguard vessel *Chase* to get rid of *Australia II*. The ploy not only worked, but put Conner up to weather of *Australia II* and in the advantageous position the American skipper was to hold from shortly after the 5-minute gun until shortly before the start when *Liberty* bore away on port from *Australia II* which was left close to the line at the pin end. Then came another starting mistake by Bertrand and his crew. The yacht crossed the line early and so had to re-cross and with Conner some 37 seconds to the good already. Bertrand later claimed that the line was biased.

While, as the two yachts approached the line some 4 minutes before the start, it had seemed as though the starboard end would be favoured, there was to be a shift shortly before the start which left *Australia II* on the better, port-hand side of the course and having regained perhaps a boat-length on *Liberty* in the few seconds after the start and when the wind shifted again. Still, *Liberty* seemed to be best placed and with Bertrand without a hope of coming back from the dead. But, Conner's policy of the previous day of ignoring *Australia II* tacks was not to pay on that Wednesday September 21. Conner remained on port tack for some 19 minutes and after some 37 minutes into the race was still marginally ahead. But after a further 6 tacks by *Liberty* and 7 by *Australia II* it seemed that the Bond boat was marginally ahead and, at the weather mark, reached after 21 tacks by *Australia II* and one fewer by *Liberty*, it was the white boat which led the cranberry-coloured one by 23 seconds. This was a sensational race already, confirming again the series as the closest since 1934 when *Endeavour* had led *Rainbow* 2-0.

Both yachts again set staysails on the second reach, but there was no change in the time margin at the gybe mark, shortly after which *Liberty* was to have a man aloft. The breeze was now around 22-23 knots, but had shifted, so *Black Knight* left her station to signal a course change to the two yachts of 185 degrees instead of the 195 degrees for the start. *Australia II* began the crucial, second beat with an advantage now cut to 18 seconds, but though both yachts took 19 tacks there was no gain by *Liberty*, covered all the way up the leg by Bertrand, who was 1 minute 11 seconds ahead at the second weather mark. It seemed like being a winning lead. It was. *Australia II* led by 52 seconds at the leeward turn, *Liberty* having done slightly better for a change on the square run. But she fell away on the last leg, when she tacked all the way up the middle. At the finish the challenger crossed the line no less than 1 minute 47 seconds ahead.

Never in the history of the Cup had a yacht come back to narrow the defender's lead to 3-2 after being 3-1 behind. And this was only the third time in the history of the Cup that a score of 3-2 had occurred; the first being when Sir Thomas Lipton's *Shamrock IV* fell to such a concluding score – there being only five races in those days – after leading *Resolute* 2-0 in 1920. The second was when Sir Tommy Sopwith's *Endeavour* stood 3-2 down against *Rainbow*. Here was history indeed, and it was not lost on the keener observers that it was only the three men who had fought relentlessly for the Cup – Lipton for five challenges, Sopwith for two and Bond for four – who had managed to get near to upsetting American dominance.

So the series was kept alive, with wild, enthusiastic but understandable Australian jubilation right after the success at

sea and in Newport Harbour as their great yacht returned to her
berth at Newport Offshore.

Neither skipper called for the lay-day they were each entitled
to as the fourth-race stage of the competition was passed –
perhaps being aware that it was not unusual for the
north-westerly that was forecast for the following day to be
followed by calms. It was an intriguing situation. A score of 3-2
and just two races left to be run. Of course, with lay-days and
delays because of the weather, those two races could take some
days to complete and both would have to be sailed if *Australia
II* was to win the Cup. While *Liberty* needed to win just once,
the Australians had to take the series to its full seven races – a
situation which had never previously arisen. There had been the
need to run a sixth race for *Endeavour*, but just the once, and
so here was a rare occurrence. It was the first time that there
had been a sixth race for 49 years.

There had never been any doubt about the potential of
Australia II and her crew but, nor for that matter, had there been
about the potential of *Liberty* and Conner and his men, who had
never lost more than 2 races in a row all summer. With a protest
flag flown by *Liberty* removed during the race and a possible
protest by *Australia II* withdrawn there was no problem about
the race starting on time the following day. By then it was
known that the trouble with the jumper strut on *Liberty* was
that the ram had bent at right angles during turning. It bent
again within 3 minutes of the start, thus preventing Conner
from tacking until 19 minutes into the race, the time that
Bertrand needed to get back into the race.

Sixth race

The brisk north-westerly of 18 knots would be expected to
favour *Liberty*. The weather was cold but by late morning bright
with a blue sky. Both boats left decisions on headsails late.
Australia II had her headsail set as she came around the *Black
Knight* and into the starting area and when *Liberty* set her
genoa, just a minute into the 10-minute period up to the starting
gun, it was clear that both she and her rival had chosen
moderate-weather mainsails and No 4 genoas. The two yachts
passed one another some 2 minutes into the pre-start section of
the race, *Liberty* to leeward of *Australia II* which followed
astern towards the US Coastguard vessel, *Chase* – some 276 ft

long – and the craft which Conner had rounded the previous day to 'lose' the pursuing Bertrand. As he neared *Chase*, some 4 minutes having elapsed since the warning gun, Conner was to try the same manoeuvre again. But *Liberty* then bore away to come up to lee of *Australia II* and remained in this position, slightly astern of the Bond boat, for fully 2 minutes as *Australia II* occasionally came head to wind, her sails flapping to cut off *Liberty* from passing her. *Liberty* then tacked away to port, again to have her route blocked by *Australia II*, which remained slightly ahead and to weather until some 2 minutes before the starting gun.

Then, 1½ minutes before the gun, *Liberty* got on top as *Australia II*, again approaching the line too soon, bore away so that her American rival could round up to weather of her and come between her and the committee-boat end of the line which at that stage seemed the favoured one. *Liberty* crossed the line on port, was able to tack on top of *Australia II* and enjoyed a 7-second advantage which, in the conditions seemed likely to end yet another Australian challenge for the America's Cup.

It was some 20 seconds into the race that Conner tacked on top of Bertrand and some 20 seconds later that Bertrand passed astern of *Liberty*. After 1½ minutes, *Australia II* tacked on to starboard while *Liberty* remained on port, before crossing *Australia II* after 3 minutes. The Australians then remained on a long starboard tack, covered rather late by Conner, who later tacked back onto port, leaving Bertrand on starboard. This was essentially the point where Conner was accused of not covering his rival. At any event, it was the beginning of the end for *Liberty* in that race. After 5 tacks and 27 minutes into the race, *Australia II* was ahead, Conner covering too late to shut out Bertrand despite a series of quick tacks. Altogether *Australia II* took 15 tacks to reach the weather mark where Bertrand was ahead by 2 minutes 29 seconds. The distance at the gybe mark was 2 minutes 28 seconds to *Australia II*, which gained substantially to 3 minutes 46 seconds ahead at the leeward mark – Conner blaming different wind strengths for the widening of the gap. It was a substantial windshift, of which there were a number of between 30 and 35 degrees during the day, which helped Bertrand to get ahead in the first place and which was to allow him, as leading yacht, to reinforce his position during the race. His lead at the second weather mark, after just 5 tacks by each yacht, was 3 minutes 22 seconds.

Not only did the wind die to around 7 knots at a couple of stages but it also backed to give a fetch for perhaps 75 per cent of the second weather leg for which the bearing had been 295 degrees. It should have been 260 degrees to have been a beat after a quarter of the way up the leg. This practically ended Conner's chances. He had no option, because of the fetch, but to follow in the wake of *Australia II*, which gained also by the run having become a beam reach. There was a similar shift of wind on the last weather leg which, as it also became a further fetch meant that there were just 4 tacks each by the two yachts. *Australia II* then crossed the finishing line 3 minutes 25 seconds ahead of *Liberty*.

If there was wild excitement after the win on Wednesday by *Australia II* it was as nothing compared to that of Thursday when, as the world that had suddenly discovered yachting through the America's Cup of 1983 now knew, the Australians, against the gigantic weight of history, had levelled the scores 3-all. It was a monumental feat and Dennis Conner now faced what no other American skipper before him had – a vital seventh race.

The seventh race forced by the historic win of *Australia II* was scheduled to take place on Saturday September 24 because the challenger's crew had called a lay-day for the Friday. The event had by now become *the* sporting contest of 1983. The eyes of the sporting world were now on Newport, Rhode Island, with the possibility at last of a challenger ending what was the longest unbroken sequence of victories by any club or country in any sport. The New York Yacht Club were well aware of the threat. Bill Ficker's comment was that the seventh race would be 'the most significant yacht race in history'.

The Australians decided to call a lay-day to check equipment – severely tested in the heavy weather of the sixth race – and to give the crew some relaxation after two hard days of racing. It made sense in one way; the two points were very valid. But it did not make sense in that the Australians had got the Americans on the run and what they needed to do was keep them on the run. Bond acknowledged at the post-race Press conference that despite two wins in two races – a previously unknown achievement at such a stage in an America's Cup series – the third win in a row would be far from easy. He was, said Bond, conscious of the great competition offered by *Liberty*, and his crew would face it with great seriousness. Bertrand was similarly confident, though he recognized that the race would be 'very tough'. He said: 'We have developed a lot of confidence and learnt how to sail against *Liberty*.'

What the Americans at the Press conference preferred were the words of Conner, looking tired, but with a more confident voice. He said: 'It will be very exciting to be involved in the race of the century. I hope we can find a way to prevail as we have for 132 years. Somehow, I think we shall pull it off on Saturday.' He pointed out also that he and the crew had been sailing together for five years, since before they had met and trained and defeated *Australia* in 1980. In that time and during all the practice and training and trials – they had never lost more than two races in a row.

Conner, with a bag of golf clubs over his shoulder bright and early on Friday morning, looked cheerful and confident as he set off for a round of golf with some New York Yacht Club members. Bob McCullough, who had chosen him and *Liberty* to mount the defence, was also calm and relaxed on the Goat Island Marina Jetty where *Fox Hunter*, the selection committee's headquarters was berthed, as he chatted with passers-by and well-wishers. There had, said McCullough, for long been arrangements for just such an eventuality as *Australia II* winning the trophy. It had not had to be worked out merely in the light of the 3 all score. There was, though, an electric atmosphere over Newport; everyone had an opinion and a favourite. They had put 50 cents on *Liberty* – to be patriotic – because a friend had put 25 cents on *Australia II*. Others were alarmed that 'their friends had suddenly come out as Australian supporters', or had remarked evidently to the chagrin of loyal American supporters of the America's Cup, that 'they hoped the Australians would win'.

But what a prospect for Newport, for the United States, for the yachting world and the sporting world. If *Australia II* won and carried off the America's Cup, the end of the New York Club's impressive 132-year reign would be rather like the Tower of Pisa collapsing. Even if re-built – or even if the Cup were regained – it would never be the same again. This, the Yankee American, the true East Coast New Englander, seemed to understand. Its loss would certainly devalue the trophy and the New York Yacht Club. The loss of America's Cup was unthinkable, to many Americans.

And so came the scheduled day of the last race: Saturday September 24. An ideal day in every way, save the wind. A clear sky, crisp day, bright sunshine but a north-westerly air which died before all of the estimated 1,500 spectator craft found their way out to the America's Cup buoy. The failing wind forced the race committee to postpone the start some 2 minutes before the scheduled time of 12.10. There had been something like a 40 degree windshift as the yachts began their manoeuvres from the warning gun. The winds remained shifty and very light and there was no further attempt at a start. Racing for the day was called off at just after 1.50 p.m., too late for the routine of 10 minutes for the course signals to be hoisted before the warning gun and meaning that the necessary 20 minutes to the starting gun had expired.

Now it was the turn of the defender to call for a lay-day, which would be Sunday, meaning that racing was not due to resume until Monday September 26. Since 1,000 lb or so of ballast had been removed from *Liberty* on the Friday night when the yacht had been re-checked by Mark Vinbury and a new rating certificate issued, the lay-day could be used to replace ballast for expected heavier weather or to enable Conner to check the tune of the boat further before meeting *Australia II* for what would be the last time. The lack of a race on Saturday was, though, a great disappointment to the thousands who had gone afloat for the day and who, if they intended again to catch the final race, would have to pay upwards of $50 each to go with charter companies.

Bond threatened after the abandoned race to protest *Liberty* if there was a further change of ballast and a new or amended rating certificate issued, on the grounds that not more than one alteration should be allowed for each race. His argument was that the race scheduled for the Monday was the same one that should have been run on Saturday. It was a futile argument because he had agreed to the conditions of the Cup challenge round which included a clause allowing for alterations to be made during the series. *Liberty*, looking in a very sorry state of repair considering that she had been described at the start of the summer as the best-looking 12-metre in Newport, did go to the yard at Cove Haven on the Sunday but, in the event, did not have any alterations made: the view was that the weather would be very similar to that of Saturday. Conner, therefore, left things as they were. The claimed 920 lb of ballast previously removed according to Johann Valentijn, the designer – would allow for about an additional 30 sq ft of sail area in the spinnaker.

It emerged on Sunday that a diver had been spotted in the vicinity of the Australian dock on the Saturday and it was alleged that close examination had revealed that a string of plastic bags had been drawn across the entrance to the dock. The implication was that this would become entangled in the keel and slow the yacht in the seventh and vital last race to the series that had become the most historic of all America's Cup contests.

Seventh race

But all of this, the frogman, the ballast, the protests, the delays – aye, even the political manoeuverings of the New York Yacht Club all those weeks ago – were quickly forgotten as on the following day, Monday September 26, what was to match the billing as 'the yacht race of the century', got under way. No better conclusion to the best America's Cup series could have been scripted by any movie maker; it had practically every ingredient necessary for a great drama – which it proved to be. The spectator fleet began to make its way out to the course – the smaller and slower craft first, the bigger, faster ships later – even before the two 12-metres, with their regular attendants left Newport Harbour at around 9 a.m. It was another glorious day; clear, only a few clouds, and to get warmer as the crispness was eaten up by the sun, but not yet hot enough to bring in the forecasted 10-15 knot south-westerly breeze. It seemed, though, that at least Conner had correctly chosen to keep *Liberty* in her light-air mode.

Reports from weather observation points up and down the New England coast which were transmitted from the local weather centre to *Black Swan*, the tender to *Australia II*, re-emphasized the lack of a breeze offshore. There was little more than 7 knots at any point on the coast and some, like Nantucket, reported nil velocity.

The course signals for the seventh race were hoisted promptly at 11.50, showing a bearing to the first mark of 200 degrees.

Conner again gave a passive peformance, steering *Liberty* dead downwind from the 10-minute gun and, when first tailed by *Australia II* after just 3 minutes, 'running away' until, with 3 minutes to the starting gun, the American yacht ended up on the quarter but to weather of the challenger. But as the clock came down to just 2½ minutes to the gun the race committee signalled a postponement. The race committee had just been informed of a 40 degree windshift at the weather mark.

When the course signals were next hoisted, at 12.45, the bearing to the first mark had become 205 degrees and, happily, the breeze remained at around 6-8 knots for the start at 1.05 p.m. It was a start accredited to the American yacht, by 8 seconds, which started at the committee boat end of the line on port while Bertrand chose – and was partly influenced by Conner – to take a starboard first tack towards the pin-end of the line and out into what it transpired was, early on, at least, to be the more favoured port-hand side of the course. Again Conner had managed to get the position he wanted and yet again he had suffered as a consequence as Bertrand got the better break on the early part of the beat. Conner, starting on that fateful Monday in American history from the starboard side of the course, had also been more aggressive at the start, engaging *Australia II* within just 2½ minutes into the starting sequence. After heading downwind for just a minute, Conner turned towards the centre of the course to meet his rival head on. *Liberty* gybed and *Australia II* tacked away from the encounter with the result that, 3 minutes into the sequence, *Liberty* was to weather and move slightly ahead of *Australia II* as they headed diagonally away from the starting line on a course that would have taken them well to leeward of the committee boat. *Australia II* then took what, from the 200 yards or so distance of the privileged spectator boats, seemed the risky tactic of trying to cross ahead of *Liberty*. But Bertrand accomplished the manoeuvre without protest or danger and the two boats ended up on opposite tacks, *Australia II* to weather of *Liberty* and sailing parallel to the starting line towards the pin-end of the line. *Liberty* was heading in the opposite direction. *Australia II* then turned to tail *Liberty* as she set off now on a diagonal course back towards the committee boat but on a heading which would have taken the Americans across her stern. This after 5 minutes.

The position then was that *Australia II* came to leeward and

alongside *Liberty*, still on an unchanged heading; so it remained
for slightly less than a minute. At this point *Liberty* tacked
downwind through 45 degrees, with *Australia II* again trying to
squeeze through to leeward. But with the yachts tacking and
gybing away from the encounter the resulting position was that
Liberty remained to weather of her opponent but now on a
diagonal heading to a point some way to leeward of the pin end
of the starting line. And 3 minutes remained before the start.

If the yachts were pointing to 7 on an imaginary clock-face,
they then came round to be facing, first, 9 and then 10, and so
they remained from just after 3 minutes until one minute from
the starting time when they reached the line from two-thirds
along it towards the committee-boat end. Just half a minute
before the gun Conner, as expected, came round onto a port
tack towards the committee boat and Bertrand, to leeward of
Liberty, went off as described on a starboard tack towards the
better, left-hand side of the course. It was 3½ minutes before
Conner chose to tack *Liberty* onto starboard to cover an
Australia II already benefiting from the shifty south-south-
westerly. Half a minute later, *Australia II* came on to port and
just a minute later, *Liberty* tacked back onto starboard. The
implication was obvious; Conner was behind and he was trying
to recover some lost ground by going back onto starboard·in the
hope that the next shift would come from the right-hand side of
the course. When, after 23 minutes, *Liberty* came back onto
port, she was to cross under *Australia II* which, because of being
caught out by a dummy tack by *Liberty*, failed to cover for 2
fateful minutes. Conner had got across to the left and what he
clearly believed now to be the more favoured side. The two
yachts next came together after 30 minutes when *Liberty* was
clearly in the ascendancy and *Australia II* was forced to tack
away again as Conner continued his then rewarding tactic of
looking for windshifts rather than being over-worried about
cover. The result was that the Americans were 29 seconds up at
the first weather mark. This was after 11 tacks by the defender
and 8 by the challenger.

It was enough of a lead at a first mark to give those on *Fox
Hunter* grounds for belief that their reign would long continue.
It was apparently confirmed when *Liberty* lengthened her lead
to 45 seconds at the gybe mark. It was then, perhaps, that
Australian hopes were renewed and American fervour tempered

a little as, with the wind shifting and making the second reach much more square and slow, *Australia II* pulled back to be just 23 seconds adrift at the leeward mark.

On the second weather leg each boat tacked 7 times. At the second weather mark the bearing had been altered to 195 degrees as the breeze shifted through 30 degrees. The American yacht had now built what surely would be an invincible 57 second lead.

No, no, no, a thousand times no! is what every Australian who witnessed the race will echo for ever and ever. From this mark there were just two legs of the course to go: one to leeward and the final beat to windward. A 12-metre nearly 1 minute ahead, as was *Liberty* that day had only to play the cards right. Then, in the light wind on a warm afternoon in late summer off Newport, Rhode Island, Dennis Conner, well in the lead with most of the race over, made a legitimate yacht racing move. But it lost America the cup.

Worried by the previously demonstrated ability of *Australia II* to catch *Liberty* on a dead downwind leg, Conner gybed over to the port side of the course, looking for a fresher breeze. In doing so, he failed to cover the challenger who went to his right, the side which on the first and second weather legs had so proved the saving side for the American 12-metre. It was not the first time on a downwind leg that Conner had gone to the left side and lost out as a result. To make matters worse Bertrand got two windshifts while Conner got only one with the result that *Liberty* was 21 seconds astern at the leeward mark. On the last beat *Liberty* made 45 despairing tacks, but was 41 seconds behind at the finish shortly after 5.21 p.m. on Monday September 26, 1983. *Liberty* was beaten 4-3 and *Australia II* had won the America's Cup.

It brought the wildest scenes ever seen on Rhode Island Sound, the graveyard for so many America's Cup hopes in the past, 6 of them Australian and 5 of them British. Here was jubilation and total chaos as Alan Bond, Ben Lexcen and Warren Jones, the three giants behind Bertrand, went aboard *Australia II* under wild, oscillating tow from *Black Swan*. Every conceivable type of craft, from large ocean cruising vessels to inflatable dinghies, tall ships to motor-cruisers of more than 100 ft all converged at maximum speed it seemed on the most distinguished of all 12-metres – the brainchild of Lexcen, or, as the lapel badges proudly worn by so many in Newport proclaimed: 'Lexcen's Lightning'. It was bedlam and mayhem. Never can there have been wilder scenes anywhere. The sirens, claxons and horns heralding the vast procession from the course out to sea to the wharves of Newport – past tens of thousands of well-wishers on vantage points ashore – finally came to an end off the dock where Bond's boat had been cradled with her keel shrouded for more than three months.

It was here that the scenes of jubilation and congratulation, champagne toasts and hugs and congratulatory kisses, became even more ecstatic as those who had suppored the Australian yacht and those who merely went there for the excitement, swelled the numbers and began a vast, never-ending string of parties all over Newport which were to continue long into the following morning.

They are the familiar scenes which accompany any great sporting success, the wild rejoicing scenes which come with many triumphs, the result of partisan passions being released at some great pleasure brought by triumph. They happen everywhere and they happen often. There had never, though, been scenes like this to mark the winning of the America's Cup. It had only been won once – by a relatively young nation against the leading yachting country of the day. It had been retained and there had been rejoicing and shock for the losers then. But never like this, with Australians and their flags flocking to congratulate their heroes who had achieved the 'impossible'. They had won the 'unwinnable' America's Cup. They had beaten the 'unbeatable' New York Yacht Club. They had conquered the 'unconquerable' United States yachtsmen at the American game of the America's Cup in their own Rhode Island state backyard.

It was an historic triumph to end all historic sporting triumphs. It had never been achieved before; it would never be achieved again after such a long spell, for sure. The Australians would never keep the cup so long or they would keep it for ever. And no-one there in Newport or afloat on Rhode Island Sound that day would ever see such an America's Cup victory again. It could never occur. Not after such a span. Recovery of the trophy by the Americans, if it happened, would be sweet, but it would hardly be the same. No, this was the end of the America's Cup as a 132-year tradition. It was, as I wrote for the *Daily Telegraph* that day and which I repeat without apology because I feel it to be as true now after the fray as I did then in the thick of it: 'The end of a sporting legend. The conquest of the last great pinnacle of sport.'

The America's Cup races September 1983

Date		Running score Challenger	Defender
Tuesday 13	Not started: lack of wind	—	
Wednesday 14	*Liberty* wins	0	1
Thursday 15	*Liberty* wins	0	2
Friday 16	Australian lay-day	—	
Saturday 17	Time limit expired	—	
Sunday 18	*Australia II* wins	1	2
Monday 19	US lay-day	—	
Tuesday 20	*Liberty* wins	1	3
Wednesday 21	*Australia II* wins	2	3
Thursday 22	*Australia II* wins	3	3
Friday 23	Australian lay-day	—	
Saturday 24	Not started: lack of wind	—	
Sunday 25	US lay-day	—	
Monday 26	*Australia II* wins	4	3

At Marble House

The next day the America's Cup was presented to a challenger for the second time only. It was swiftly arranged and quickly done in a short but moving ceremony with no precedent.

The night of the final race, the Auld Mug was unbolted from its pedestal in the New York Yacht Club, 37 West 44th Street, packed in a black box and conveyed by armoured truck to Newport. The surrender of the cup took place at midday on the terrace of Marble House, which had been built in 1892 for William K. Vanderbilt. Close by, in the sumptuous Victorian mansion, was the personal trophy room and America's Cup museum established by the Vanderbilt family who had helped to defend the Cup for a hundred years.

After the disputes of the summer, the Commodore and members of the New York Yacht Club acted with style and grace. Robert Stone first presented Alan Bond with the forty inch bolt which had secured the cup. Then he picked up what was once known as the 100 Guineas Cup, 8lb 6oz in weight and 2 feet 3 inches in height and handed it to Peter Dalzeil, Commodore of the Royal Perth Yacht Club. Stone said, 'We turn this over to you. I don't think there is any other country we'd rather see have the cup. But we'll be back to get it. Take good care of it.'

For Australians it was a day of history for their country. Alan Bond was able to say, 'This sporting effort has united Australia: all of the people in our country were behind us. It has shown that we can pull together as a nation; a young nation that has to build a heritage.'

Others had their say or their thoughts at this emotional moment. For John Bertrand, it was 'the fight back of a lifetime, the fulfilment of a dream'. Dennis Conner said, 'There was nothing we could do', but Ben Lexcen said of him, 'Dennis saved the Cup last time and he deserves the credit for almost saving the Cup this time'. Bob McCullough did not attend.

For other Americans – and for those of other nations too, who had sailed in or supported this and previous campaigns – came four words from Halsey Herreshoff, navigator on board the defender and grandson of Nathanael Herreshoff, who between 1893 and 1920 designed yachts which successfully defended the Cup five times: 'The unthinkable has happened'.